SISTER GUMBO

URSULA INGA KINDRED

SISTER GUMBO

SPICY VIGNETTES FROM BLACK WOMEN
ON LIFE, SEX, AND RELATIONSHIPS

MIRRANDA GUERIN-WILLIAMS

ST. MARTIN'S GRIFFIN NEW YORK

www.stmartins.com

Book design by Victoria Kuskowski

Library of Congress Cataloging-in-Publication Data

Kindred, Ursula Inga.
    Sister gumbo : spicy vignettes from black women on life, sex, and
    relationships / Ursula Inga Kindred and Mirranda Guerin-Williams.—
    1st ed.
        p.   cm.
    ISBN 0-312-32679-3
    EAN 978-0312-32679-1
    1. African American women—Social conditions.   2. African American
    women—Sexual behavior.   3. African American women—Interviews.
    4. Man-woman relationships—United States.   5. Sex—United States.
    6. Sex role—United States.   I. Guerin-Williams, Mirranda.   II. Title.

E185.86K57   2004
305.48'896073—dc22

                                                            2004040959

First Edition: August 2004

10 9 8 7 6 5 4 3 2 1

CONTENTS

RELATIONSHIPS

SEX

SELF

ACKNOWLEDGMENTS

We'd like to make the following acknowledgments:

God, who inspired us to write this book.

Mary Julia Quiett (Mama), our maternal grandmother, who was never at a loss for words, and who blessed us with our mother, Barbara Dean Quiett-Guerin-Harris-Hilliard.

Mother, we love you. Thank you for the sacrifices you made when we were young and for your advice (even when we didn't listen). Thanks for always being honest and for making us laugh so much. And thanks for your encouragement.

Our husbands, Wade and Jerome, and our children, Jazmyn, Alvin, Guerin, and Justin, we love you more than you know. Thanks for your patience and support while we were interviewing, writing, rewriting, editing, re-editing, etc.

The ladies we interviewed (you know who you are). Thank you for being totally open and for sharing your stories with us. This book would not have happened without you.

Our sisters in "Suede," for all the sleepovers and talks long into the night.

Special thanks to all of the following who sold books and/or helped us to sell books by radio, from home, over the phone, on their jobs, and out of their trunks. We love you and are so grateful for your support. Without you, we would never have sold so many copies of the first release of *Sister Gumbo*, and we would never have caught the eye of our wonderful agent Jenny. (Jenny, you're wonderful and so is your mom! Thanks for believing in us and for shopping our book around to all of the big publishing houses in New York!)

To our cousin Sedric M. Miles, thank you so much for the

ACKNOWLEDGMENTS

beautiful cover art on the original *Sister Gumbo* that caught the eyes of so many people. You're a wonderful artist! Mother, Daddy, Tommie, Uncle David Quiett and his staff at the Southern University Student Union, Aunt Pearl Henry, Aunt Gladiola Miles, Aunt Idell Hawthorne, Jackie and Jerome Hill, Charlotte and David Hopkins, Gretchen and Donald Malone, Dawania Quiett, A.J. and Debra Jones, Alvin and Dee Miles, Claudette and Wilbur McIntyre, Kim and Sam Kindred, Jodye Newton, Denise Washington and Miki Turner at the *Fort Worth Star-Telegram*, Kenny and Laura Grimes and their friends and family, along with the Black Cowboys at Lil' Henry's in Beaumont, we had a ball!, Emma Rogers at Black Images, Til and Milton Pettis at Jokae's, Sonia Williams-Babers at the Black Bookworm, Vera and Jennifer at Community Book Center in New Orleans, Alvester and Glenda Gibson at House of Knowledge, Terry (Tariq) at Afro Awakenings Books, Sonya and the Thomas and Hall Art Gallery in Dallas, the K104 Morning Team and the 105.7 Morning Team in the Dallas/Ft. Worth metroplex, Bobby Patterson and Paul Turner at KKDA, Tony B. at 94.5 KSOL, *Rolling Out* magazine, Beatrice and Davage at LeaTouche' Hair Designs, Peggy Heinkel-Wolfe and *Eclipse* magazine, TCU and the Pink Bag Luncheon group, members of the North Texas-Mid Cities Chapter of the National Association of Blacks in Criminal Justice (NABCJ), American Airlines Employee Resource Group, *Southern Digest* magazine, all of the independent African American bookstores and book clubs, all of our co-workers and friends who bought books for themselves and for others, and last but not least, all of the brothers and sisters who loved our book and spread the word to their friends and family.

INTRODUCTION

What could a book titled *Sister Gumbo: Spicy Vignettes from Black Women on Life, Sex, and Relationships* possibly be about? Well, let us tell you, it's a book about the gumbo of women's lives.

Just as gumbo is only as good as the ingredients that go into it (the shrimp, crab, sausage, onions, garlic, spices, etc.), *Sister Gumbo* is good for the same reason. It has life ingredients based on experiences with men, love, sex, advice, infidelity, and all the other day-to-day stuff we deal with as we go about the business of living as women.

Sister Gumbo began when we two sisters originally from Louisiana decided to interview several of our close friends, women of all ages and walks of life, about their experiences. Once we told them of our desire to write a book and that their names and other identifying characteristics would be changed, they seemed to enjoy opening up and speaking honestly and directly. We found that most women don't mind talking about their lives as long as they know they're not being judged.

We wanted to write a fun and enjoyable book, and although there are other books already out there dealing with this subject, we feel they are often too analytical or clinical. Our desire is that each woman who reads *Sister Gumbo* will be able to reminisce, laugh, cry, agree, and maybe even disagree with these women, without having to determine why she lived her life the way she did, because after all, it is her life.

We hope to make light of the fact that even though we as women sometimes make bad decisions and may not be proud of some of the things we've said, done, or endured, our individual experiences enable each of us to create our own gumbo. We often draw from this rich stew to help another sister just when she thinks no one understands what she's going through. Hence, *Sister Gumbo: Spicy Vignettes from Black Women on Life, Sex, and Relationships* exists to make it easier for you to feel free to tell it, even if it doesn't always feel good, because your story may help someone else.

So now that you're relaxed and ready for a good read, turn on some soft jazz, pour yourself a nice glass of wine, sit down in your favorite space with *Sister Gumbo,* and enjoy.

MOTHER'S GUMBO

BARBARA QUIETT-GUERIN-HARRIS-HILLIARD

5 tablespoons cooking oil

1 cup flour

2 yellow onions, finely chopped

1 bunch green onions, finely chopped

⅓ cup green peppers, finely chopped

3 cloves garlic, minced

2 (15-ounce) cans tomato sauce

5 cups water

2 lbs. shrimp

2 lbs. crab

1 lb. smoked sausage

In a large pot over medium heat, sauté oil, flour, onions, green pepper, and garlic until flour browns.

Add tomato sauce and water and bring to a boil. Lower heat and cook for 45 minutes.

Add shrimp (deveined), crab, and sausage. Season to taste. Cook an additional 15–30 minutes. Serve over rice. *Yield: 12 servings.*

RELATIONSHIPS

RELATIONSHIP (ri-la-shan-ship) noun
The condition or fact of being related.
Connection by blood or marriage; kinship.

As bad as physical disease is for the eyes, there is another disease which can ruin your relationships. It is the "I" disease where your conversation contains the words "I," "me," "my," and "mine," every eight to ten words. If these words were removed from most people's conversation they would have nothing to say.—SIDNEY MADWED

Intimate relationships cannot substitute for a life plan. But to have any meaning or viability at all, a life plan must include intimate relationships.
—HARRIET LERNER

A successful marriage requires falling in love many times, always with the same person.
—MIGNON MCLAUGHLIN

God could not be everywhere and therefore he made mothers.—ANON

The best time to make friends is before you need them.—ETHEL BARRYMORE

A friend is one who knows us, but loves us anyway.
—FR. JEROME CUMMINGS

PAST

AYOKA, THIRTY-SOMETHING

Ayoka is a buyer for a major retail store and travels at least two weeks out of the month. A classy woman with lovely honey-brown skin that needs little if no makeup, Ayoka has full lips and shoulder-length hair that most of the time she pulls up in a French twist, and the fact that she appears to be at peace within herself makes her even more attractive.

Her town house was both cozy and classy and we conducted the interview in the living room, sprawled on her tan leather sofas. Her "power" color was purple. She had purple chenille throw pillows on the sofas, purple vases on the fireplace, and purple high-backed chairs upholstered in suede surrounded the dining table. Exotic white candles stood among the vases on the fireplace and the color of the walls was a soothing eggshell beige. The living area merged into the kitchen where the cabinets were blond wood and kitchen appliances were brushed chrome. Atop the stove sat a handmade purple teakettle.

We dined like queens on Chinese food and sipped on one of her favorite wines. Ayoka had been separated for two years and was in the process of getting a divorce, so we asked her how her life had been going since she and her husband split.

As we got comfortable on the sofas Ayoka hugged one of the purple pillows to her chest and started to talk.

"Since our separation my life hasn't missed a beat. I haven't had to use a lot of money out of my savings but I did use some to furnish this town house because I didn't want the debt. The only reason I don't buy a new car right now is because I want what I want, and I don't want my soon to be ex-husband acting like he can take it away. I don't know if he could do that but I don't want to take a chance and give him any more leverage than he already thinks he has.

"I got my eye on this cute little two-seater BMW and it's just a matter of getting my divorce finalized before I get it. I already got the loan set up and it's been preapproved, I'm just waiting till that day comes and you know where I'll be the very next day? At the BMW dealership, that's where." Ayoka laughed and clapped her hands together like a little girl.

"I'm going to keep my other car so this is just going to be my midlife car, and of course it will be black because I love the look of black cars. They're so classy, especially when it's a luxury car like a BMW. One of my neighbors has one and I stand in my window and just stare at it all the time thinking, 'Yeah, I can picture myself riding around in a car like that.'

"On the other hand, I've talked to several people about my soon to be single status and the picture doesn't seem too pretty, mainly because of my salary which is in the low six figures. I was talking to this guy at work who's about thirty-eight and just married, and he tells me, 'You're going to have to face it, potential prospects for a woman of your financial standing are going to be slim to none. You're not going to meet a man compatible to you because if he's making that kind of money, he's probably already married or has some other issues.'

"I said to him, 'Well, there are no issues with me so why would a potential mate have issues?' He said, 'You're a woman and you make extremely good money and that's unusual because most of the time it's the man who is expected to be the primary breadwinner.

" 'A man wants to be able to offer the woman something and unless he's some kind of a pimp daddy kind of guy, which I know you wouldn't be interested in, the sex isn't going to be the major focus of that relationship. You're not going to be thinking that just because he makes good love to you that you're going to be paying for this or that. I can look at you and tell you're not that type. That man will have to come up with something equal to or more than what you have so you might want to face the fact that you may end up by yourself. You may have to settle.'

"I wouldn't even care about him making less money than me," Ayoka said. "He would just need to be secure in himself; regardless of what I make or what he makes and regardless of what I'm bringing to this relationship or what he's bringing to this relationship. Insecurity is what turned out to be a problem in my marriage. My husband was insecure because he didn't think I needed him. He always had this impression in the back of his mind that I could do without him. I never perceived it that way, but that's what our marriage grew to become.

"My husband made it an issue for both of us because it got to the point where if I wanted a car I'd tell him, 'I'm going to buy a new car, you're welcome to come help me pick it out,' but it was never, 'I need a new car, let's get the budget out and see if this is feasible or not.'

"I wouldn't mind having a man who wants to be in charge," Ayoka continued. "But if his major purpose in life is to bring me down to his level so I can be as miserable as he is, then I want no part of it. That's the mind-set my husband had and it was horrible. I don't want a 'yours and mine' relationship. I just want to be able to put my check in our joint account and let him pay the bills.

"I don't intend to marry anybody who's not trustworthy either, and that's why he'd have to prove himself to me. He'd have to prove that he was secure within himself before we could even get to that point. I don't have anything that I worry about financially, period. I know that God has blessed me and I'm afraid that if I'm not more humble that it could all be taken away from me. I've gotten so spoiled, I just do what I want to do, and don't think a lot about it. Yes, I make a good salary but on the other hand, I've made a lot of sacrifices too, so I think I deserve to do what I want to do."

SADIE, FIFTY-SOMETHING

I met with Sadie in her café, which was appropriately named A Cozy Little Café. For the past ten years she's owned this wonderful little place where I frequently eat lunch. I've seen women throw their weight around when they're in positions of authority, but Sadie does it with such class that her staff, comprised of about ten percent black women and ninety percent black men, in every different hue and height, seem to enjoy being ordered around by her.

A Cozy Little Café is the first black-owned and -operated upscale café I've ever been in. With jazz playing softly in the background and walls covered with pictures of people like Ella Fitzgerald, Count Basie, Duke Ellington, and The Original Savannah Band, I felt right at home and proud, sort of the way I'd felt when I visited Sylvia's, that famous restaurant in Atlanta.

Sadie greeted me at the door, a tradition she's kept over the years with each and every customer whenever possible. She was wearing a beautiful black suit, pearl pumps, and her usual bright smile. She hugged me and started talking to me in that fast Louisiana dialect as soon as I got inside. Sadie is a serious red-bone with short, curly, golden brown hair—good hair, as we often say—and beautiful light brown eyes.

"Sit down, baby, and excuse the 'church clothes.' I'm only dressed this way because I had a meeting this morning and I haven't had time to change yet," she explained. "Would you like some juice or coffee?"

"I'll have some coffee, thank you," I said while admiring her attire. "I love that suit." She motioned to a waiter and told him to bring a pot of coffee, two cups, and plenty of cream and sugar, since we both drink it the same way—a little coffee with a lot of cream.

"Thank you, baby," Sadie told the waiter. "I hope you don't mind if I slip my shoes off. I like to look good, but I like to feel good too, and right now my feet are killing me."

"Go right ahead," I replied. "I certainly know that feeling."

"So, you and your sister are writing a book, huh? What do you want me to talk about?" she asked.

"Talk about how you were raised and go from there," I suggested.

"Okay, to start with, I was the seventh of eight children, but the eighth one, a baby girl, died at birth. Since I ended up being the youngest and the last girl, after my mother had five boys in a row, I was treated a little bit special by my daddy. We were extremely close. I think he favored me over the other kids, which was wrong, but that's just the way it was, and I favored him over my mother. We were a close-knit twosome, and the boys protected me hundred percent.

"I was never allowed to date, and I was never allowed to have company like most teenage girls. Whenever I went out, I went out with my brothers to places where other teenagers went to dance. My parents owned a small café, so I would spend a lot of my time there because that's where they were most of the time." Sadie motioned to her surroundings. "A lot of the decor I have in here came from their place. No matter where I went, I had to get permission from both my parents, and one of my brothers would be there to take care of me and walk me back home.

"Put that over there, darling," Sadie said, winking at one of her sexy young waiters and making him blush. "I was a tomboy, so it didn't bother me to have my brothers along.

"It wasn't until my junior and senior year in high school that I realized I didn't have the freedom that other girls had. They could go out on dates and ride in cars with boys and I was never able to do that, so I had to slip out a couple of times. You know, you got out and did your little thing with the little boys, the normal teenage stuff that kids do. A couple of my girlfriends slipped out one time too many and got pregnant, which scared me to death because I loved my father so much I didn't want to take the chance of hurting him that way. Especially since my sister had gotten pregnant and had to get married at fifteen years old, then had another baby by the time she was seventeen. By the time that baby was born, she was separated and had moved back home, but to make matters worse, she ended up getting pregnant two more times by her boyfriend. Now remember, she was separated, not divorced, and had the nerve to get pregnant by another man, twice.

"That in itself was a big thing because you just didn't do that back then, so Daddy put her out. It was terrible, just terrible, and I'll never forget the look on her face when Daddy packed her shit up and told her she had to go. Then her husband filed for divorce, so she didn't really have anywhere she could go. Mama and Daddy took custody of her two older kids to make it easier for her. Daddy said she was unfit to be a mother since she'd gotten pregnant by another man, so he didn't want her raising them anyway. I was still very young at that time, probably about ten years old, so I grew up with her kids. She rented the house right across from ours and her boyfriend moved in with her. He was a light-skinned black man with blue eyes and blond hair. Daddy would hardly ever let her two oldest children go over to visit because he didn't like the boyfriend, so she always had to come to our house. It was a terrible thing.

"Because of what happened to her, I was scared to do anything wrong. I didn't want Daddy to think badly of me; I wanted to remain his favorite. My sister was family, but it was clear to me that she wasn't loved the way I was. Daddy would hug me and say, 'Hey, Miss Sadie, how's Daddy's baby?' But with my sister it was like, 'Hey, how you doin'? Y'all doin' okay?' He treated her like family but not like close family. They never did get close because Daddy felt that any woman who'd do something like that wasn't a good woman. Now, men could do that kind of thing all the time. He did it himself. But quiet as it's kept, I knew Mama was a cat, too. I just kept my eyes open and my mouth shut."

Sadie noticed the head waiter trying to get her attention. "Okay, sweetheart, you can just leave those liquor receipts on my desk," she said with another flirty wink. Damn, she had a way with these men. They just grinned and bowed at her every word, and you could tell she enjoyed the flirting as much as they did.

She gave me her attention once more. "Honey, these young men are something. They love older women and I love young men. They work hard for me, and it don't cost me anything extra to be nice.

"As I was saying, Daddy was a good-looking man, looked like an Indian with green eyes. He had a pocketful of money all the time and this straight black hair that he'd slick back. The women would just go crazy over him, young and old. I think he always had girlfriends but I found out that Mama had a boyfriend too, a man she'd known all her life who had been married to her best friend. I guess before this man's wife died, they'd all been good friends. His wife died at a young age, you know how some women died young back then. I guess she was like thirty-one or thirty-two at that time. Anyway, she died and Mama used to date her husband—I know this for a fact.

"I never saw them together, but I remember that whenever she'd get mad at Daddy she'd say she was walking to the bus station so she could catch the bus, and I'd watch her. The first couple of times it happened I was running and crying because I thought my mama was leaving. When I got close enough to see what was going on, I hid to watch and see if she got on the bus to leave, but there was never a bus. Instead, a man whose face I couldn't make out would be there in his old coupe and they'd take off going toward town. When I saw that I figured Mama was okay and that he was probably taking her somewhere to cool off and would bring her back home later that night, but she didn't come home that night. She had relatives who lived about thirty miles from where we lived and she'd stay over a few days. Then Daddy would go make up with her and bring her back home. I started paying attention to this cycle, and I figured out what was going on, but I'd never tell my daddy because I knew better. He would've killed her because even though he was a soft-hearted person, he was deadly if you made him mad.

"At the café when people were acting ugly, he'd say, 'Look here, don't do that. Just leave. Leave right now.' But when he said, 'God-damnit, I said leave,' you knew he was going to pull a gun and shoot at somebody because he was really mad when he used that word. He hardly ever cursed, so even at home, when he said 'damnit' all of us would get up from the table because we knew he was mad and things were going to get bad. Mama—and Lord knows I'm just like her—was kind of quiet, but she could curse like a damn sailor when she got the slightest bit pissed off.

"When I finished high school I moved to Los Angeles with one of my brothers. I met my husband a year after I was there. I was young and not real street-smart, but I knew a good man when I saw one, so we got married five months after we met. It was wonderful for the first fifteen years while I was at home raising the children, but when they got old enough to take care of themselves in the evenings, I decided to go back to school and that was a problem because my husband felt threatened.

"I still went anyway, and by the time our oldest child was in high school, I had my degree, and had given a lot of thought to opening and running my own business. But when I mentioned the idea of a café, he hit the roof and told me he didn't understand why I couldn't just be happy as a wife and mother. He said he'd always tried to make things comfortable so I wouldn't have to work. He couldn't under-stand why I wanted to start my own business.

"I'd enjoyed raising my children, but I didn't want to go through life not having achieved anything on my own and always being dependent on him. Marriage is not a guarantee for a com-fortable life, and the café was supposed to be a family business; I wanted the kids to learn how to run it so they'd have a sense of what it was like to be self-employed and make their own business decisions. It's good that we encourage our kids to go to college and get degrees, but we also need to teach them to bring some of that knowledge back to their own neighborhoods.

"I used to think this café would be the end of our marriage, but we've been together so long now, what's the use in either one of us starting all over again? Of course, we've had our ups and downs and both of us have done our share of wrong, but it all came together once we both matured. After I'd been married for a while I realized I wasn't going to find everything I was looking for in one man. That's just not possible.

"I had to look at the things that were most important to me and just deal with the rest because there is no perfect mate," Sadie said. "I think women go into marriage thinking he'll eventually want to do everything it takes to make us happy, that he'll change in the areas we want him to change in, but usually that doesn't happen. We're not perfect, and neither are men, but we have to mature to the point where we can deal with that and learn to concentrate on their strengths rather than their weaknesses. Bitching at a man all the time won't change him, it will only make things worse, believe me.

"I'm not saying women should lower their expectations. I'm just saying that love and marriage is only what you make it. Sometimes you have to give a little more than you get, but in the long run, it will all work out, as long as you've got a decent man.

"My husband and I had our fights when we were young, but I learned from my parents that loving someone means you try to work things out. Love keeps you around and keeps you going, even through the bad times. If your man has good family values and he's a good husband and father by your standards, then you might have to put up with some shit every now and then. If you can pack up and leave when you get into a little argument because he says something like, 'You bitch too much,' then you weren't in love anyway because you'll take a lot if you love your man. You'll take an ass whipping if you know you've done something wrong. I don't care what these women are telling their girlfriends. Some of them know they've had their ass whipped and they deserved it.

"Some women are always talking about what they will or won't do. 'Girl, I'd leave his ass if he even thought about hitting me. I don't have to take *no* shit off *no* man, and I don't know why you're staying there putting up with his shit.'

"I know better than to say what I won't do because I've taken plenty of shit from my husband and he's taken plenty from me. That's what love is all about. You know you need each other, so you don't just walk away from a relationship when you've invested your time and energy, just because you have a little spat.

"Now that I'm old enough to look back on all that, I'm glad we worked through our hard times. I think I made some good decisions and my life has turned out pretty well. I enjoyed staying home with my children for as long as I did, but I'm also happy that I stood my ground and followed my dreams because when I look around and see what I've accomplished, I can say I'm truly proud of myself."

PORSCHE, THIRTY-SOMETHING

When I drove up Porsche had already parked her brand-new Jaguar under a huge oak tree and set up everything like she owned the damn park. I'd brought along some of my famous low-fat walnut chicken salad and some fruit because I claimed to be on a diet, but here she was sitting on a blanket with a basket full of grapes, summer sausage, crackers, two types of cheese, and two bottles of wine on ice. I should've expected that, since Porsche always lived up to her nickname, "the original material girl." She even brought some wineglasses with saucers and napkins as well, and I was happy to indulge in the wine and enjoy the beautiful day.

We'd decided to meet at the park because Porsche, although very educated and proper at times, could be just as loud as she was professional, so meeting her at some nice restaurant for dinner or at a club for happy hour just wouldn't work.

As I walked up, she was grinning, satisfied with herself and her setup, and ready to talk, since she'd already had her first glass of wine. "What's up, girlfriend? I was just sitting here trying to decide what all I want to tell you." She laughed. "You know I can talk."

"You sure can, and I imagine that wine won't hinder you either," I replied. "How long have you been here? Looks like you tried to start without me."

"Oh, about thirty minutes or so. I couldn't wait to get out and enjoy the sun. Isn't it a beautiful day?" I agreed, and after spending a few minutes talking about the book idea and what was going on in our lives, Porsche cut up some of the sausage and cheese, poured herself another glass of wine, and began.

"When I was about six months old, my mother gave me to my grandparents and I lived with them until an aunt and uncle of mine who were in the military returned to the States. By then I was around two, I guess, and I lived with them until I graduated from high school and went to college. My real parents did have other children who lived with them, but I was the sixth of seven children and just happened to be the one they couldn't afford to raise or some shit like that, but we'll get into that later.

"From what I understand, my father never finished fourth grade and my mother didn't finish high school, so my immediate family was relatively poor. They lived in the projects, and my sisters and brothers didn't have a lot of the things I had. On the other hand, my aunt and uncle were pretty well off, and they gave me everything, materially, that I could ever want. But because my aunt wanted to do what she thought was right, she sent me to spend every summer with my real family, and that's where the madness began because those were the worst summers of my life.

"They never accepted me because I was different. If someone who'd never seen me before walked up and asked if I was their sister, they'd say, 'No, she ain't no kin to us. She just some girl we know.' And that really hurt my feelings. They used to call me 'baby shit yellow' and they'd make me and my younger sister compete against each other all the time. And believe it or not, my mother participated in it.

"One summer when I was seven years old and my sister was six, they asked us to spell 'ice,' a really easy word. My sister couldn't spell it, so they asked me to, and when I did, they beat me up because I could spell 'ice' and she couldn't. I'll never forget that.

"Another time my younger sister and I were fighting because they made us. I punched her in the nose and it started bleeding. Do you know my mother whipped me for punching her, and for winning the fight, even though she'd sat there and watched them instigate the whole thing? By this time I knew for sure they were crazy as hell, but I still didn't understand what was going on until years later when my father died.

"He wasn't around much during the summers when I was there; I had no relationship with him at all and only called him by his last name, Jackson, even though the other kids called him Daddy. But then, I called my mother by her first name, even though my sisters and brothers called her Mama, so that doesn't mean a whole lot, right?

"Well, my mother died a few years before, and when Jackson died I went to his funeral. I felt nothing for him at all, but I went back home to be with my so-called family. Everything was fine during the funeral, but afterward when we got back to the house and there was just us kids and close friends, I was talking with three of my four sisters and one of them brought up the fact that Jackson might not be my real father. I figured that would make sense because I don't look like anyone else in my family, and the fact that they'd kept six kids out of seven made it seem even more true. So, I asked my oldest sister and that's when the shit hit the fan. She got all upset and started crying, saying she didn't know why I would start some shit like that at a time like this. Then she had the nerve to say that every time I came home I made everyone else feel uncomfortable.

"She was screaming that I always had the best of both worlds and they never understood why I just couldn't be satisfied with that, and then accused me of being the 'golden child.' Imagine that." Porsche made a face at me.

"Still, I tried to explain my perception of my family life and tell her how I always felt like I was nobody's child with no immediate family and no one to call Mom and Dad, but she just didn't want to hear it. By this time my brothers had come from outside because of all the noise. They sided with her, of course, asking, 'Why did you even come to this funeral? You weren't really our sister anyway. You lived with our aunt and uncle.' Like I'd made that choice.

"So, I cursed them all out, and then ran outside to try to get myself together. While I was walking around the backyard, sniffling and minding my own damn business, a very good friend of my mother's came over and started trying to calm me down.

"When she finally got me to stop crying long enough to listen, she said, 'I really wish you'd asked your mother about your father while she was alive because she told me that Jackson wasn't your father.' Of course I was speechless after she dropped this bomb but she continued telling me how it happened. You know black folks can keep secrets real good when they want to, and I guess that's why it never got out. She said that my mother, two other girlfriends, and she had gone to the beach one summer in 1955 to hang out because they all had small children and needed to get away. They met a group of guys and spent the whole day drinking and partying, and one thing led to another. By the time the evening was over, a few of them ended up making out on the beach and my mother was one of them. By the time she gave me the rest of the details, I was just floored because now it all made sense.

"I asked her if she would come back in the house with me and explain this to my sisters and brothers because after all, both of our parents were dead now and there was no reason to hide the truth anymore. So she agreed and had a long talk with all of us.

"After a long silence, one of my sisters spoke up saying, 'Oh, my God. That explains it. Now we know why Daddy was always telling Mama stuff like, "You know what you did, you know what happened," every time they got into an argument.'

"I was just numb, still trying to figure out how my mother, even though she had a hard choice to make, could just give me away rather than face up to her mistake. Even though it was very obvious that she chose to ignore what she'd done, I still did not want to believe this was the reason she'd given me away like I didn't matter at all. She chose to give me away rather than have him walk out on her.

"As I sat there, listening to everybody try to make sense of this crazy shit, I reflected back on my life with my aunt and uncle. It was okay for the most part, except that they had a daughter who hated having me around. She was several years older than me and had been their only child until I entered the picture. She was very angry with me for taking all the attention that used to be hers, and was constantly saying, 'Get away from me. I don't want you here because ever since you came you've been getting all the attention.'

"Therefore, during the school year I had to deal with this fool being jealous and a real bitch, deal with my other crazy ass family during the summer, and here I was a child who had nowhere and no one to turn to. I don't think anyone even considered how I must have felt.

"I never was told that I could address my aunt and uncle as if they were my parents because they didn't want their daughter to feel insecure. And when I was old enough to discuss my feelings with my aunt she'd say, 'Baby, we give you everything, how can you feel like you're not loved?'

"I tried to explain that having everything except somebody I could call Mom and Dad, or somebody I could call when my back was against a wall, had been hard for me. I tried telling her that never in my life had anyone said they'd be there for me, and I needed to hear that. You know, having things is nice, but that's not what makes a child feel loved. Every child needs to know someone is there for them, no matter what.

"I guess I really should be thankful because I could have been raised in the projects with my sisters and brothers who had little hope for a future because my parents weren't giving them any. But I was lucky because my aunt and uncle taught me to be strong, instilled good work ethics and morals in me, and sent me to college. They would always say, 'That which does not kill you will make you stronger.' So hell, maybe that's how I survive.

"They never adopted me and one time I got up the nerve to ask my aunt why they hadn't. She said they tried, but my parents wouldn't sign the papers. Ain't that screwed up? She said that I was seven years old the last time they brought it up and she had a knockdown drag-out fight with my mother and they didn't speak for almost a year. Afterward, she just gave up. My uncle was retired military, so I could've gotten all kinds of benefits since they were raising me anyway, but for some reason, my parents wouldn't approve of it. They didn't want me but didn't want anyone else to have me either.

"With all that happened, I can't believe nobody saw how I was being affected. I finally realized my mother didn't care about me when she went on a weekend trip with her ladies' club one summer while I was there, and she came back with souvenirs for everybody but me. We were all excited and jumping up and down and shit when she opened her suitcase and started passing out stuff, but when she got to me she just said, 'Oh, I forgot you were even here.'

"That was hard, and it was also hard to go from an upper-middle-class neighborhood to the projects every summer, because I still had all my nice clothes and they had used clothes that they had gotten through this white lady, so they used to take my stuff without even asking," Porsche recalled. "The last time I went was the summer between my tenth and eleventh grade year of high school. In the community where they lived, there was a summer youth work program where they got jobs for all the teenagers, so I got a job working with the little kids at the community center.

"We'd taken the kids to the high school football stadium to play, and there were some boys there who didn't work at the center, and my brother was with them. They were standing by some concrete bleachers and they were like, 'Hey, come over here.' Since my brother was standing over there I went. I didn't think anything of it. Well, they grabbed me and pulled me behind the bleachers and started pushing me around between themselves, talking about how they were going to find out what I was all about. I tried to get away, but one of the bigger guys grabbed me and the next thing I know, one had his hand over my mouth, one was holding me down, and the other one was taking my clothes off. I was literally about to be raped while my asshole of a brother acted as the lookout, because they had me naked all the way down to my panties. Then, all of a sudden, my brother said someone was coming, and they stopped and ran off, just laughing like it was the funniest thing they'd ever seen.

"I was scared to death, but what was worse, my own brother just stood there and did nothing. I know he would have been ready to fight if that had been one of my sisters, but I guess he didn't feel the same way toward me. After that I thought, 'This is crazy. I am not subjecting myself to this kind of cruelty.' And I decided if they didn't want me in their crazy, dysfunctional ass family that was fine with me.

"I didn't even tell my so-called mother what had happened. Instead, I called my aunt as soon as I could sneak to the phone, and told her I was never going to spend the summer there again. I told her what had happened, and she asked to speak to my mother. About ten minutes later my mother told me to pack my shit. She said I was a liar and that I thought I was too good to stay there, so I left on the bus that night and never went back for the summer again.

"I graduated from high school two years later and went to a college as far away from home as I could, and for a while I was successful at getting away from those skeletons in my past. I got my master's degree, got married, and completed med school, but my family didn't even come to my graduation. Actually, I only see them about every four years or so because even though they know the truth, they're still crazy as hell. They will never acknowledge me as part of the family, as if I'd want them to anyway, and I refuse to spend my whole life trying to fit in with people who want to hold a grudge for something none of us had any control over."

"It is clear to me that all the things that happened during my childhood and the things I found out about my mom and dad had a major impact on my decisions about marriage and having children. I always wanted to get married, but as you well know, I don't have the best marriage in the world and I know my childhood played a big part in my deciding not to have children. I didn't feel comfortable with the thought of being a mother when I never knew what a real mother was supposed to do. I'm a damn good physician and I worked my ass off to get the education for that, but children don't require a degree, nor do they come with a handbook, so I wouldn't know how to nurture a child because that's something I never experienced.

"Besides, that's the reason there are so many screwed-up people in the world already; people have kids when they know good and damn well they don't have what it takes to be a good parent. If your parents weren't worth a damn, then they probably didn't teach you how to be a good parent either. How could they? You should just spare some poor, little, sweet child the expense of being born if you know this in advance, and choose another road in life."

MARCELLA, FORTY-SOMETHING

Marcella, a strong Venezuelan woman, was raised in Trinidad and has a beautiful accent. Listening to her always makes me long for the beaches and clear blue water of her childhood home, and when she speaks of her life in Trinidad, where we Americans spend millions of dollars to vacation, one can only wonder why she chose to leave such a beautiful place.

Marcella invited me to her home for the interview, and when I walked in, the first thing she did was tell me to take my shoes off and "get com-for-ta-ble." You know how people from the islands who have that accent seem to pronounce every syllable in a word? Well, she still does that even though she's been here for over twenty years, but I find it alluring because you'd think she was born and raised right here in America, until you hear her speak.

Her place was small, spotless, and filled with many beautiful pieces she'd brought from Trinidad and other surrounding islands on her frequent visits, and she could tell you anything you wanted to know about each piece. The pride with which she spoke was obvious and again made me wonder why she chose to move to America. I silently decided that if she didn't tell me why, I would ask.

"I was born in Venezuela, South America, but we moved to Trinidad when I was six years old because my father was a schoolteacher and got transferred there, so even though I'm really Venezuelan all I know is Trinidad because that's where I was raised.

"My father was a heavy drinker. But back then in Trinidad when a person who was well known got drunk, they would take him to a jail cell, leave him to let him sleep it off overnight, and then take him home. My father died when he was in jail because he had cirrhosis of the liver and no one knew.

"That left my mother alone to raise all of us, which she did by ironing white people's clothes to support us. There were four of us and, O Lord, a lot of hard times, a lot of hunger. I remember it as plain as day. Let me tell you something—we walked to school maybe a good five miles a day, back and forth. And in the evening time, when Mommy didn't get any work, when we hit our door coming back home from school we didn't know if there would be food in there for us or not. Sometimes we'd have food, sometimes we didn't, so we'd drink coffee, eat bread, and go to sleep. I remember one time Mommy bought some bread because that was all she could afford, and she fed all of us and didn't eat one piece herself because she wanted us to have enough. There were times when my baby brother would sit down and suck his thumb and go to sleep hungry. He was just weak because he was so hungry.

"Things got a little better as we grew up because all of us started working. I started washing people's clothes and baking for money, and I learned to cook by watching Mommy. The railroad was really big there and we used to cook food and sell it to those guys who worked on the railroad, so that helped a bit.

"When I was fourteen years old, my mother went to work one day and didn't come home that evening. I was the oldest and we were in the house hungry for a whole week, so we finally started thinking that she'd abandoned us because times were so hard. We were there by ourselves with no food, no nothing, but in Trinidad your neighbor is your friend, so we would just eat at a different house every day. If they had food, we'd have food. If we had food, we shared. Everybody shared just like a little African village.

"Finally, my godmother called the police and they put a missing person's report out on my mother. When the police finally located her, they told us that she'd been on her way back home from work and the driver of the taxi she was in fell asleep at the wheel and ran into a parked truck that was full of lumber. Mommy had been in the hospital for a whole week unconscious. No one knew who she was or nothing. When we went to see her, she was still unconscious; she stayed in a coma for a whole month. She had terrible head injuries, a broken jaw, and she'd lost all her front teeth. It was just terrible. She was lucky she even lived.

"So, my godmother took care of us, but I had to quit school for a whole year because my baby brother was like nine months old. Then when my mommy got out of the hospital, she couldn't work at all, so I continued to wash and bake bread for people. We had a thing you call sweet bread so I would bake sweet bread and make dinners for people, and we used the money I made to take care of everybody in my family. The neighbors really started helping us because they felt sorry for us. They were giving us food and that was really a blessing, but we were still poor and had to struggle.

"Anyway, Mommy stayed sick for a long, long time. She didn't remember anything, and she was peeing on herself, and it was like I was the head of the house by the age of fifteen. Then, finally, when I was about seventeen and about to finish high school, Mommy got well and things started to get better. I got my first real job as a maid, going to people's houses to clean and everything, and that's also when I met my son's father. I was ignorant about sex, so I got pregnant by the time I was nineteen, but we didn't get married, even though my mother begged me to marry him. I didn't really love him, so I wouldn't marry him because I didn't want to spend my whole life being miserable. I'm glad I didn't marry him because he started doing some really crazy things right after I found out I was pregnant.

"I had my son and shortly after that, I was working for this American couple who were getting ready to come back to the United States. They asked me if I wanted to come, but I told them I didn't know nobody in the States, so why would I want to go there? After they explained the wonderful opportunities I'd have, I decided to go with them. I sent my son to stay with his father's mother until I could get on my feet, and I followed the couple to New York.

"Once we arrived and got settled, they told me I could continue to live with them, but they no longer expected me to work for them. They were only helping me to be nice, and I was very fortunate to have them do that for me. I found a job working for another family, taking care of their children and cleaning and cooking for them. But I didn't like New York because the family I was staying with was different. I wasn't fast and I didn't use drugs or anything. I'd never even been exposed to drugs.

"Well, one day they left a whole bunch of stuff on the coffee table, and I was like, 'Why do they have all that grass and dirt on the coffee table? What is all this?' I figured they were really nasty, and, girl, I vacuumed all the stuff off the table, stuff that just happened to be marijuana. I was twenty-one years old, and I didn't even know how marijuana looked. I thought the kids had just brought dirt in from outside and put it on the coffee table. I dusted everything off and cleaned the house and vacuumed the marijuana off the table—like maybe two pounds of it—and when they came home they had a fit.

"See, at home we did different things for fun, like go to the beach and play like kids because that's what we were, kids coming up. I didn't have all that other stuff to worry about.

"A lot of people back home get high but my mother is very old-fashioned, so we didn't know nothing. Even when I started my period, all she said was that I'd become a young lady. I was outside and had sat down to eat some soup, but when I opened my legs and saw this red stuff I thought the soup had messed my stomach up and caused me to bleed. I didn't know nothing about a period and I was thirteen years old.

"I didn't like the situation at the house where I was working so I wrote this friend of mine in Trinidad who had a brother in Rhode Island, and he said I could come there and stay, so I did and he and his wife and kids were a real nice, decent family.

"About a week after I got there, he started helping me to get information on the many schools available, and I just couldn't believe it. This country offers many opportunities and that's the reason Caribbeans, Africans, Indians, Asians, Iranians, and all these other foreigners come here and end up more educated than people born here. Americans take education for granted, but most foreigners will get here and find a way to educate every last one of their children.

"Just go to a high school graduation ceremony. You'll notice that when the awards and scholarships are being given out they can hardly pronounce the names. The majority of the children receiving scholarships are foreign. You seldom hear them call many Smiths, Joneses, or Shaquita whatevers—and when you do, it's usually for an athletic scholarship. I don't understand that, especially for black American parents because they have had to struggle so hard. You think they'd encourage their children to excel in school so they won't have it as hard as they did, but many of them don't even mention the word 'college' until the child is a senior in high school.

"Shortly after I moved to Rhode Island, I started going to this school they call OIC, an adult educational center they have up north where you get your GED, and they help you find jobs and stuff. I had my high school diploma, but since I wasn't raised in the States, they helped me to take a few courses I needed and then I got a job through them. During that time I met this girl from Texas and we became real good friends. After about two years she told me she was going back home to Texas, and asked me if I wanted to come with her. I didn't have anything holding me in Rhode Island so I worked and saved enough money for a ticket, and I've been in Texas every since."

EBONI, FORTY-SOMETHING

Eboni looked as cool as a cucumber with her new short haircut. She'd lit a few candles earlier and the scent of eucalyptus was all over the room. She turned the jazz music down low so we could talk, but then her phone started to ring. When she didn't answer, the person on the other end wouldn't leave a message; they just hung up and called right back repeatedly. She finally gave in and answered it, snapped at him that she was too busy to talk, and told him she'd call him later. Looking at her you'd never think she was well into her forties because she had the figure of a woman twenty years younger. If she was wearing some kind of body shaper beneath that dress and it made her look that good, I was thinking, sign me up for one right now because it was doing one hell of a job. Only if you looked real closely could you see the fine lines etched across her forehead.

Eboni's living room looked like something out of the *Architectural Digest*. It was spotless and perfectly decorated with taupe leather sofas covered with oversized pillows. Authentic pieces of African woodwork and black art were strategically placed throughout the room. On her dining-room wall there was a beautiful rug made from Kente cloth and straw. She'd purchased it during her honeymoon on the Ivory Coast. Even the lamps and tables looked like they were made especially to go with her other furniture.

Although the furniture was obviously too large for the small condo she'd recently moved into, it had probably fit perfectly well in the half-million-dollar home she'd left a year ago.

When I complimented her on how beautiful and cozy her place was, she forced a smile and said, "Oh, thank you. I guess it'll do. Would you like something to drink?"

Since Eboni was newly divorced, I guess "cozy" wasn't exactly the right word to use. She seemed a little down, which was unlike her. I knew about the divorce, but this had been her second marriage, and even though the divorce had been final for six months, it seemed as if she was still dwelling on it.

I didn't press the issue or ask any questions about what had happened. I figured that would come up once she loosened up. Instead, I let her talk about her childhood and teenage years, hoping that reminiscing on better days would bring back good memories to help cheer her up.

"I was the oldest child, and I had a good childhood because I got everything I wanted," she began. "I was the only child for six years and when they had a second baby, my brother, I was very jealous. I couldn't stand the fact that he was getting any attention because I wanted it all. One day, when he was about a year old, I walked him outside and put him in an ant bed, thinking the ants would take him down into the hole. But, child, when those ants started biting him and he started screaming and hollering, my mama and daddy came running outside and my daddy whipped my ass all the way back to the house while my mama was trying her best to get those ants off my brother. I thought they were being mean to me because all I wanted was to be their only child. I really didn't think I'd done anything wrong.

"Now, I loved my mama, but I was really close to my daddy. Even though he made it obvious that he hadn't wanted a daughter, I learned to make him happy by trying to do anything a boy could do because I felt that way I could win his heart. He was a big black man with a beautiful smile that I adored, so I learned to cut the yard, climb trees, whatever, just so I could see that smile. But then he came to expect me to do these things, which kind of bothered me because it was making me tough. When I became a teenager, he got mad at me one day and said, 'You should've been a boy 'cause you're always out to get what you want,' and that didn't make sense because he'd made me that way by being so hard on me.

"My mama gave me love, but Daddy taught me how to think like a man because he was really hard on me. If I fell down and skinned my knees and started crying he would say, 'What you cryin' for? Cryin' don't help nothing. Get up and clean your face and quit actin' like a baby.' And I would do it. One time I fell off my bicycle and broke my arm, and he threatened to whip me if I didn't learn how to ride without falling off.

"My grandparents lived in East Texas, in the country, and me and my brother went down there every summer to visit. I must admit, now that I'm grown, that it was a beautiful place. But as a kid, we were bored because there was nothing to do but sit out on the front porch and wave at the few neighbors who passed by or go swimming in our cutoff shorts and T-shirts with our cousins.

"They had what you call a tank that we swam in, but they also stocked catfish and perch in there and we actually ate them. Whenever we wanted some fresh fish we'd just take our cane poles and go catch some for big mama to clean and fry, and you talk about good eating. I think that was the best fish I've ever eaten.

"They also had chickens and hogs and stuff, and one summer when we were down there and had just come back from swimming in the tank, my grandpa and daddy were catching chickens for dinner. We stood there and watched while they caught those chickens and wrung their necks. Then my daddy told me to catch one after it slipped by him, so I ran after it and caught it, but I was scared to death. I held it out in front of me for one of my cousins to take, but my daddy said, 'Gal, go on and wring that chicken's neck. I know you ain't scared of a little old chicken.' Of course, I couldn't show that I really was scared, so I had to do what I was told.

"Even today when I think about it I want to cry. I closed my hands around that chicken's neck and I could feel the softness of its feathers and the warmth of its body. I started swinging it around, like Daddy and Grandpa had done, but I guess I was swinging it around too slow and Daddy thought I was playing, so he hit me on the shoulder with his razor strap and told me to quit playing. I wanted to cry so bad, but instead I closed my eyes and started swinging the chicken around faster and faster. It seems like I swung it around forever until I heard my daddy finally tell me to let it go. When I opened my eyes, the chicken's head was in my hands."

Eboni looked straight through me. "You just don't know how that felt. I've always tried to put that out of my mind, but every time I have to cut up a chicken, it takes me right back to my grandpa's farm, standing in the yard with all that blood on my hands.

"The things Daddy taught me made me strong, but that also made it hard for me to show affection because he didn't show much affection toward me. I feel affectionate, but it's just hard for me to show it. I knew my daddy loved me because he spent a lot of time with me and taught me things about life. But I never felt like I had his unconditional love, and I was always trying to prove myself to him so he wouldn't think I was weak, but I never understood why he felt that way about me, and I didn't ask.

"You know how it was when we were coming up. Our parents didn't feel they needed to explain anything like that to us," Eboni recalled. "They were the parents and we were the kids, so we just did as we were told. We lived on the rough side of town, so I guess Daddy wanted me to learn how to stand up for myself. Besides, I had to be my brother's protector because he was always running his big mouth and getting into something, and I had to fight for him.

"One time he was fighting this boy and the boy put a sleep hold on him. That's when you put pressure on a certain part of a person's body and make them pass out. Well, I thought the boy had killed my brother and I got scared. I was scared and mad because I knew I had to go home, but I couldn't go home without my brother. So, I picked up a brick and hit the boy in the head and his parents threatened to file an assault charge on me. When my brother came around and I took him home and told Daddy what had happened, all he said was, 'Did you kick that boy's ass who was messing with your brother?' I said, 'Yes, sir.' And he said, 'Well, you done damn good.'

"As I started to mature, I also started filling out. I'd never been heavy because I was such a tomboy and was so active, but I never gave any thought to the fact that one day I would have breasts and hips, let alone a well-shaped ass.

"Well, one day when I was about thirteen, a boy, who I'd secretly liked, squeezed my butt as I was passing him in the hall. I turned around and swung at him so hard that I almost fell down, but I missed. Then I got so mad I wanted to cry, but it wasn't because he was laughing at me, it was because when he touched me I had this funny feeling inside that I'd never felt before. I didn't understand what was going on with my body, so I just cursed him and walked away.

"When I got home that day and started to change clothes, I looked in the mirror at my reflection and there I was, a young lady. I had changed without even noticing it myself, and then I really did start crying. My mama heard me, so when she came into my room and I told her about what had happened at school, she just laughed and took it as an opportunity to explain the facts of life. From that day on, I struggled with my femininity because on the one hand I wanted to be tough, but on the other hand I began to look at boys differently. I really started to like them.

"I began to talk to boys more, as friends at first, and by my freshman year in high school I had my first boyfriend who convinced me to try out for cheerleader. Of course my parents didn't feel I was old enough for a boyfriend, and they let me know right away that being a cheerleader did not mean I was going to be allowed to hang out at school or anyplace else unless I was practicing or cheering. As my daddy put it, 'Just go ahead and tell all them little hardheaded, slick-ass boys that being a cheerleader don't mean you can take company or date or anything else, so they won't make the mistake of knocking on my door.'

"Boys came by anyway, but we had to act like we were buddies and I had to act rough so my daddy wouldn't think anything was going on. If a boy wanted to kiss me, he'd pay my little brother, who was always conveniently nearby, to go around the corner for a few minutes and be the lookout while we were kissing. Really, the only time I got to do any socializing other than at school was when I went skating on Saturday evenings. That's where I would get to be with my so-called boyfriend, but even then my parents would pick me up at 7:00 P.M.

"Still, I was determined to have my fun, so I started sneaking and doing things. I started lying about where I had to go so I could be with my boyfriend, and, baby, I was screwing every chance I got. They didn't really let me go on a date where a boy could come to the house and pick me up until I was a senior in high school, but by then I'd already figured out how to do what I wanted to, even with an early curfew.

"On my first real date I got pregnant because I was seventeen and thought I knew what I was doing, trying to use that damn withdrawal method. I figured that shit must be for old folks because it's almost impossible to get a seventeen-year-old boy to quit in the heat of the moment. Of course, my parents were devastated and from that point on, I felt like I had to prove myself to everybody. Here I was, a straight-A student, a cheerleader, my daddy's heart, and I'd made the worst mistake I thought I could make. All I could think about when I found out was that Daddy had told me over and over again, 'Don't be out there making mistakes with your life 'cause mistakes are for weak people.'

"Even though I got pregnant, I've never viewed myself as being weak. I finished high school before my baby was born, but I still hadn't learned anything because I compounded the situation by getting pregnant a second time when my son was about thirteen months old, and then I thought my daddy would die for sure. He talked about me so bad that I thought I'd never get over it. But again, it only made me stronger."

BIANCA, THIRTY-SOMETHING

I couldn't wait to get to Emel's, the dinner club where I was meeting Bianca. It had been a long, busy day at work. I was starving, and I always looked forward to ordering their blackened cajun shrimp salad, so this interview came at an ideal time for me.

Since it was still early, barely 4:00 P.M., the place was fairly empty and quiet when I arrived. Emel's has several cozy little nooks and crannies you can hide in if you're looking for a little privacy, and it would be a while before the evening crowd started showing up.

As soon as I was seated and had ordered my drink, Bianca showed up looking all chic. I just don't understand why this girl doesn't have men falling all over her. She's a single, professional woman in her thirties, has no children, and has a wonderful personality. She recently moved into her own custom-built home and drives a beautiful Land Rover. But she says that's part of the problem. She says the only kind of guys she seems to meet are the wrong kind. Either they have nothing and want a sugar mama, or they feel intimidated because they think she has too much and doesn't need a man.

"Hey, beautiful," she said as she walked into the room with that gorgeous hair flying behind her. "I'm sorry I'm late, but you know how that traffic can be."

"Girl, I just barely got here myself, so you're fine. You look so pretty. Where in the world are you coming from in those cute boots and that short skirt? I wish I could wear something like that."

"The mall, girl," she replied. "You know Foley's is having a Red Apple Sale, and I couldn't miss it. I worked through lunch and then left early so I could beat the crowd, and I'll probably go over to the club for a little while when we finish, so I had to be dressed for the occasion. Did you already order something to drink?"

"Yeah, I'm having my favorite—rum and Coke, and I've already told the waiter what I want to eat because I'm starving. He'll be right back with my drink so you can order then. Isn't this place nice?"

"Very nice," she agreed. "This would be a good place to have dinner with a date."

Bianca started talking as soon her drink came. She was telling me so much so fast I had to interrupt and tell her we should just go ahead and start before the food came, so we did.

"Okay, you know I'm from Pasadena, California, and I was an only child. My mother didn't work outside our home when I was a kid, and my dad was an engineer for an architectural company, so he traveled a lot. Therefore my mother and I were very close because we were always together. She made friends with a few of our neighbors, but I can't recall her ever really being close with anyone besides me. When Dad was home, he was either working on his next project, watching TV, or sleeping, so he didn't spend much time with me or with my mother, and I used to feel sorry for her because she seemed so lonely at times.

"Mother kept me busy with dance lessons and modeling classes because she grew up poor and always said she wanted to make sure I was 'well rounded,' but to me most of that stuff was boring. Our weekends were full of dance recitals and plays and stuff like that, and she was happy as long as we were running around all weekend. I felt she was trying to keep herself occupied because by having me involved in these things, she didn't really have a life.

"As soon as I started middle school, I told her I didn't want to take ballet anymore. I was tired of going to recitals and I just wanted to hang out in the neighborhood and be with my friends on weekends. So she let me stop, and then enrolled me in African dance at the local black arts school where all the black girls went, and I loved it.

"Let me tell you about my hardworking dad before we go any further. When I was about seventeen years old, I found out my dad had another woman and another daughter in Denver, Colorado, and the other daughter was already ten when I found out.

"It was a trip the way it happened, because the woman actually came to our door when he was away on business, and told my mother everything. We were sitting down, getting ready to eat dinner one evening when the doorbell rang and I went to answer it. There was this little white woman who looked like she used to be attractive with a little girl, who looked like she was mixed, standing there looking pitiful. She asked for my mother, and I told her I'd go get her, and she said, 'Tell her that her husband's other wife is at the door,' just like that.

"My mother was acting all calm and cool. But I was like, 'What does she mean his other wife?' I was ready to kick her ass just for ringing the doorbell, but my mother gently grabbed my hand and squeezed it, indicating that she had the situation under control.

"She invited the woman in and offered her some dinner, and let her sit there and cry and tell her little sob story. But Mother kept a straight face and ate her dinner the entire time. Then, when the woman got through, my mother put her fork down, looked right in her face, and smiled and said, 'Honey, I already knew all that shit you just told me. This ain't no surprise.

" 'I know who you are and where you're from. I know what day that baby was born, and I know your address and just about everything else about you. But you know what? I know what my last name is too, and I know that I live in this nice house, I don't work, and I ain't gonna work unless I feel like it. And even though my husband might've been stupid enough to have an affair with you, he's not fool enough to divorce me and move in with you permanently because he knows that if he does, I'm taking his ass to the bank.

" 'I'm taking this house, half of his current income, half of his retirement, and all of his dreams because he should have thought about who he married before he went out there and got you pregnant. I'm from the old school, see? As long as my husband is taking care of me and my child financially, and I'm living easy without having to worry about anything, I don't really give a damn what he does when he's supposedly working all over the country.

" 'So even though I feel a little bit sorry for you, I can't help you because you knew he was married in the first place. I am not about to conspire with you to run down a black man, especially when that black man is my husband. And as far as I'm concerned, we never had this conversation.'

"Then my mother politely walked the woman to the front door while patting her on the back, and told her everything would be alright, while I sat there in awe of her.

"Here I was, thinking my mother was a proper little lady who just didn't want to make waves, when she had already planned our future without so much as lifting a finger. I'll tell you, that really taught me how much strength a black woman can have.

"I wanted her to whip the woman's ass for even having the audacity to come to our house. You know, white women can be bold. But she made me swear that I'd keep this to myself, and I felt like if she could be that patient and that strong, so could I.

"About five years ago, she finally filed for divorce. I guess she got tired of the game she'd had to play for so many years. She moved to Phoenix and bought a nice little condo and a brand-new Acura with the money she'd saved," Bianca laughed. "She also has a boyfriend who's ten years younger than she and he just adores her. She's happier than I've ever seen her.

"I sometimes wish I was more like my mother. I made a lot of mistakes when I was younger, and I think I'm still paying the price for that." She tried to tug her short skirt down so the waiter wouldn't trip and drop the drinks he was carrying because he was so busy staring. "I started having sex when I was sixteen and haven't stopped since. Matter of fact, it's been one of my favorite pastimes in life.

"Unfortunately, when I was sixteen I didn't do any of the things I should've done to protect myself, so by the time I was seventeen, I got pregnant. This was during the late seventies and my mother had always been very open with me about a lot of things, but she wasn't open enough to say, 'When you think you want to start having sex, come talk to me. Maybe there's something we can do.' She probably felt like she might have been condoning it if she'd offered to take me to the doctor to put me on birth control.

"I was very thin as a teenager because I'd been dancing since I was a little girl. When you're in dance, you don't even think about gaining any extra weight. Because I was so slender I was able to hide my pregnancy for three months, almost to the point where it was too late to have an abortion. When my mother found out about it, she asked, even though it was a year too late, why I hadn't used any birth control. But since she hadn't discussed birth control with me, I wasn't aware of all the options out there."

Bianca had ordered some of Emel's famous hot wings, and she bit into one before she continued talking. "I was in this career enhancement program in high school, so I went to school half a day and worked as a receptionist at this small insurance company the other half. One day I was at work in the bathroom crying, and my supervisor, a black lady, came in and asked, 'How far along are you, Bianca?' She was the kind of woman you could tell anything to, so I felt comfortable telling her the truth. I was so amazed that this woman who barely even knew me could see what kind of trouble I was in right off the bat. I told her about my pregnancy and how I had kept it a secret from my mother. I cried even harder when she said I had to tell my parents because they needed to know what was going on.

"That same day I went home and told my mother. Of course, my dad was out of town. I can remember the exact day and time I told her. She was in the kitchen cooking my favorite meal—chicken fried steak with gravy, mashed potatoes, and green peas. She was seasoning the steak with salt and pepper when I walked into the kitchen and was about to roll it in flour when I told her. I just blurted it out, 'Mother, I'm pregnant.'

"She dropped the bag of flour on the floor, it burst, and flour went everywhere. She ignored the mess and turned off the skillet that had just begun to heat with oil, and looked at me, devastated. She had that 'What did I do wrong?' look in her eyes. After all, she was a stay-at-home mom and had enrolled me in dance and music lessons, and took me to plays and museums to make sure I got a well-rounded education. This wasn't supposed to happen to us. Her whole face froze as she sat down, and her hands began to tremble. Then she was talking to herself, saying she didn't understand how she hadn't seen the signs.

"She bought me a pack of Kotex every month and she thought I'd been using them because the empty packages always ended up in the trash. But all along, I'd been wrapping the unused Kotex in tissue and throwing them in the trash."

Bianca caught the waiter as he was passing by and asked for more ranch dressing for the hot wings. "After my mother got over the initial shock of my pregnancy she said, just as bluntly as I'd announced it, 'You don't need a child. What in the world are you going to do with a baby? You're only seventeen years old, blah, blah, blah.' I knew I didn't need a child and that I wasn't willing to put my life on hold to raise one, but my decision to go ahead and have an abortion was based on her telling me straight out, 'I am not going to help you raise a baby, so you do what you have to do.'

"The abortion was expensive because I was so far along. It cost almost $600, and my mother had to borrow the money from a great-aunt so my dad wouldn't find out and blame her. I don't know what excuse she gave my aunt. I just know she didn't want to take the money out of the family account because she was afraid my dad would get suspicious.

"A week later we went to a clinic in Dallas and they did a sonogram and then gave me a local anesthetic. By that time I was sixteen weeks along but the technician wouldn't tell me whether it was a boy or a girl. All she asked was, 'Where in the world is your baby? You don't even look like you're pregnant.' I'll never forget lying on that table because at sixteen weeks, I knew my baby was fully developed. The whole time I was there, a Lionel Richie tape was playing—the one that had 'Penny Lover' on it. To this very day, whenever I hear that song, I have to hold back tears.

"It wasn't long after I had the abortion that my mother asked me if I thought I should go on the pill. It was a year too late, but at least she'd finally asked me. When I didn't say no like she clearly wanted me to, I think she was hurt. It was like I hadn't learned my lesson. She thought I chose to take the pill because I wanted to continue having sex. But in reality, I was choosing not to get caught up in another situation where I might have to abort another baby."

Bianca offered me the last hot wing. "I guess what I'm telling you is this: If I had to do it all over again, I would've waited to start dating, and to start having sex, because once a girl has sex for the first time and enjoys it, it's too easy to say yes to the next guy you really care about. Even when you know it's a dead-end relationship and sex won't make it any better."

DATING

SADIE, FIFTY-SOMETHING

"I did get married when I was young, but I was single for a little
while too. And just because I got married young, that don't mean
anything, because I'm still a woman and I still made mistakes and
did things I probably shouldn't have. You know what I mean? I
like men, period. I don't give a shit what color they are. I've had
them as black as this suit, and I've had them as white as a damn al-
bino. Color doesn't matter to me. What matters is that a man treats
me right.

"I used to date a black man who was so sexy and so beautiful I had
to pinch myself to make sure I hadn't dreamt him into being. He was
a professional man and had more things going for him than he knew
what to do with. He had the perfect job, the perfect house, the perfect car, and the perfect dick, but he treated me like shit and I put up
with it because I was young and didn't know any better. He made it
clear he wasn't the settling-down type and whenever we went out,
he'd show up late, if he decided to show up at all, then he flirted with
other women with me standing right there next to him.

"We were at a party one time and I'd left the room to go powder
my nose or something, and when I came back he'd disappeared.

I thought he'd gone to the bathroom, too, so I waited about ten minutes before I started searching for him. I stepped out front to make sure his car was still there, and then I went out back and walked around to the pool, but everyone had gone inside. As I headed back toward the house I heard this whispering and giggling coming from the pool house. Then I heard his voice.

"Well, of course I went to investigate, and there he was groping this woman's ass with both hands, and she was kissing him like her life depended on it. He acted all embarrassed and apologetic when I cleared my throat to let him know I was standing there. Then he had the nerve to blame the woman for coming on to him. I was so through with him after that I didn't know what to do, but I had to be cool because he was driving me home.

"After that, I decided to date somebody who didn't seem so wrapped up in himself, so I started seeing this guy I met at work. He was white, nice-looking, and pretty low-key with a dry sense of humor. He'd been after me for some time, but I was worried about what my brother would say, so at first I didn't want to date him. But then after that other asshole I was dating messed up, I decided I'd try it and I must admit, he was nice to me and very thoughtful. If I even mentioned that I liked a certain book or album, he'd go out and get it. And when we went on a date, I had his undivided attention. It was like no other woman even existed when I was around him, and that was a wonderful feeling. So, I learned that color doesn't matter. All that matters is how you're being treated."

MARCELLA, FORTY-SOMETHING

"Now as far as your question on interracial relationships, I think they're fine, but it's not for me. I told my son years ago that if he wanted to go that way, fine, but I wouldn't feel comfortable with it because every time I watch *Roots*, I get sick to my stomach.

"The only problem I see with it is that black women are being shortchanged because there aren't enough black men to go around as it is. Take the high school prom, for instance. When it's time for a young black girl to go to her prom, there aren't enough guys to choose from but the white girls will have more than their share because they can pick from the white guys and most of the black guys, too. It happens all the time. Then we have the cases where a black man is lucky enough to finally make some decent money, and nine times out of ten what does he do? Go get himself a white woman.

"I know people have the right to choose as they like, but if a black man wants a white woman just to be able to tell somebody he's got a white woman, who cares?" Marcella arched her eyebrows and shrugged one shoulder as she adjusted her bra strap. "Now, if that man sincerely loves that woman, he doesn't care how she looks, doesn't care how big or little she is, and he just loves her for who she is and not for the color of her skin, I don't have a problem with that.

"The same thing goes for the woman. If she really likes a man because he's nice to her and they have a good relationship, then no matter what anybody says, if that's who she wants to be with then that's who she needs to be with. I'm forty-something years old and I've never been in an interracial relationship. But if I met a white man who treated me the way I want to be treated, and if I liked him, not because he was white, but because feelings were there, I wouldn't care what color he was.

"Really, black people are still color-struck from back in the days of slavery. My son is fair-skinned, but he likes dark-skinned women. As far as he's concerned, the darker the better. But if he'd married a white girl that would have been fine with me as long as she treated him right. His stupid-ass father, on the other hand, doesn't feel that way. When my son sent his dad some pictures of him and his fiancée, you know what his dad called me and said? He said, 'I don't mind him getting married to a black woman, but does she have to be *that* black?' I can't believe that we as people still feel that way, and all I could do was just shake my head.

"His father is a black man but he is very, very light-skinned.

My son married her anyway, and, honey, let me tell you, that dark-skinned daughter-in-law of mine is treating my son like the King of Egypt, do you hear me? She treats him much better than his light-skinned father ever thought about treating me."

BIANCA, THIRTY-SOMETHING

"The pool of eligible men out there seems to be getting smaller and smaller, so I can't find Mr. Right. I just broke up with Thomas after eight months because, although he was nice, he said I make him feel inferior. You remember that surprise birthday party I gave him? Well, I set it up and paid for everything because he said he'd never had a birthday party in his life. I felt like we'd been together long enough, and I thought it would be a really nice birthday gift.

"During the party that asshole grinned and stuck his chest out all night, then when it was over and everybody had left he told me he didn't appreciate me trying to make his friends think I was his 'sugar mama.' I was like, 'Sugar mama? Hell, I'm only a year and a half older than you in the first damn place, so how could I be your sugar mama? I don't have to try to impress your friends; I just threw a party for you because I thought that's what you wanted.'

"Needless to say, we couldn't keep it together after that. I hate to feel like I have to change who I am just so a man can accept what I have. That's so stupid."

Bianca sighed heavily. "I was engaged when I was twenty-two, and I broke it off even though I was still very much in love with the guy. I will probably always love him. When we first got together, if I wanted to go somewhere with my friends, he didn't have a problem with it. As soon as he put a ring on my finger it was like he'd placed a noose around my neck. He didn't want me out of his sight, and I couldn't go anywhere without him. He began acting like he owned me, but I was young and I wasn't about to let him put shackles on me.

"Finally, I'd had enough. I told him that I refused to be locked in a cage, and I broke up with him." Bianca turned her eyes toward mine. "That's when I found out how crazy he was because he tried to kill both of us. He left that night, but he wouldn't stop calling me all that next day. 'I just want to talk to you,' he kept saying. At first I was hanging up on him, but because I wanted to see him too, I finally said okay and agreed to let him come over that night. When he got there we sat and talked for a while, and I told him the relationship just needed to be over. He said maybe we could both relax if we went for a drive, and since it was getting late, I thought if I'd just ride with him for a little while he'd calm down. But once we got on the freeway he headed out to an area that wasn't very busy and started pressing down on the gas. He was making the car go so fast that it started shaking and I was really getting scared, but I didn't want to let it show. Finally, he said, 'You really gonna break off this engagement?'

" 'Yes.' I told him. 'I love you, but I can't stand being with somebody who's so jealous.'

"Then he got this crazy look in his eyes and said 'Okay. Do you see that bridge we're heading toward? If you don't change your mind by the time we get to it, I'm going to drive right off of it and kill us both.'

"I didn't believe him, and even though he wasn't slowing down, I just laughed and said, 'No you're not; you're not going to kill yourself.' He said, 'Watch me,' and pressed that gas pedal all the way to the floor. At that point, I got really scared and told him, 'Okay, okay. I'll marry you. Please don't do this.' He stepped on the brakes, barely missing the on-ramp to the bridge.

"That ride back to my house was the longest ride I'd ever had. When he finally pulled into my driveway and stopped, I jumped out of the car and screamed at him, 'You stupid-ass motherfucker. I don't ever want to see your ass again.' I ran into the house and before I could get inside and lock the door he had caught up with me. The next thing I knew he'd closed and locked the door and had his hands around my neck and was choking the shit out of me.

"I don't know if he was really trying to kill me or what, all I know is I remember seeing stars and then it started to get dark. When he realized he was actually choking me he stopped and started shaking me so I could get my breath. Once I got my voice back I told him to leave or I was going to call the police. He left, I guess he was scared, but I still called the police anyway because I wanted to make sure that crazy motherfucker didn't come anywhere near me again.

"Since then I've met and dated lots of guys. Some of them I really cared about, but I haven't been in love with anyone like I loved him. I guess I'm scared because sometimes men put on one face when they're trying to get you, and then when you fall for them they show their true colors. I don't intend to end up dead or in some dead-end relationship just because I'm in a hurry to get married. I'll just have to be patient until the right one comes along."

PORSCHE, THIRTY-SOMETHING

Porsche sat straight up when the question arose regarding interracial dating. "Oh, that is one of my pet peeves," she said. "White girls are a trip. They'll flirt with your man like you aren't even standing right next to him, and he'll eat up the attention like he's won the lottery or something. I'm sorry but that shit just pisses me off. What's so bad about it is, he tries to blow it off by saying some shit like, 'She wasn't even doing anything. Why you wanna act like that?'" Porsche held her freshly manicured hands out and looked at them. "What I'd like to know is how his ass would act if a white man came up to me and started telling me how nice I look or how good I smell.

"And don't go to a club that white women frequent. I mean, they can be the only white face in the entire place and be just as comfortable as they please. I don't care how she looks, you can bet some brother is almost going to break his neck trying to get to her side to ask her to dance. He'll probably step over a few sisters to get there, too. I've seen that shit with my own eyes. I was at happy hour with some friends last week and none of us are bad-looking women. We were all sitting around the table and these two black guys almost broke into a race to see who could make it to this white woman to ask her for a dance." Porsche shook her head in exasperation. "Now, I know for a fact that white men like black women just as much, but you won't ever see them step all over a white woman to ask a black woman for a dance. You'll never see that shit."

Now Porsche was fanning herself and frowning. "Let's move on to something else, girl, because that subject makes me hot. It's a damn shame that after all we've been through as a people, we still have to deal with shit like that. It really isn't even worth talking about because it's not going to change anyway."

ALICIA, FORTY-SOMETHING

"I see dating as an opportunity for two consenting adults to spend quality time together and get to know each other in a social setting. You date because you want to get to know that person and find out that person's likes and dislikes, and you want to take this opportunity to let them get to know your likes and dislikes as well. A lot of the time, people make the mistake of putting up a front and trying from the start to be something they think that other person wants them to be. That's a waste of time because eventually, the real you is going to come out and if the real you isn't what that other person is interested in, then the relationship is doomed to fail from the start.

"It can be something as simple as acting like you can barely eat one meal a day so on the date you only eat a small portion of your meal, when in reality you could've eaten your dessert and his too but you don't want him thinking you're some kind of glutton. You might even pretend that you love watching professional basketball games when you know for a fact that the only thing you know about the sport is that it involves real tall guys chasing a ball around the floor and getting paid very well to do it. When you pretend to be something you're not while on a date, it's a total waste of time because eventually your true self has to come out.

"My favorite date was with the guy I'm seeing now. He was my high school sweetheart, but I'd been divorced for about a year or so and he got my address from a close friend of mine. She'd told me that she saw him at the grocery store in a neighboring town a few weeks ago and I was like, 'Oh, I would love to see him again, it's been years.' Then one day shortly after our conversation, my doorbell rang and I peeked out and recognized him right away. I was shocked to see him standing there and to me he still looked as wonderful as ever. I flung the door open and he was holding an armful of roses. Before I could say a word, he handed them to me and said, 'I fell in love with you thirty years ago, the first time we met. I heard that you were no longer married and I just thought I'd take a chance and stop by to see if we could maybe pick up where we left off, I would like to start seeing you again.'

"In my eyes, this man could do no wrong from that point on. He was as different from my previous husbands as the day is to the night. He liked to go out and do the fun things I like to do like camping, boating, fishing; you know those fun outdoorsy type things. My last husband never liked doing stuff like that; he was more into hanging out with the fellows at a sports bar and cheering on his favorite team or maybe having his friends over for a game of cards.

"We talked for hours that first day and caught up on old times. We sent out for a pizza and I had cold beers in the refrigerator so we just sat at my house and talked and talked and it made me feel good to know that the major reason he had come to town was to see me. His focus was on me and that was very flattering. After we made a date to see each other the following weekend, he headed home and even called me on the way home. Then when he got home he called me again to tell me good night, and we've been inseparable ever since.

"I've only had one horrible date since my separation and it was with a guy from Africa. The only things I knew about him was that he was cute and he was funny and I wasn't seeing anyone yet, so I thought it would be nice to go out with him and see what he was all about. I'd met him through a friend of a friend and he asked me out to dinner.

"Dinner was okay but there were just too many obstacles for that relationship to even think about working. We had a language barrier and a cultural barrier and physically, he just didn't do it for me. He was cute but there was absolutely *no* chemistry between the two of us whatsoever, and of course, that date seemed to drag on for an eternity. We sat through drinks, waded through our appetizers and main course, and finally finished dessert. I just couldn't wait to get out of there.

"To me, dating is like a mini-relationship. You can say anything you want to say and be whoever but I always show my true colors when I'm dating. If it doesn't work out then no harm, no foul. If you both end up liking each other then you'll see one another again and again. Sometimes it may only end up being a friendship, but it's still a new relationship. If you find that you don't like one another, there are no obligations, he can go his way and you can go yours and then you can just start the cycle all over again with someone else.

"The worst thing about dating is being more interested in or liking a guy more than he likes you, but that can be true in a marriage too, can't it? I never liked those dates where you go out with this guy you're really interested in, you both seemed to have a good time, and then for the next several days you wait for a phone call that never comes.

"Why do guys always leave you with that little 'I'll call you' line when they know before the date is even over that they won't be calling you back, ever. Haven't we all picked up the phone receiver to see if there was a dial tone, like somebody might have come in while you weren't looking and turned the ringer off. You find yourself thinking, 'Hey, my sister's bad little kids were just over for a visit yesterday, they might've done something to the phone,' but of course when you pick it up, everything seems to be working fine, he just decided not to call.

"I hate waiting by the phone, hoping that he'll call to say hi or call to say that he wants to see me again and I won't make the first move and call and ask him out because I'm old-fashioned. When I was coming up girls didn't call guys. I'd always been taught that if a man is interested he will let you know he's interested, there's no reason for me to have to make the first move. Unfortunately, the longer it takes for him to call the more you start questioning yourself asking, 'Am I not cute enough, am I not skinny enough, am I not interesting enough, is my hair the wrong length, do I laugh too loud?' You start wondering all kinds of things but once he finally decides to call after maybe four or five days have passed, and he says something funny or asks you out again, you forget all about those crazy doubts until it happens again.

"I don't think that men and women define dating the same. I think women view dating as an opportunity to get to know the man better. Women view dating as, 'This could be my potential mate.' To me, personally, dating is like window-shopping, while I think men see dating as a test drive and when I say drive I mean they expect to sample the merchandise. The only problem is, you can't allow every guy you date to have a sample because then you're like a used car and none of them will want you."

CHEYANNE, FORTY-SOMETHING

When asked how she felt about interracial dating, Cheyanne pursed her lips and looked at me, "I'll tell you straight up, I'm not for interracial dating or relationships. My nephew got a white girl pregnant and when I found out I was like, 'Oh, hell. He's already got enough problems in this world just being a black man; now he done gone and got a white girl pregnant.' My sister had a fit. And what about the child? Society always has to put people in a box, but there is never a box that mixed children can choose. Maybe they want to check Asian and Black, but they don't have that option because they can only check one box.

"Then you get people who treat you badly because you're mixed—blacks as well as whites, because you know we can be just as prejudiced as they are. I know because I was mean to my light-skinned cousin when we were little. I was always onto her about thinking she was better than everybody else because she had light skin and bone-straight hair. I didn't realize at the time that it wasn't her choice that she looked the way she did." Cheyanne shrugged her shoulders. "I'm embarrassed by it now, but I was really hateful to her. And as a child, I myself was teased about my lips. Now the tables have turned. People are paying to have shit injected into their lips to make them look like mine—and oh, by the way, they're no longer called big, they're called full. Can you believe that?"

MISS NORA, SIXTY-SOMETHING

Miss Nora is a lady I've known since I was a child. She moved into the house next door to us, after divorcing her second husband and leaving Arkansas with her two daughters. She kept us kids cool and happy many a summer day with her Dixie cups and homemade ice cream. When I entered her home and followed her into the kitchen, my eyes immediately went to her kitchen counter where she used to keep a box of ice cream cones, an ice cream dipper sitting in a little bowl of clean water, and a jar full of the change she earned from selling her confections to the neighborhood children.

She noticed me looking around as we continued toward the garage and commented, "You remember eating my ice cream, don't you? Well, I'm still making it, and those Dixie cups too. The only difference is I charge a little more now because I'm on a fixed income and this little change helps. I only charge fifteen cents a scoop, but they like my ice cream better than what they sell in the store and it gives me something to do."

Right away I could see that Miss Nora hadn't changed a bit, she still had not one, but two deep freezers, I felt right at home. "Look in here, baby," she said. "All these vegetables are from my garden. I've got some mustard greens, crowder peas, squash, lima beans, and black-eyed peas in this one here. My friend brought me these catfish he caught last week. I've even got a 'coon that I bought from a man down the street. See?" She tugged at the freezer bag so I could get a better view. "The feet are still on it. They have to sell them to you with the feet on so you can be sure it's a 'coon.

"And I see you turning up your nose, but you young people don't know nothing about good food. I'll bet if I cooked this 'coon with some sweet potatoes and you didn't know what it was, you'd be licking your fingers." She laughed.

"Even though I live by myself," she continued, "I like to have food in my freezers because I came up through the Depression and going to bed on an empty stomach is no fun, even when you're on a diet. We were always taught to keep plenty of food on hand for those hard times, and I like to have extra food because I cook for my senior citizen friends who can't cook for themselves anymore. I do other things for them, too, like take them to the doctor, help them get their medicine, or go to the store for them."

We went back to the kitchen table. "Child, I could talk all day, so let me get started. I'm too old to be keeping secrets, so I don't have nothing to hide. Let me tell you how it was back in my day, when I was out there dating. See, I always got a good man because I didn't go with a man who had no job and no money. That's crazy. If a man can't take care of himself, what can he do for you? See, that women's lib stuff did us some good, but it also put us in the position where we have to compete with men, and I don't like that. Men don't see women the same way anymore, and that's the reason they don't treat us like ladies.

"They've gotten so used to us taking care of ourselves that they don't know how to take care of us. Some of them don't even want to know how. It's not necessarily the way they're being raised either—it's just that some women are weak, many have low self-esteem, and since there appears to be a shortage of men, at least a certain kind of man—some women will do anything to get a man. They give them money, buy their clothes, pay their car notes and their rent. Some even let them move in rent-free, and I never thought I'd see the day that things would get to that point.

"And these young men walking around with their pants hanging off their ass—what's that all about? I sure hope they don't think it looks good. Back when I was young, a man wouldn't dare dress that way, and if he did, my mama wouldn't let him in the front door. Lord, it's just unbelievable. Don't these girls understand that accepting a man who acts like he doesn't care about himself gives him permission to treat her like he doesn't care about her either?

"When I'm checking out a man the first thing I look at is how neatly he dresses and how good he smells. I like a man whose shoes are so shiny you can see your face in them, and whatever he has on, even if it's cutoffs, must be neat and clean. His body must also be clean because if I'm getting with a man and he takes off his clothes and I can smell him—and he smells bad—that knocks me away. I can't stand that. Some men will put cologne on right on top of funk, and that's a damn shame.

"I passed by one the other day who was handsome as he could be, but he reminded me of some of the men I used to ride the bus to work with back in my younger days. After wearing the same clothes all week to work, some of them would come back on Monday and get on that bus with those same dirty clothes on.

"Don't get me wrong; I don't have a boyfriend right now, but I still love men—good-looking, tall, solid men—especially one tall enough to pick me up and hold me in his arms. I love pretty teeth, a pretty complexion, and a well-groomed head of hair. And you know what? It doesn't make no difference what his skin color is to me, as long as he knows how to give me the best of everything, because I always give my best. I also think it's important that a man be grounded spiritually. Otherwise, he can't be a good leader, and I'm not interested in a man who's too worldly. I'm not talking about a fool who wants to recite scripture while we're making love or nothing crazy like that, or someone who thinks he's holier than everybody else. But I do like a man who attends church regularly and has a spiritual sense of how a man is supposed to treat a woman.

"I don't like cheap men. The men I dated knew they couldn't go to no Kmart or Lerner's to buy my clothes. I always made it clear that I don't wear cheap clothes, I don't drink cheap drinks, and I don't wear cheap perfume. Honey, after what I went through with those two husbands, I knew I'd have to set my standards high in order to be treated the way I thought I should be treated.

"Love is a wonderful thing, but I don't believe in making a fool of myself over it. When I was a young girl, my grandmama told me I should never love a man so much that I couldn't walk away if things got bad. She said, 'If a man loves you and cares about you, that's nice, but you can't put that in a cash register. And being in love or making love won't buy you no clothes or anything else you need. If he ain't giving you any money, he's going to give it to somebody else, so go ahead and get yours. If he's got something left to give another woman, that's fine, too.' So, being in love has never really been an issue with me. If a man is good to me and we enjoy each other, I don't think I need to fall in love or anything like that. From what I've seen, love is just too complicated anyway.

"A long time ago I used to go with this guy who was a manager at McDonald's. He always gave me money, but when it was time for my daughter's graduation from college, he didn't have much cash so he brought me some of everything that McDonald's sold. I got on the phone, called my friends, and had them call people. Child, people came over and bought all that stuff from me. Big boxes of stuff like hamburger patties, french fries, and apple pies. I had over $1,800 when I left to go to my daughter's graduation. I appreciated the fact that even though he didn't have enough money to give me, he cared enough about me to help me get it. He was good with money, but on the other hand he was very jealous.

"He got mad at me one time because I was out partying and he couldn't find me. He went to my house and took all my clothes, wigs, bras, and panties, and put them in his car. Then he took the car somewhere and parked it. Then he came back, climbed on top of my house, and waited for me. When I drove up, he jumped off the roof and was holding a machete—scared me to death. He took that machete and swung it at my dog, cutting one of his legs off, and then threw him over the fence in my neighbor's backyard. When my neighbor heard all the noise and came running outside to see that dog, she almost died.

"It just goes to show you that even the good ones can get crazy. But as long as I have a choice, I'd rather have one who's crazy about me and good to me at the same time than be with some fool who doesn't have anything and still has the nerve to try to treat me bad."

AYOKA, THIRTY-SOMETHING

"I haven't thought about dating in such a long time because I have a steady boyfriend, even though he's married, I consider him my boyfriend. If I had to, I guess I would define dating as spending time with a man who was just a friend and someone to hang around with. I wouldn't want it to be serious, not at first anyway. He would definitely have to be my friend first.

"My ideal date, and I've thought about this a hundred times, would be something really nice because I have a champagne taste and I love dressing up and going out to nice places. I would love for my date to pick me up and fly me to Rio de Janeiro, just out of the blue. I mean, it would be one of those dates where he'd call and say, 'I'm coming over to get you and taking you to Rio for the weekend, and you don't need to take anything but your passport.

" 'Once we get there I'll buy whatever you need, so don't even take an extra pair of panties. We'll be going to the opera, then to dinner and out dancing, we'll spend some time on the beach, and

I'll take you shopping and get you an outfit for everything we're planning to do. The hotel has a salon and everything so you don't even need to get your hair done until you get there.'

"Everything would be my option including having my own room if that's what I wanted because a real gentleman wouldn't say, 'I flew you over here and spent all this money showing you a good time, so you know what's up tonight, right?' That wouldn't even be an issue. Sometimes my boyfriend treats me like that. We may not fly anywhere, but he'll surprise me with a no-limit shopping trip, or an envelope full of cash to spend however I like, and there are no stipulations or strings attached. He's just sweet like that.

"Since I've become single, I've tried to date a little because I realized I needed to get out and explore my options. I finally had one of those horrible 'dates from hell' when I was set up with a minister from my friend's church, and that just about did it for me. They both belong to this huge, very popular, Bible-teaching church, where they really teach you how to apply the Bible to your daily life. Since he was one of the full-time associate ministers on staff at this church, I figured he would be a really great guy to date. From the conversations we'd had, he appeared to be nice, smart, articulate, funny, and financially stable. He'd been divorced for a while and he was older than me by about ten years.

"We talked on the phone more than a few times before I finally met him at a restaurant close to where I live. I'm always careful about inviting men to my place if I don't know them, and I wanted to be close enough to get back home if things didn't go well. We were sitting there talking, and he said, 'I can't believe you're almost divorced and somebody hasn't scooped you up already,' which of course was pleasant to hear. But thirty minutes into the conversation he started talking about me moving to his little hometown. It turned out that he'd had a baby with some woman he used to date in the little country town where he was from, and the child is about twelve years old now. He bought the woman a house down there and takes care of all of her bills and stuff, but he never wanted to marry her.

"The problem is, she's very ill and is probably going to die, and he needs to move back there to take care of his daughter. So, he was talking about how he could see me and him getting married, working out together, then growing old, and retiring together, and I'd just met him. Then he slid around in the booth and placed his hand on my leg, and I was thinking, 'Oh, hell no. This fool obviously thinks I'm desperate for a man or something, but he is sadly mistaken.'

"I gave him a few more moments of my attention before I shot his plans down and told him that I do have a career and a life. But he acted like he didn't even hear me and went on to say I could just give my job up and let him take care of me because he was from the 'old school.' I just sat there and let him keep talking, looking at him like he was crazy as hell, and I guess he was getting annoyed because he'd planned this wonderful life for us and here I was not responding, acting like I didn't even appreciate it.

"He kept talking and talking, and finally he said, 'I can't believe you. I'm an intelligent, good-looking, churchgoing man who could take care of you, and I've got women at church and everywhere else running behind me, but I'm choosing you and you're sitting here looking at me like you don't have a clue. I'm a man of God and He reveals things to me. He could have placed someone else in your life by now, but the reason He hasn't is because He was saving you for me. If you'd just listen to what I'm saying, and give it a chance, I know everything will work out. I can even move in with you while I get everything set up back at home, and we could spend that time getting to know each other.'

"Well, bringing God into the conversation didn't work because I'm still sitting there looking at him like he's a fool. So, he tries to go the other route and moves his hand up on my leg a little higher, squeezes for emphasis, and says, 'I'll tell you what, why don't you take me home with you tonight so I can show you what you're missing.

When I get through touching you up you'll be ready to marry me tomorrow.' And that was enough. I held one finger up, told him to hold his thought, finished my cocktail, picked up my purse, and got up and strutted right out the front door without even looking back. I was not about to sit there another minute and listen to his bullshit when it was obvious that all he was looking for was a place to lay up while he got his shit together. And I'm willing to bet he doesn't even have any money, talking about he's financially stable with those cheap-ass shoes on. Give me a break.

"So, for the record, I do not like dating and I don't really want to do that part of the relationship thing, but there's no other way to meet or get to know a person unless you date. I'm just too tired and it takes too much effort. It's not worth all the trouble because you meet so many guys who come across as really nice, and then you go somewhere with him and he's the craziest thing you ever met. Hell, I may even check out Internet dating or a dating service because I really don't have time for the bullshit.

"Most men, notice I didn't say all, but most men, still don't define dating the way women do. They think that all dates lead to sex, even if all they buy you is a cheeseburger. Seriously, even mature men who are not naive enough to think it will happen on the first or second date expect to be jumping up and down in your coochie by the third date. With all the stuff going around these days, a few dates just isn't enough time for me to get that intimate with someone."

VICKY, FORTY-SOMETHING

Vicky is originally from New Jersey. A slender woman with shoulder-length black hair and hazel eyes, she's about five feet nine inches tall, with a slim waist and legs that seem to go on forever. Her basic outfits consist of short black skirts, black tights, and vivid-colored T-shirts. Today the shirt was a cobalt blue. She was the only one at the table even making an attempt at eating healthy, which is probably why she looked so good in that skirt and tights.

Vicky is the divorced mother of a girl and a boy ages nine and eleven. The children were currently spending spring break with their father so she was enjoying her temporary freedom. Just getting out with friends to have a drink or two, eat Mexican food that was so good it made you want to slap somebody, and talk about some of her life experiences wasn't something she got to do very often.

Before we got started, we had the waitress take our orders because we didn't want any interruptions. Vicky ordered Latino Stir Fry, which is a meal that consists solely of stir-fried vegetables, but me, I had to have meat so I ordered the chicken fajitas. After all, how fattening could chicken be? I chose to ignore the calories in the chips drenched with salsa that I popped into my mouth every minute or so and told myself that I wasn't calorie counting today, which of course is why I can't lose these extra pounds. But regardless of all that, I was going to eat some Mexican food today and I was going to enjoy the hell out of it.

To start things off, we ordered a round of frozen margaritas and asked for some warm corn tortillas and butter. Baby, you haven't lived until you've eaten warm tortillas slathered with butter, a sprinkling of salt, and salsa. Heaven . . . We did say no to the queso when the waitress offered it as an appetizer. I was going off my diet temporarily but I hadn't completely lost my mind and I knew if I'd said yes and she sat that hot bowl of melted cheese in front of me I probably would've hurt myself.

Vicky was excited about being interviewed so she began talking while we waited for the margaritas. "Let me tell you what I think about dating. Dating is what you do with someone you want more than just friendship with, but that doesn't mean it has to be serious, and I think men should pay for the date because I'm old-fashioned. Even if I weren't old-fashioned I still think men should pay until you get to know each other better. Once the relationship becomes serious and you two are dating each other exclusively, I think it's okay to buy dinner for him on special occasions or bring dinner over, or make dinner at your house. Also things like buying movie tickets or tickets to the theater, or buying the tickets if you invite him to your company Christmas party is okay.

"Of course, I was married for twelve years, so dating was weird and very scary after I got my divorce, because I never even thought about dating while I was going through it. That was *not* a priority for me nor was it something I was looking forward to. I actually didn't think I would even want to date, but I did, and I do, and it's nice most of the time. Really, dating has made me feel better about myself because it lets me know that men are still interested.

"The best dates I have are not the ones where I dress up and go to some fancy restaurant. It's the simple ones, like picnics in the park, that I enjoy the most. You know, packing up a picnic basket and going to a nice park, and sitting there on a blanket drinking a bottle of wine, talking and laughing, and getting close and personal. And let me mention that just because you're dating doesn't mean you have sex with that person right away, not in my opinion. Of course for some people, especially men, sex and dating go together, but I think as you mature that shouldn't be the case. Besides, if I had sex with every guy I dated, I'd just be a little whore I guess. But sex is not the only thing I'm looking for in a relationship, so I like to take my time and see where things are going before I get involved sexually.

"I have had a few bad dates, although I've not had many of those kind, and they're usually not with someone that you date over and over again. It usually happens as soon as you open the door and look at him, or sometime during the first date with him, and you know right away that you don't want to see him again. I know instantly when I see somebody if I'm interested in them or not. For instance, I like tall men, and one time somebody fixed me up with this blind date. When I asked what he looked like my friend said, 'Oh, he's tall, probably about six-one, real nice, never been married, no kids, just a nice guy.' So I said okay and when this guy came to my door—you had to see him with your own eyes; he was about five-five, which is shorter than I am, and I probably weighed more than he did. He had his pants pulled up to his chest, and was just standing there looking crazy as hell, and here I was about to go out with him, damnit." Vicky grimaced.

"He did turn out to be kind of nice, but he was just too weird for me. I found out that he'd been married twice, had two kids who he had custody of, and he liked to go out and drive these big trucks through mud—I think you call it 'mudding.' He asked me if I'd like to go along with him one day, and the hair on the back of my neck must have stood straight up. Before I answered, I was saying to myself, 'I don't think there's a chance in hell that you're ever going to be coming to my door again, buddy,' but I responded nicely, in the negative. Then I sat through the rest of the night thinking, 'I cannot wait to get home and away from this Poindexter-looking weirdo.' I'm just picky, and I know I'm picky, but I don't care. I don't want to settle for being with anyone who doesn't suit me. If I end up alone, then that's fine because at least I can say I didn't settle.

"Now, back to sex on the first date, I haven't had any dates with guys who just came right out and started the night off trying to take me to bed, and I guess that's because I am so picky about who I date. But I did go on a date with one guy who was a pilot for one of the major airlines. He made a lot of money and had been with this company for about thirty years, so he was well established. Well, during dinner, he started going on and on about his dogs trying to have sex which I thought was very inappropriate for a first date. To make matters worse, it was a double date and the other guy, who was his friend, was just as obnoxious. He started acting stupid, and talking silly, and laughing all loud as if discussing two dogs having sex was really funny. Thank God I'd driven my own car and met them there, because by 9:00 P.M. I could not stand him or his friend for another minute. I stood up and said, 'You know what? It's been very nice to meet you and thank you for dinner, but I have to leave,' and I just walked out.

"Who in their right mind would sit there and talk about dogs trying to have sex, in front of two ladies they hardly even know?

Damn fool was probably into bestiality and wanted to see if he could get a willing partner, you never know these days.

"So far I've only dated one guy who I was really crazy about since I've been divorced. He was a big guy, he kind of reminded me of Mr. Big on *Sex and the City*. When I first saw him I thought he was the most gorgeous man I had ever seen in my life. I am telling you, I just went crazy over him. He used to come to my office and talk all the time, and I was instantly attracted to him but I never said a word, even though I'd been separated for about six months at that time. He knew I was separated and that I was in no hurry to date, so we just talked off and on at work for about seven or eight months. We'd talk about divorce and all that kind of stuff, and during that time my sister became very sick and he was right there talking to me and helping me through it. I wanted to fly home to see her, but my soon to be ex-husband had taken all the money out of our savings account and I was flat broke.

"He offered to pay for whatever I needed. That made me even more crazy about him, but he had no idea. Later, when we started dating he told me that whenever he used to come into my office, he'd get flustered, and that's the reason it took him so long to ask me out. Of course that made me feel good because I didn't know he felt that way. He said, 'Women never make me nervous, but you made me so nervous that I used to sweat each and every time I would come to your office. The first time I saw you I knew that you were the woman for me.'

"I'd love to have a wonderful end to this story, but even though we really cared for each other we ended up breaking up because we both had different ideas for what we wanted in a marriage. He'd been married before, but had been divorced for a long time, and had never had any kids. When we first started dating he was still dating other women, which was fine, but after a while we started to date exclusively. He really wanted to get married and have children of his own, even though he loved my children, but I was almost forty years old and didn't want to have any more kids. He kept telling me how much he cared for me, but he really wanted to have a baby. I'd had such a hard time with my pregnancies that I'd had my tubes tied after my last child was born because the doctor suggested that I not even try to have another baby.

"I even thought about having my surgery reversed, but I just couldn't do it. I mean, what if I died trying to have another baby? What would happen to my children? I had to consider that because the doctor had already warned me, so my choices were very limited, if I had any at all. It broke my heart to have to give him up, but it just wouldn't have been fair for me to marry him knowing that I could not give him what he wanted. He ended up marrying the first girl he dated after we broke up and even though he's been married a couple of years they haven't had any babies yet.

"I still see him whenever he visits my agency and I still enjoy talking to him when I see him, but my heart doesn't flutter the way it used to. I know he belongs to another woman and I would never want to put someone else through what I went through, so married men are not on my list of available men.

"I guess I would have to say dating is fun because I get to do all the different things that I wouldn't normally do by myself. Things like going to a really nice restaurant and just sitting and talking all night, or doing that picnic at the park thing, I like that. But what I dislike is when the man you're dating wants you there all the time. You know, at first they say, 'I don't want to get all involved and clingy,' but then if you're not right there when they want you to be, they get upset about it. Some of them want to see you too often or want you to give them all your attention, and I just have too many other things to do in my life. I don't want to be involved with a man who wants me to give him all of my attention because there are other things I need to do. I have my children, and I have friends who I like to see, and although I like to date, I don't want that to be the only thing I do. I'm a mature woman and I don't need to be right under a man all the time, and many of them aren't used to that. I don't know what it is, but I think some of them are used to needy, desperate women, and I'm not that type.

"In my opinion, men definitely do not define dating the way women do. At least not all men. For a few of the men I've met, dating means, 'I'll take you out for a drink and a wonderful dinner, and then we'll go back to my place and have sex.' If that happens, I'm not going anywhere with him, and I'm never going on a date with him again because, as I said, I'm not looking for that kind of man—that's not a date to me. That's foreplay that he paid for, and I'm not for sale.

"I don't want to feel obligated to have sex at the end of the evening just because a man spends money on me. I think that's very immature. Don't get me wrong, I like sex just as well as the next woman, maybe even more, but just because we go out doesn't mean that's going to happen. I might not feel like it, or it might not be the right time, you know? Sorry, but with me it's not happening.

LADY, FORTY-SOMETHING

The interview with Lady was conducted at a local bookstore. It was a rainy day so there wasn't very much traffic in and out. We found a quiet spot in front of a huge window where we could see shoppers dashing out of the cars and into the store and vice versa. I dragged an empty bench over to face the one bench sitting against the window and there we sat and laughed and talked for about two hours. Every now and then we had to remember where we were and lower our voices. Luckily the area we'd chosen to talk in was the Genetics and DNA area. There seemed to be fewer browsers there than anyplace else in the store, at least until one woman stood there a little bit too long and tried to add her two cents to our conversation. We didn't really mind because at least that let us know that what we were talking about was interesting.

The light that filtered through the window was bright, but tempered a bit due to the gray rain clouds that every now and then decided to let loose with a quick summer shower. As the sunlight attempted to push its way through the clouds, I was reminded of that old saying: "If it rains while the sun is shining, that means the devil is beating his wife because she burned his corn bread." It was cool inside the store, and the misting rain that had greeted us upon our departure from the car made it even cooler.

Lady works as an administrator at an alternative high school and is a self-confident and extremely sexy sister who wears her locks with pride. She's also proud of her shapely legs and she never goes anywhere without wearing heels that are at least three inches high, and the skirts or dresses she wears just barely brush the top of her knees, no farther. In my opinion, Lady's best asset is her eyes. She has the most beautiful dark brown flirty eyes I've ever seen, and she can talk with those eyes better than anyone I know. She said those kind of eyes run in her family. Her mama and both of her sisters have those same expressive eyes and for some reason they always seem to be in some type of trouble with the opposite sex.

As we got comfortable and placed our wet purses and umbrellas on the floor beside us, Lady went into a fit of laughter when I told her the first thing we were going to discuss was dating.

"Dating? You want me to talk about dating? Oh, my goodness," Lady sputtered between laughter. "The people in this store are going to put us out and we haven't been here a good ten minutes yet." She pulled herself together acting like she was about to get all serious.

"Okay." She pressed her glossed lips together. "Well, first of all I shouldn't even be talking about dating because as you know, I'm married. But I'm gonna talk about it anyway 'cause I do date. What that means for me is when you and the person you're seeing go out to eat or go to the movies or just go hang out at the park or something. You know what I mean, when you just get to hang out and spend some quality time with a person you care about. One of the

ways you get to know a man you're interested in is to date him."
Lady aimed those expressive eyes my way.

"Now that's what I think dating is but sometimes that's not what
I've experienced 'cause niggas be trippin'. I haven't been to na'n
[Ebonic translation—not any] park and I haven't been to na'n
movie. All he wants to do is go get a movie from Blockbuster, order
some food to eat, and sit there and get full before we fuck, and we
do that every Monday, so how is that a date?" Lady raised her arms
in question. "That shit just irritates the hell out of me.

"I guess in his mind that's dating because I'm married and I
don't have no business being out there anyway. We have gone to a
couple of clubs but they were way off somewhere in another part of
town because he says he can't be going where people might know
him. Hell, I'm the one who's married so if anybody is worried about
being seen, it should be me. As far as I'm concerned we're just seeing each other. We're not going on no damn date because eating,
watching TV, and screwing isn't a date, okay?

"The guy I dated before I married my husband knew what dating
was. He used to do so many nice things for me, but we ended our
relationship because he just wasn't ready to commit. He used to
send me flowers and cards just out of the blue. Not every day or
once a week, just every now and then when I was least expecting it. I
did the same thing for him, but some men just seem to be stupid or
something because they don't have a clue as to how to date a *lady*, and
you know that's what I am." Lady smirked.

"I hope at least a few men will read this because most of them
just don't have a clue. Men, listen up. If a woman sends you cards,
even if it's once every quarter, then that's a good indication that
she likes cards as well. She must be thinking about your crazy ass or
else she wouldn't be buying you a card, right? And if she sends you
flowers for whatever occasion, as some women do for the men they
really care about, then she probably would like for you to send her
some every now and then too.

"This man I call myself seeing gave me some sorry-ass excuse that he can't send me cards or flowers because I'm married, and I'd like to know what the hell that has to do with anything. I have an office, my husband doesn't work with me, and if he sent flowers to my job with a note, who would know who sent them? Nobody, so that shit don't wash. I also have a P.O. Box, so if he sent me a card, who's to know as long as he doesn't put his name on it? That's just a bullshit excuse.

"I think the problem is that when you're dating a guy who's single, and you're already committed or married, he gets the impression that all you're supposed to want from him is sex. I guess he thinks that since I'm in another relationship I already have somebody to send me flowers and buy me cards. Well my response to that is he's got a girlfriend who can send him flowers and cards too, but I'll bet she doesn't. That works both ways. If I'm going to meet his needs he needs to make it worth my time just like it's worth his time, and sometimes it's not worth my time because I end up more frustrated and pissed off than I would be if I weren't involved with him.

"At first I wouldn't tell him how I really felt because I thought he might get pissed off and stop calling or seeing me, but you know what? Damn that, I started telling him how I feel anyway and I figure if he doesn't call, good, maybe he doesn't need to call. If I can't tell him how I feel, I don't need to be involved with him, it's simple as that. I don't care whether he's married or single or what. After all, this relationship was more his idea than it was mine in the first place, and now that I'm into it he's acting like he's got his foot in the door.

"That's what men do once they think they got you where they want you. They stop the chase but they need to realize what they did to get with you is what they need to keep doing. I just don't understand why they think they can just cut off the romance once you start to care about them." Lady sighed.

"When we first started seeing each other I enjoyed the chase. I'm a woman and I like that. The compliments, the phone calls, the 'I want to see you, I want to get to know you,' that kind of stuff. But it's like once you become interested and let them know it, you don't get that anymore. I guess in order to keep that from happening you can't let them get too familiar, you can't start saying, 'I miss you and I can't wait to hear from you' and all that, but I like telling him that because that's how I feel. I think it's so immature for two adults to hold their feelings back from each other.

"I don't mind telling him how I feel about him, but just because I do he shouldn't assume that I won't cut his ass off tomorrow. For real. It's not that serious and he needs to understand that. But oh, baby, one day he's going to say the wrong thing and it's going to be over and when it is, it'll be his loss.

"On my birthday, I have to remind him that it's my birthday, even after being involved with him for three years. But when it was time for his birthday, he started talking about the shit at the beginning of the month, and his birthday wasn't until the twenty-ninth. Nevertheless, we made all these plans for what we were going to do on his birthday, and do you know that fucker had the nerve to cancel on me? Shit, that's what I get for trying to be so nice, but I really thought we were on the same page, and I thought he was more mature because he's almost six years older than me.

"Another issue I have with him is the sex. I'm not in this relationship with him because I'm looking for sex and I want that to be clear because for some reason, men think when they give you sex, especially if they *think* they're giving you good sex, that the moon and the sun just rises on their ass and that's bullshit too.

"When will they learn that dick is easy to find. Good dick, bad dick, big dick, whatever kind of dick, it's all out there for the taking. All you got to do is keep some condoms on hand and you can have all the sex you want, so they should never be stupid enough to think they're doing you a favor by having sex with you. Hell, I turn down more offers for sex than he could even imagine.

"So, now that I've told you what I think about dating you probably understand why I say I'm not going down this road anymore. I was very reluctant to get involved in the first place because of the things I'd heard about being with a single man. This is the first, and I hope the last time I'm having an affair because it's not worth it. If he was doing something for me that my husband wasn't doing, it would be different.

"He's supposed to make my life tolerable but that's not the case because he isn't giving me anything I don't already have at home. He doesn't send me flowers or cards, and he doesn't leave sweet notes or anything else on my car to let me know he's thinking about me, so if all he's doing is adding more frustration to my life, why am I even being bothered? All he's doing is wasting my time, and like a dummy I'm letting him. I swear, sometimes we need to have our heads examined and I say we because I know I'm not the first woman who's been involved in a one-sided affair." Lady made a motion with her hands like she was shooing a fly. "It makes no sense at all."

CRAWFISH ÉTOUFFÉE

½ cup butter or margarine

1 large onion, chopped

¼ cup celery, finely chopped

¼ cup green pepper, chopped

2 cloves garlic, minced

1 pound peeled crawfish tails

1 teaspoon salt

½ teaspoon ground black pepper

½ teaspoon onion powder

¼ teaspoon ground white pepper

½ teaspoon hot sauce

1½ tablespoons all-purpose flour

¾ cup water

½ cup green onions, finely chopped

¼ cup fresh parsley, finely chopped

Hot cooked rice

Melt butter in a large skillet over medium heat. Add onion and next 3 ingredients; cook, stirring constantly, 5 minutes.

Stir in crawfish and next 5 ingredients; cook 5 minutes. Stir in flour; cook, stirring constantly, 2 minutes.

Stir in water gradually; cook over low heat 20 minutes, stirring mixture occasionally.

Stir in green onions and parsley; cook 3 minutes. Serve over rice. *Yield: 4 to 6 servings.*

MARRIAGE

MARCELLA, FORTY-SOMETHING

"I was a good wife, probably because I was taught that women are supposed to do certain things. Some women think that when they come home, cooking and cleaning is beneath them. I feel like that's part of your duty as a woman and as a wife. When you get married, those are the things you're supposed to do. That's what makes a home a home, you know what I mean? And washing—to me washing is a woman's place. That's the way I feel about it. I wouldn't want nobody else washing my clothes anyway.

"Well, I married this guy and I was trying to be a good wife, but I knew it wasn't going to work out because although he was a nice person he was very jealous of my son, and I refused to put any man in front of my son. He started being verbally abusive to him because he didn't like him, and then we started getting along bad. He even started talking crazy to me, acting like he had no manners.

"He would tell me, 'Fix my plate,' and not ask me properly. So I simply would not fix his plate or do anything else he told me to do because I was his wife, not his servant, and I refused to let him treat me otherwise.

"I ended up hating him because he beat my son when he was six years old. It was a terrible, tragic thing and I left him because I'd rather be homeless than with some man who doesn't like my child.

"See, what happened was there was this car in our driveway and my child always liked to play by himself inside the car. I was gone to work and my husband worked nights, so he told my son to stay inside while he slept. But when he woke up my son was outside in the car playing with his toys, and he got angry. I understand that he should not have gone outside because he'd told him not to. But he was only six years old. I didn't mind him spanking my child, I really didn't, but he beat him with the buckle of his belt, and I don't think that was necessary.

"I didn't know what had happened right away, but at night when he took his bath I'd always run his water and then go to the kitchen and cook dinner while he undressed and got in the tub and played for a while. Then I'd go in and wash his back and make sure he'd bathed himself correctly, because he was a little child.

"When I went back in there this particular night and I saw all these marks and bruises, girl, listen to me, I went dumb. I literally lost my voice. It was completely gone. Completely. I got so mad that it was like I went into a coma for a few moments. When I finally came to my senses later that night, I packed our stuff. I did not give him a chance to explain because you don't do that. You do not hit a child like that, I'm sorry. And what made it even worse was that he was such a sweet child, he didn't even tell me what happened. Honey, he had marks on the back, the legs, the hands, the sides, everywhere. Everywhere, do you hear me? How could I lay down with my husband again after that? I couldn't. And I know what the consequences would have been if I had stayed with him. I'm sure he would have done it again.

"I had no family here and it was a good thing because if I'd had someone here who could take care of my child, I would have given him up for adoption and then killed that son of a bitch. That way, when they took me to jail, my son would've been taken care of by my family.

"I seriously would have done that because I was so angry I couldn't see any other solution," Marcella said. "But then I decided that fool wasn't worth me spending the rest of my life in jail over, so I just left before he had a chance to do it again. You know, I hate him still to this day, and he's the reason I never remarried. I just couldn't bear the thought of being with someone who would do something like that again, so I've been single ever since."

EBONI, FORTY-SOMETHING

"I ended up marrying the first man I thought I was in love with, because I had very low self-esteem when I was younger. He was a wonderful lover, but the marriage only lasted about two years because we fought all the time and it was just wearing me out. Sometimes I felt like I had to be his mother, like I was raising another child. I had to nag all the time just to get him to do anything, except have sex of course. And I felt like I had to constantly pump up his ego, which was draining me.

"I think a man should be confident enough to know who he is without a woman having to constantly praise him. The funny thing is, when I met him, I thought he was very self-sufficient and that attracted me to him. But then he started acting like he couldn't do anything unless I told him to. Then when I did he'd say I was bitching, so I couldn't win either way. I guess I should have realized that good sex alone wouldn't make a marriage work.

"After we divorced, I stayed single for many years, often dating men who gave me money or bought me things that I thought would make me feel good about myself. I guess I was looking for the one man who could make me feel special, just like every woman does. But I was going through the men as fast as I was spending their money, and sometimes I'd have two visitors in the same day, which made me feel like I was turning tricks.

"I was trying so hard to find someone who really loved my kids and who would be able to give them the things I felt they needed.

You know, when you have your children out of wedlock, you want them to be better than regular people, so I thought if I had a man with money, my kids could have all the things that regular people had, and then they wouldn't have to be ashamed of having a mother with no husband. I didn't even consider how dating all those different men would affect them.

"I finally ended up falling in love with a man who did have money. He had his own trucking company. But I soon found out his company was just a front for the drug business he was running, and like a fool I married him anyway. The next thing I knew, he had me flying across the country to pick up drugs and money, and I was living a life I never dreamed I could get accustomed to. I still can't believe I did some stupid shit like that, but I was just crazy in love with him. What else can I say?

"With two Cadillacs in the driveway, a beautiful home, and both of my boys driving their own cars to school, everybody was happy. Even when the boys finished high school and left the house, my husband and I were still very much in love. What I felt for him was totally different from what I'd felt for any other man.

"He took me to some of the most beautiful places I've ever seen, bought me furs and anything else I wanted, and after twelve years together I still couldn't stop smiling when I was on his arm. I couldn't wait for him to come home in the evenings so we could spend time together, and even when he worked late, I'd still have his dinner waiting for him. Making love with him was a feeling I can't even express or try to explain because it was so unique from what I'd ever experienced. Just being in his presence made me happy."

Eboni paused, trying to gather herself for what she was about to say, and I waited, afraid to say anything that would make her change her mind. The rumor was that her husband had just packed all his things and left her one night, but no one knew why. When she finally found her voice again she had tears in her eyes.

"He came to me and said he had fallen in love with my first cousin, and that they'd been having an affair for the last two years."

"See," she said very quietly, "I loved him so much that I didn't even notice he wasn't loving me back the same way. I wasn't paying attention to the fact that he was late on the same nights every week—he'd always had meetings on Tuesday, Thursday, and Saturday evenings. So I just thought he was doing what he always did. I hadn't even wanted to question why we made love less frequently, I attributed it to him being tired and getting older. And even though at some point I thought he could be having an affair, I guess I didn't really want to confirm it because then I'd have to make a decision, and what decision do you make when you love someone so much? I figured if he loved me like I loved him and something was going on that it would pass. Hell, I guess I was just in love and in denial and he knew it, so he took my love for granted.

"We didn't even try to work things out because when he told me what was going on, he didn't even ask me how I felt or what I wanted to do. As a matter of fact, he'd already filed for the divorce when he told me the truth, and our house was up for sale the next day. I wasn't working, so he had complete control of our finances and I didn't know what to do. Shit, I didn't even know where the money was anymore because he gave me money whenever I asked for it and took care of everything else himself.

"I could've gone to the police about his business, but then I would have implicated myself and they would have seized everything, so my ass was stuck and I knew it. I just had to take the cash he gave me, which was substantial enough to help me get my life together, and move on from there, I had no options.

"So, here I am starting all over again. It's hard but I'm trying to learn to be happy with myself and with my life. I realize now that what I thought I needed to make me complete was to be in love and have a husband and a life full of stuff. But I'm finding that true happiness comes from within and you should learn to be happy with yourself whether you're in love or in a relationship or not."

"I'm not knocking love and marriage because I'm a true romantic. My parents stayed together, and even though I'm sure they had their problems, they kept it to themselves and they never disrespected each other. At least not in front of us. They were a team and that's the one thing I was never able to accomplish in my marriages, but I still think marriage can be good.

"Even if I never get married again, that's okay. I'm having a lot of fun dating and as long as I'm happy, that's fine with me."

PORSCHE, THIRTY-SOMETHING

"I plan to get out of my marriage as soon as I can get some more things in order financially. Me and my husband just don't have anything in common anymore. I'm not in love with him, and the only reason I haven't already left is because my boyfriend isn't available. If he was single, I'd leave home tomorrow."

"I used to love him, I guess, because I always thought when you loved a man you genuinely cared about him. And that's the way I used to feel. I really cared about what happened to him and I cared about his feelings.

"But now"—she paused, clicking her tongue and tossing her braids back—"I don't even buy his ass a greeting card because I can't find one that would express my true feelings. The days of me thinking he's everything I need are long gone, and not too soon either.

"He never helped around the house, wouldn't wash my car or help me keep it up, and I even had to start paying someone else to take care of our yard. So, since he wasn't willing to do things for me, I wasn't willing to meet his needs either, and you know when you stop giving a man sex, all hell breaks loose."

"He needs to realize that I'm a woman. I want to be taken care of if I'm fucking, even if he is my husband. I truly don't understand why any woman would have sex with a man unless he's doing something for her. I got this cellular phone, my pager, and the down payment on my Jag from my boyfriend, but I do nice things for him, too, so he doesn't mind giving me gifts. Besides, after what I was going through with my husband when I met him, I let him know in advance that my shit is good, but it's not free, and I'm not giving it away just to get a good feeling.

"I just don't understand women who complain that their man won't even buy them a birthday gift, but then wants to screw any and every time he feels like it, just because he feels like it. I think that's just absurd and also very selfish because a man should enjoy doing things for his woman if he cares about her. And you know what else, if he doesn't give you what you want, you'd better learn to ask for it because otherwise, he might not know what you need.

"A friend of mine who'd been single for years had become accustomed to making her own mortgage payment. Even after she got married she continued to pay it until she finally woke up one day and asked her husband, 'Why don't you ever help me pay the mortgage?' Do you know what he said? ' 'Cause you never asked me to.' Can you believe that?

"I guess we all live and learn and some of us learn faster than others. As for me, it didn't take me long. I know I only have one life to live, and I plan on living it to the fullest and doing whatever it takes for me to be happy. If I don't, no one else will, right?"

MISS NORA, SIXTY-SOMETHING

"I married a man I really cared for when I was eighteen, but I was never in love with him. I really liked him and he was good to me at first, but he was seven years older than me, and I just wanted to get married because that's what everybody else was doing. By the time I found out marriage wasn't everything I thought it was supposed to be, and that he was running around on me, I'd already had my first child. Since I didn't want my children to have different fathers, I stayed with him until I'd had my second one and decided I wouldn't have any more.

"Being married was okay at first, but you know when you have a husband he expects you to have sex with him, even when you don't feel like it, and that used to get on my nerves. I didn't mind all the other stuff I had to do as a wife, but sex was a chore and he used to get really mad if I wouldn't give him what he wanted.

"Other than that, I loved cooking for and taking care of a family, and since I never finished high school, I didn't work outside my home because, for number one, I didn't want nobody else raising my girls, and I never knew I was capable of doing anything else. I'm not saying there's anything wrong with staying at home though because I enjoyed it. I never worked until I divorced my first husband, but I didn't need to because he took good care of us financially. He liked to run around, but he cashed that check every week, kept a few dollars for himself, and gave the rest of it to me so I could take care of the bills.

"Now, after we had that second baby, that's when he started to change, and I guess I started to change too. I was getting tired of always being at home while he was gone on the weekends. He started to drink a lot and when he was drunk he would sometimes kick me out of bed, call me all kinds of names, and start accusing me of doing shit I wasn't doing. I'd warned him time and time again that one day I was gonna act like I'd lost my mind and just shoot him because I was getting tired of that, but he didn't believe me. Sure enough, he started that shit up one night when I was dog-tired, so I jumped up, went into the other room, got my pistol, came back, and shot his ass."

Miss Nora picked up her cup of coffee, black with a single teaspoon of sugar, and calmly sipped it as if telling a story about shooting somebody was just a normal everyday occurrence. She continued. "Fortunately for him, he caught the bullet in his thigh because I was aiming between his legs. We divorced after that little episode, and I got a job cleaning house and cooking for a white family. About a year later I met another man whom I married, but I didn't love him either and he used to hit me, too. He blackened my eyes, kicked, and cursed me the same way my first husband did. I don't know why some women are attracted to the same kind of man over and over again, you'd think we'd learn."

Miss Nora offered me a slice of lemon pound cake that she'd baked just that morning. Of course I wasn't going to say no because I remembered how good her pound cakes were. I was in heaven as she poured me a glass of cold milk to wash down the cake.

"I quit working because he wanted me to stay at home," said Miss Nora. "But although I enjoyed being at home during the day if my girls needed me, and I liked having a home-cooked meal ready when they got home, I wanted to get out sometimes, too. He was always going out on the weekends, so one Saturday evening I told him I wanted to go out, too. He said I couldn't go with him because he was going out with his friends. So, I got a babysitter to stay with the girls and went out with my girlfriend.

"We went to a club called Maxine's, and I spotted him as soon as I got inside the door. He motioned for us to come to the table where he was sitting with another guy, and said, 'Hell, I didn't think you were serious, but I guess you found my ass, didn't you?'

"I didn't even respond. I was just glad to be out somewhere. Later on I got up to go to the bathroom and this woman followed me inside. She must've been drunk because she had the nerve to tell me she was seeing my husband. I didn't get mad at her; I got mad at him. When I got back to my table, I told him what the woman had said and he got to cursing and carrying on like he'd lost his mind—acting like I was the one who had done something wrong. Then he started calling me names, and what did he do that for? Something went all through me because before I knew it, I'd jumped up, grabbed an empty beer bottle off the table, and started wearing his head out. He never even had a chance to get up out of his chair."

Miss Nora placed a piece of cake into her mouth and chewed. "My girlfriend was begging me to stop hitting him. She said he was going to bleed to death, that I was going to kill him, but I didn't care. I wanted to kill him. In fact I even screamed at the top of my lungs, 'Let the motherfucker die. He's called me names for the last time.' Then I threw the bottle down, picked up my purse and my drink, and got ready to leave his ass sitting there bleeding right there in that club.

"Then he started to beg and plead with me, saying, 'Baby, don't leave me. I won't hurt you no more. Please take me to the hospital.'

"I was like, 'Take you to the hospital? Hell no. The only thing I'm going to do for you is go home, get my gun, and come back and kill your goddamn ass.' I don't get mad easily, but I'd taken all I was going to take. I thought my grandmama must've turned over in her grave a thousand times for all the shit I'd taken from this fool.

"I think that was the beginning of the end of that marriage because after that I went out every weekend, and he couldn't handle me being out there like he was, even though I wasn't out there with no man. I was just out having fun with my friends, but every time I went out, he'd end up jumping on me when I got back home. I tried to defend myself, but he always caught me off guard and I was tired of him hitting me.

"Even though I was always taught that you should stay with your husband no matter what, as long as he's taking care of the bills and everything, it just didn't make sense to stay with him if we were going to be fighting all the time. Those words my grandmama used to say, 'Always love yourself,' stayed in my head. But how could I love myself if I was staying with him and letting him beat my ass all the time? Since I knew in my heart that I didn't deserve to be treated that way, I knew it was time to go. So that's what I did.

"For the most part, I've had a good life. The only thing I regret is the foolishness I put up with when I was younger from the men I married and the men I dated. But I guess we all do that. I can say that I learned from my mistakes. There were times I had to struggle, and I had to have sex with some men who I really didn't care that much for because I had children to raise and you know how that is."

TAMIA, THIRTY-SOMETHING

"I've been married twenty years and I like being married because my husband makes it pleasant. I know from listening to my girl-friends talk that I have one of the good ones, he does everything. He's not one of those helpless men who don't even know how to use a stove or washing machine. He cooks as good as any woman I know, and I'm glad because I can't cook at all. At this very minute, he has a ham hock boiling with onions, garlic, and red pepper in preparation for a pot of red beans, and once he finishes cooking, all I have to do is go in there and clean up. He doesn't mind cooking and I don't mind cleaning, so we have the best of both worlds.

"If I have to go out of town on business, or if I just don't feel well enough to do it, he'll wash clothes, and clean the house, and then go and buy groceries. He just pays attention to details, and a man like that impresses me. I don't think our marriage would have lasted this long if he was a selfish or lazy man, he doesn't have a lazy bone in his body. Now, he'll sit down and drink a beer and watch a football or basketball game on TV, but you can best believe that he's taken care of business before he does.

"Most importantly, he takes great care of me and our children, and he's not afraid to tell us or show us how much he loves us. He's never been the type of man to say, 'Oh, I can't do that, cooking is woman's work,' or 'I'm not going to fold those clothes 'cause wash-ing is a woman's job.' He does the things that men normally do around the house, but he never complains when I ask him to help me do something. I think the reason a great many marriages have so much discontent is because a lot of times one partner doesn't pull their share of the load. The yard might need to be mowed once a week, and the trash taken out once a week, but dinner has to be prepared every day, dishes have to be washed every day, and laundry done every other day if not every day. A woman can get awfully tired and feel put upon when she's doing all of that and all her husband is doing is mowing the yard once a week because he doesn't feel that he should help out and have to do"—Tamia made quotation marks with her fingers—"so-called woman's work. That kind of selfishness can cause a lot of bitterness in a marriage.

"I try to make it a point to let my husband know how much I appreciate what he does and he does the same for me. It's easy to take one another for granted after you've been married a long time, so I work on that. I know you should never say never, but I sincerely believe that if something were to happen to cause our marriage to break up, I would never get married again because I know I would never find a man like my husband. That's the honest to God's truth," Tamia said sincerely. "He's caring, giving, loving, and he doesn't mind hard work, so what more could a woman ask for in a man?

"The only problem we've ever had was when he was so protective of me, because I was so young when we got married. As I got older, his protective nature started to make me feel smothered, because I felt the need to assert my independence, which is quite difficult to do when you marry young and have allowed this one person to be your protector for so long. I went directly from home to marriage and being that young, the last thing you think about is needing your own space. It was difficult for him to accept the fact that I was a grown woman and not the teenage girl he married, but we worked through that and our marriage is even better because he came to understand my needs.

"I've heard it said that in every relationship one person is the giver and one is the taker and I would definitely say that he's the giver in our relationship and that also means he's the stronger one. I'm still a bit selfish but not nearly as much as I used to be, having kids and being married changed all of that." Tamia smiled. "I'm sure I could be less selfish, and I do try to work at that, but there's not really anything he needs to do different to make our marriage better because he does everything already.

"The only other issue we have is that it's kind of hard to keep romance in a marriage when you've been together so long and I know that we both need to work on that. Sex can become routine and it's hard to be spontaneous when you have kids in the house. You want to be all into it when making love to your husband, but your mind is halfway in the room and halfway in the hallway, and you're wondering if you made sure that the door was bolted because you don't want to be caught in the act. That causes you to feel somewhat inhibited, and that can make sex more of a chore than anything else.

"I don't want my kids' hearing nothing that sounds like it's even related to sex coming from my room. You can call me old-fashioned if you will but that's how I am. I didn't hear it coming from my parents' room when I was growing up so I try to respect my children the same way. I remember making up my parents' bed one time and a pair of my father's underwear was under the covers, and that just grossed me out, so I'm careful with things like that where my children are concerned. I mean, they know how babies get here, but they don't want proof that their parents are still actually having sex, so even though I still enjoy the act once we get into it, we can't have that swinging from the chandelier, jumping off the headboard type action anymore. It's just more subdued. Maybe when the kids are all grown and gone we can get freaky again." Tamia grinned. "Maybe we'll start when we're able to buy that summer home in the islands."

AYOKA, THIRTY-SOMETHING

"Even though I'm going through a divorce I think marriage is wonderful but I wish that we received more teaching as young adults on what marriage is really about. In the culture I grew up in everybody just acts like, 'Oh, well, you'll figure it out when you get into it or as you go along.' Marriage is a lot of work and I think it's worth it but I just really, really wish that people would realize, and this is from a divorcee, that divorce is not an option. When you get married, it's about the promise. I think the institution of marriage should coincide a lot more with the word, with God and the Bible. If you've got that foundation when you go into a marriage you'll have a whole different perspective and I didn't.

"When I got married I didn't know anything about what the Bible said about marriage and what marriage was supposed to mean. I really believe that couples should seek counseling, even if they're not affiliated with a church, they should get some type of counseling before marriage.

"I think marriage is a good thing and I would do it over again, but I'm an idealist and I want a perfect marriage. I know there will be fights and disagreements but I really want somebody in my life who, even after all that stress, when I look at him I can still say, 'I love him soooo much, I can't imagine my life without him.' I never had that. When I was with my husband it was more like, 'I hate him.' And I meant it. I tell any young girl, pray for your future husband and ask God to send him to you. Otherwise, you might end up with some fool you wish you'd never met.

"If you asked me what I liked about my marriage," Ayoka stated, "I'd have a hard time thinking of anything. We've been married for fifteen years and separated for two and there was nothing I liked about that marriage. We never got along, not even during the early years. The reason I got married was because I was pregnant and I'd always been taught that I had to uphold a certain image, so being an unwed mother wasn't an option. There was no question that he was the father because he was the only man I'd been with at that time." Ayoka took a deep breath. "I don't know why he got married but he obviously wasn't in love with me.

"From the very start the marriage was unhappy, it seemed like whatever I wanted was the exact opposite of what he wanted so it was a mess. I was never in love with him, but I was physically attracted to him because he was rough around the edges and I'd never been around guys like that. I grew up in a small town where the boys just acted like boys, they weren't trying to push up on me and they weren't street. Then the guy I dated in college was very reserved, kind of a mama's boy while my soon to be husband was bad, he was rough. He knew things and was doing things I had never experienced, and he had more street-sense. It was totally a good girl, bad boy thing between us.

"He taught me a lot of stuff when we first met because I was so naive and I didn't even know much about him because I had a job so we could only hang out on the weekends. Then his roommate moved back to Nevada and he asked me if he could move in with me and I said yes as long as he paid the rent. We moved in as platonic friends only, and to me it was a convenience, because I was thinking that if some lunatic was watching my apartment they'd see a man going in and out. Also, with him there, the apartment would be occupied more. I worked during the day and he worked at night.

"We'd dated a short time a while back before he moved in, but eventually that bad boy thing gets old, he was just so ungroomed and I noticed that at the very beginning. We stopped dating because we were not compatible and I told him it was because the world he was from was too different. It even came to the point that I was embarrassed by who he was around my coworkers.

"For example, we were going to a company party, something like a congratulations for a promotion for one of my coworkers, and I asked him to get a card so we could put a twenty-dollar bill or something in it. Come to find out it was a sympathy card and when my coworker opened it and read it aloud, I could have gone through the floor. Unfortunately I didn't read the card before handing it over to my coworker.

"Then the first time we went out to a nice restaurant, a place where you had to wear a coat and tie, and they had three forks and two spoons, I remember him saying, 'They gave me too many forks, I don't need all these forks.' I told him, 'Shhh, you start at the end and work your way inside.' And this was basic stuff that people who have lived for twenty-two years should know but he was clueless.

"It was during dinner at this restaurant that I realized we were from different backgrounds. We were eating and he would take his fork and his knife and just hold them the entire time. Then when he ate, he would cut and stuff, cut and stuff, and I remember saying to him, 'You will *not* eat like that if I ever take you home to meet my family. You will *not* do that.' So we kind of broke up after that.

"We didn't see each other for a while after that, but one day I had a flat tire and I didn't know anybody else to call. Even though it had been three months since we last spoke when I called him and asked for his help he didn't even hesitate. He didn't say he had something else to do, he was right there to fix it. He was so nice and I remember thinking, 'Maybe I should give him another chance, maybe he's a diamond in the rough.' I thought if I introduced him to the nice and what I considered normal things in life he might just be alright. But instead of him receiving and trying to learn about the nicer things, he would just refuse to participate and then I got pregnant and that was that.

"I never loved him the way a wife should love a husband. I cared but I don't ever remember feeling that anticipation you should feel if you haven't seen each other in a week and can't wait to get home.

"Now I'm just glad to be able to go to bed at night and not have someone bothering me. I could not *stand* to have sex with him. It's wonderful to know that I can go to bed and not have to fight with someone because I don't feel like having sex. I used to tell him all the time, 'You start making love when you get up in the morning; you start making love when you tell me I look pretty even though my hair is still standing up from sleeping all night. You can't ignore me all day long and tell me to get out of your face every time I try to have a conversation with you and then expect me to come to bed at night and try to be romantic,' but he never understood that. That's how I know he never loved me because even if he didn't understand, if he actually loved me, he would've made an effort."

Ayoka bit down on her lip and closed her eyes for a moment. "I've asked myself a thousand times what finally caused me to take that step toward divorce because even though we were miserable with one another, I could have stayed with him, if I'd been willing to put up with his shit. We never had money problems. We had 'my money,' and 'his money' and there was no problem as long as the bills were getting paid. He never knew how much money I made and I honestly didn't know how much he was making either. Everything was separate and I think that had a lot to do with the failure of the marriage. We never were a 'we' "—Ayoka made quotation marks with her forefingers—"not even with the money.

"My daughter told me recently that one time she asked her father why he'd married me. She was looking for a romantic answer like, 'It was love at first sight, blah, blah, blah.' Well that wasn't the answer he gave her. He told her, 'I married your mother for economic purposes only. I knew we could have more together than I could have by myself,' so to me that's more than enough proof that he wasn't in love either.

"It was just a bad marriage. I can remember something as simple as going to Disneyland being a terrible experience. He would go but he would make the outing miserable for everybody just by being mean. He'd say, 'We're only going to get one bag of popcorn not four bags,' and then he'd eat it all or at least most of it and the children would be saying, 'We want some popcorn,' and he would gripe back, 'I'll hand it to you in a minute.' I could've afforded to buy all the popcorn I wanted but I didn't want to fight about it so it just got to the place where we stopped with the family vacations. I would just take the kids myself because I always say if you can't afford to buy something as cheap as popcorn, then you don't need to be at a theme park in the first place." Ayoka grimaced and rolled her eyes.

"The kids and I were laughing about that recently. At least now we can laugh but for a long time we couldn't. My son said that he'd been scared to death of butter knives for a long time and that was because when he was little and we'd go out to eat, my husband would always yell at him if he even thought about touching a knife. He would just make dinner crazy. He was constantly saying, 'Don't touch that knife. Don't touch that knife.' " Ayoka shrugged her shoulders in confusion. "Hell, it was a butter knife, it wasn't even a steak knife but I guess he thought the child would cut his hand or something. When he was about twelve he used a real steak knife for the first time and he cut his finger. I can't imagine why that happened, can you?" Ayoka smirked. "There was always some drama in that household.

"Even when we were talking about getting a divorce I asked him, 'Name two situations in our entire marriage that you can remember that you thought was a good experience for us.' I was just trying to get him to name a time since we'd been married that we could look back on and hold on to as a good time. His reply was our oldest child's birth when he hadn't even been there for the birth. He had been out of town but once again he was being a smart-ass because he knew I wasn't going to say that wasn't a happy time for us.

"I told him, 'I wasn't having a good time when I was giving birth and you know that's not what I'm talking about. I'm trying to get you to talk about activities we shared and enjoyed together,' and he got mad at me because he couldn't remember anything and neither could I. That's why I asked him that question. I was just trying to get a feel for what he thought might have been a good time.

"If I could go back and do it all over again, I know for a fact that I would've gotten involved in the church a lot sooner. I've learned a lot through my affiliation with the church I go to now about having relationships in a godly way. I really believe that could have helped our relationship to grow as opposed to having a 'You want to do this, well, no, I want to do that' type of marriage.

"I buy him books now, like those manpower books, and even though it won't help me any, he's still the father of my children. These books are written from a spiritual aspect and help men to learn how to be a good husband, a good leader, and a good father based on God's plan. I never tried that before because I didn't know to try it. I don't think he would've totally rejected that although when I did get involved with the church while we were married, he stopped going, and that was crazy because when he was going to church and I wasn't he went every Sunday.

"I put up with his shit for a long time, to this day I just can't understand how I allowed him to do me that way. I guess I'm just one of those people who finds it easier to keep the peace, shut her mouth, and take the grief.

"As a matter of fact, that's part of the reason I became involved in an affair. I was just so miserable and unhappy that I was vulnerable to any man who could love me for who I was. I'm still involved with that man but that had nothing to do with the problems in my marriage. The affair was only one small symptom.

"Even with all of that said I'd like to remarry because I'm one of those people who need companionship. I need to have somebody around. There are some people who say they love being by themselves, they love being alone. Not me. While I don't need somebody in my face all the time, asking me questions or talking to me nonstop, I do like the idea of knowing that he's in another room somewhere and I can get to him. I like the presence of him in my space. If I want somebody to talk to he's there.

"If I do get married again, there are going to be some different prerequisites next time. It's going to have to be about more than infatuation or physical attraction, that's only a starting point. Marriage takes more than 'He makes me feel good or I'm really happy when he's around,' and I wish I'd known that but I didn't. It's a choice, it's not a feeling. It's not 'I'm excited because he's cute,' you choose to love him and once you make that choice it's just that. So, if I do it again, I'll be more careful before I choose to love someone and vow that I'll be his wife 'until death do us part.' "

ALICIA, FORTY-SOMETHING

"I think marriage is wonderful, I must think so because I've been married three times so far so obviously I haven't given up on it. I was married three years to my first husband, six years to my second husband, and twenty years to my third so apparently it gets better each and every time because I've stayed married longer each go round.

"I liked the partnership that comes with being married. It's good to have someone close who knows you better than anyone else and it's good to have someone you can count on who loves you no matter what happens. You might be eight months pregnant with his child, unable to force a pair of shoes on your feet if you tried and have your hair pulled back with a rubber band, and he will still take the time to rub your feet or your back and tell you how beautiful you are. It's easier to deal with a problem if you have someone to share those problems with and I like coming home and having someone there who is just as excited to see me as I am to see him.

"One of the things that I didn't like in marriage was being taken for granted. People in a relationship should always treat one another with courtesy and respect. I didn't marry you to be your housekeeper; I married you to be your wife and your partner. Don't think that just because we're married that I'm automatically supposed to do everything for you and when I do something for you the least you can say is thank you, at least acknowledge it because I didn't have to do it. I tried not to expect much from my husbands in that respect because that way I wouldn't continue to be disappointed. The few times that one of them did do something nice I was so stunned and shocked that I probably acted more appreciative than I should've.

"I divorced all three of my husbands because of dishonesty on their part. It was dishonesty in all three cases; the dishonesty just wore different masks. The first husband drank too much and chased women, the second husband hid money and was controlling, and the third one lied about everything under the sun, even if I caught him lying he would still stand there and insist that the guitar he bought only cost $50 when I was right there holding a receipt for a guitar with his signature that said $250. All I ever wanted from them was the truth and they had a hard time telling something as simple as the truth.

"If I had it to do all over again, I wouldn't have married so young. I would've allowed myself more time to get to know me and my likes and dislikes before trying to deal with somebody else's issues. I also would've spent more time getting to know more about my husbands before I said yes to marriage. Looking back, I don't know why I was in such a big hurry, it wasn't like I was pregnant and my daddy was holding a shotgun to my boyfriend's head.

"I do plan on marrying the man I'm dating now. So what if it's the fourth time, maybe this time I've got it right. The key this time though is that there is no hurry, we know each other and we're taking our time with each other, and this time it just feels so right to me. I want this man to know everything about me and I want to know everything about him as well. After that, if he still wants to propose and if I still want to say yes, then we'll go for it."

VALEKA, FIFTY-SOMETHING

I was so anxious to interview Valeka that I'd arrived at the Pappadeux Seafood Kitchen twenty minutes early. By the time she got there, I'd already drank half of my "Swamp Thang," which is a mixture of rum and some other good stuff that's frozen, and had eaten most of the warm French bread the waiter brought over. The day happened to be gray, rainy, and cloudy, but that reminded me of Louisiana in the summertime and that was fine with me. Since Pappadeux is decorated in the style of New Orleans with colorful beads and tiny lights throughout the room, moss draped from the trees, and zydeco music playing in the background, the atmosphere along with the rain outside and the smell of seafood simmering brought back memories of home. It was perfect.

A funny little lady with a quick tongue, Valeka arrived late, as usual. I could see her in the parking lot from where I sat as she popped open a huge umbrella, and took her time prissing up the steps, through the courtyard, and inside toward my table. Wearing a size seven and all of five feet tall, she has dark, chocolate-colored skin, wears her hair cut so close that all she has to do is brush it, and is as cute and outgoing as can be.

Today Valeka was dressed in some fabulous little Fubu jeans, a teeny tiny T-shirt, and shoes to match. It was no surprise that her whole outfit was name brand because she has always, and I do mean always, dressed to impress. Even though she claims that she's a bargain shopper, you'd never know it judging by what she wears and how good she looks in it.

I'd looked forward to this interview because not only is she an interesting lady, she's also very funny, and I needed an excuse to eat at Pappadeux anyway. Seems like I'm always looking for an excuse to eat out, and doing an interview over lunch is as good an excuse as any.

Since we both already knew what we wanted, we wasted no time with the menu. The waiter, who was as handsome as could be in his black pants and vest, starched long-sleeved white shirt with a white apron tied around his slim waist, was very attentive, and we placed our order for the appetizers and main course at the same time, so we wouldn't have to wait too long to indulge.

Valeka ordered oysters on the half shell for an appetizer, while I ordered a cup of seafood gumbo. For the main course, I ordered the Cajun Combo, which consisted of blackened catfish, dirty rice, and grilled shrimp in red sauce over white rice. Valeka went for the Seafood Combo where the catfish, oysters, shrimp, and potatoes were all deep-fried. She was a size seven after all, so what did it matter?

With that out of the way, I turned on the recorder and asked her where she wanted to start. "I'll start with marriage," Valeka replied, "I have a lot to say on that subject.

"Marriage is a very sacred commitment between God and the two people involved. I think you need to be sure you're not marrying for the wrong reasons, and I think when you meet someone you should first become friends and make sure you're compatible. The two of you are supposed to 'forsake all others' like it says in the Bible, but I didn't understand that it meant you're supposed to love one another, be totally committed to each other, and be as one, until I got older and was already well into my second marriage. Forsaking all others means no one else should come before your spouse. You hear all the time that a family that prays together, stays together, and that starts with the couple.

"The reason I believe you should be friends first is that if the marriage doesn't work and you decide to divorce, you can always go back to being friends. But if you're not friends, and you jump into a marriage because of what he looks like, or for what kind of job he has, it's not going to work because you married him for the wrong reasons.

"When you become totally committed and feel that you want to get married, one way to make sure it's gonna work out is to take a trip together, and that doesn't mean you have to sleep together. If the two of you are confined in a car, or if you fly or take a train together, you'll find out a lot about that person. Many times that man's personality, his likes and dislikes, will be totally different from what you think they are, and may conflict with your personality. Of course, I'm not saying you'll find out everything you need to know, but if you take a trip with a person for a few days and they start to get on your nerves, or if you start noticing all these little things you don't think you could live with 'till death do you part,' then that may not be the person for you.

"When you're dating, you seem to like everything he likes, and even though he may have some habits you don't like, you ignore them. But those habits are not going to change just because you get married. Farther on down the road you'll be saying, 'What was I thinking? I saw that before I married him and I ignored it, but that shit really gets on my nerves.'

"You cannot change a person, nor should you try to, and I didn't learn that lesson until I was well into my forties. Once you're married and start finding all these faults, it's too late. But if you're both mature, you'll understand that while you have some of the same likes and dislikes, and some of the same goals and desires, that doesn't mean you're going to agree on everything. Mature couples realize this and deal with it, and will often have better marriages than those who try to change one another. Even after you're married, you're still an individual and you both have to allow for that in order for a marriage to work.

"In my first marriage, I had a husband who didn't have any goals and didn't expect me to have any either. His favorite phrase was, 'I'ms a gonna.'" Valeka rolled her eyes dramatically. "All he did was talk about what he was gonna do, and then he wouldn't do shit. He constantly told me that I spoke my mind too much, but I felt the same way about him. We were just not compatible at all.

"I married him for his looks, his position, who I thought he was and who I thought he was going to be, and those were all the wrong reasons. I didn't date him long enough to really know him, and by the time I did get to know him, it was too late. He was controlling and verbally abusive, and I never had a say in anything, he made all of the decisions. I had to get his permission to go to my mother's house or write a check. Whatever he said, I had to go along with or else he'd be hell to live with.

"He did have his good qualities, like he was very clean, and worked hard, but he even took being clean too far. He kept the car immaculate inside and out, and I can recall many times that if I had the children in the car, and had let them eat chips or cookies or something, I would have to stop on the side of the road before we got home and get every one of those crumbs out of that car because I knew if I didn't, I would be scolded and fussed at, just like I was a child myself.

"Before he got home from work in the afternoon, I had to make sure that the children's hands and faces were clean, that their clothes didn't have any spots or stains, that dinner was prepared and the house was just right, or else I was asked, 'What the hell have you been doing all day long?'

"I was so in love and so blind, because I was young and dumb, that anything he told me, I took as gospel. I didn't know any better. He only slapped me one time, but he would put me down and call me stupid and ignorant all the time, and that hurt more than anything. Many times he would get angry and say, 'I don't know why I married you,' and all I could do is cry because I didn't know what I had done wrong.

"Once when his mother needed some money, he took her to the bank and helped her to apply for a loan in my name. I didn't know anything about it until a letter came to the house. It was addressed to both of us, so I opened it and when he got home he was furious. He said, 'If you ever open my mail again, I'll hurt you, with your dumb country ass,' so I couldn't even open the mail after that.

"I told my mother what had happened because at that point I just didn't know what to do anymore and she gave me some of the best advice I've ever received. She said, 'The next time you find something like that, shut your mouth and keep it shut. You have two eyes, two ears, and one big mouth. So always look, and listen twice as much as you speak.' Since then, I've done just that and it has helped me a lot," Valeka said.

"Even though that first marriage scarred me, I was determined to keep a positive outlook on life and on my future. So, after we divorced I went to counseling and found that I was carrying around a lot of hurt, anger, and resentment. I learned that I should not feel badly about my marriage not working out. I also learned that I was a loving, caring, and giving person, and that I deserved to be happy. So, I decided then and there that I would put my energy into going back to college, taking care of my children, and making a better life for myself so that I could be happy with or without a husband.

"I became engaged to another man about three years after my divorce, but the closer we got to the wedding date, the worse things became. He was one big baby with no goals in life except to boss other people around. He'd been a policeman for years, and he was used to being in charge and telling everybody else what to do, even to the point of telling me how to park the car. A lot of the time, when we were alone, he'd threaten to call off the wedding because he said I acted like I loved my kids more than I loved him.

"I was constantly trying to prove my love for him and I did the best I could to keep him from feeling that way, but nothing I did seemed to be good enough. I loved him, no, I was crazy about him, but when I realized that marrying him meant my children would have to grow up in a negative atmosphere, and that they'd inevitably be affected by his low self-esteem, that was it. I knew I could do better than that, so I said, 'To hell with this' and I broke it off. Once I did that, I never looked back because there was no reason to. It's just like chewing gum, once you spit it out, you don't pick it back up and chew it again because the sweetness is gone.

"I was single for quite some time after that, but I did finally remarry, and I've been married for ten years this time. I met my husband at church, even though I wasn't really looking for a husband. I'd become comfortable being single, but since he's totally different from my first husband, I feel it might work this time.

"We took trips together while we were dating and became best friends. We talked a lot, we did things together, and after dating him for two years, I found that he was just about everything I would want in a friend, a husband, and a lover, and we were both ready to make a commitment to each other when that time came.

"I enjoy being married to him because I can share things with him. Sometimes when I'm tired or feeling down, he has a way of picking me up and making me feel positive. As we grow older, I realize that we are all that we have, and what I mean by that is I'm really the only person he can depend on and vice versa. Your children grow up and have their own lives and their own families, they have commitments to jobs and other things they have to do, and I cannot rely on them for everything, or get upset when they can't spend time with me. Sure, there are times when I want to see them or be with them, but even when I can't, I still have him and he's always there for me.

"Even though we get along well, that doesn't mean we have a perfect marriage. There are some things I dislike about being married, but they're not major. For example, there are times when you need space, even when you're committed to someone, you need time alone and time to think.

"I like to shop or go out to eat alone sometimes, because I don't want to be rushed and I don't want to make my decisions based on what someone else thinks or wants. I can get the Bible, or a jigsaw puzzle book, and be all by myself, and when I do that, I really don't want to be disturbed. My husband always wants to be involved in what I'm doing no matter what it is, and sometimes I just don't want to be bothered, and I don't see anything wrong with that.

"Just last week I was talking about taking a trip back home, alone, and he started making decisions about where, what, when, and how we were going to do it, and I hadn't even invited him. Men have a tendency to want to be in control and run things, and I don't always like that. When you're single, you can do as you please, and you can enjoy your private, special quality time alone if that's what you want to do. So, marriage isn't perfect by any means, and people who have never been married need to know that.

"I believe we should have a personal relationship with Christ because a successful marriage only occurs when two people work together in every aspect of that marriage. I can't expect him to do everything my way, nor can he expect that from me, but we both should be wise and intelligent enough to sit down and discuss things. When there are problems, we need to discuss them because one never knows what the other one is thinking. We pick a time and place, and not at night in the bedroom before going to bed, but a neutral place, where we can talk.

"We don't have any secret or private things going on that we hide from one another because we know that would destroy the trust between us, and once that's gone, you have a real problem. So, even though we might both need space and private time, having separate, private accounts and things like that is not a good idea.

"I could always do things to make my marriage better, but one of my hang-ups is that when I want something done, I want it done now. I don't want it done tomorrow, or next week, and it really bothers me when he procrastinates. When he tells me he's going to do something, I don't appreciate it when he keeps putting it off because I feel like he doesn't care about me when he does that, and it seems like tomorrow never comes. I like for a man to be true to his word, so I have a real problem with that. I probably need to be more patient, and more tolerant, but that's something I have to work on.

"Also, I believe in telling people what I think or what I feel, and if my husband upsets me in any way, I have to let him know, I just can't hold it in. So, maybe that's another area I need to work on. I know that I'm not perfect, and I realize this is my second marriage. I can't always put the blame on him when there's a disagreement, I have to look in the mirror sometimes and be honest enough to admit when I'm wrong, and I often do that. I'm not too proud to apologize when I've upset him or hurt his feelings, but I do stand my ground when I feel I'm right.

"Now let me say this, loud and clear: He could really, really make things better if he'd stop procrastinating, and stop using the words 'I'ms a gonna.' My first husband used to say that all of the time, and I cannot stand that phrase. If I could go to the Supreme Court and have those words stricken from the English language, I would. Don't be saying, 'I'ms a gonna,' just get off your ass and do it. Don't put off today for tomorrow because we're not promised tomorrow. We're not even promised the next hour. Life is uncertain but death is sure, so if he'd stop using that phrase, I wouldn't have a whole lot to get upset about.

"As I look toward our future, I'd love for my husband and me to buy some land with a nice little house on it, where we could be away from all the hustle and bustle of the city. It would be a nice little place where we could take long walks, go fishing, or just sit out on the porch and drink a cold glass of lemonade. I don't view getting older as just giving up on life, I see it as an opportunity to continue growing and doing some of the things I couldn't afford to do when I was young with little children. I want us to grow old together, but I want to grow old gracefully.

"Now that my children are grown and gone, and my grandchildren are growing up and doing their own thing, I just want to enjoy the rest of my life doing the things that make me happy and bring me peace."

JACKIE, FORTY-SOMETHING

Jackie and her husband's dream home was no more than a year old, and they'd spared no expense in building it. A little over 4,000 square feet, the house sat on two acres of land and their privacy was maintained behind a large stand of oak trees. The decor inside was old English, with lots of dark woods and marble tabletops. An antique grandfather clock stood watch in the foyer and the floors were hardwood, covered with Turkish rugs. The kitchen took up a huge portion of space and was outfitted with professional cookware and appliances, and while the look of the house's interior was expensive, the rooms were still very cozy.

Jackie was a part-time chef in one of the hottest restaurants in the city. She worked part-time because it gave her something to do and she loved to cook, and she liked having her own money. She also loved throwing down at home for friends and family as well which she did often. Her three sons were all long grown, so the only responsibilities she had were to herself and her husband of twenty-eight years.

As a chef, Jackie always found herself fighting the battle of the bulge, so to balance that out, she'd made one room of the house into a fully equipped gym. She did her best to make it a point to visit the room at least four times a week, but the gourmet kitchen was like a magnet to her. She was forever in there perfecting already superb recipes, and it was always an honor when she called us over to sample her concoctions.

After we'd eaten a fabulous dinner that consisted of grilled steak and shrimp kabobs on a bed of yellow rice, we settled down on her wraparound porch with some ice-cold lemonade and homemade oatmeal and raisin cookies and started to talk.

We first asked her what she thought about marriage, but just watching the way she always doted on her husband, it was obvious what her response would be.

"I think marriage is great," Jackie said. "I think everybody should experience it at least once. Some people may have a different viewpoint but I enjoy being married, it's been good for me. I've been married for twenty-eight years, I'm still happily married and I married my childhood sweetheart. He is the man I shared that first kiss with and the only man I've ever been with sexually, so I learned everything from him.

"During the time we were dating, it was understood that you didn't have sex or do any of those promiscuous type things. You became friends first and I would recommend that to anyone. Be friends first, then involve your body. That seemed to work for us at least."

She crossed her legs and leaned back while toying with the silver charm that circled her neck. "I like having somebody here when I come home. I like having somebody to talk to, and somebody who will uplift me.

"My husband and I see one another as best friends. We can tell each other anything. Granted, there are some things on his job that he can't talk about but other than that we talk about everything. There is nothing we don't share.

"My parents were very strict so I couldn't do a lot of things the other girls did, I couldn't go any place I wanted to. If it was a basketball game or football game that was fine, but as far as all of the parties being held around town, if I got to go, I had to leave the party at a certain time and be home at a certain time and I had to be dressed a certain way. My mother always made sure to remind me of who I was. She would say, 'You're Dr. Howard's daughter. Make sure you handle yourself accordingly.'

"My parents told my husband the same thing when he started dating me. When he first met my mother he talked to her and asked if he could date me and she said, 'Yes, I don't mind, you seem like a nice young man, but you got to talk to her father to see what he says. Dr. Howard is the one who's going to let you know if you can date Jackie.'

"You're looking at me like that's odd, but you had to have permission from a girl's parents to date back then, if she was a decent girl. Remember how boys used to ask, 'Give me a chance,' or 'Will you go with me?' Well, he had to ask my parents just to be able to do that. Just like a man would ask your father for your hand in marriage, just to be able to date me he had to ask. It was the respectable thing to do.

"Not that he was used to that." Jackie laughed. "He said he'd never met a girl whose parents made him go through all that so it was a new experience for him. It was one he was willing to go through but it was something different. I know that's old folky and people don't even do any of that stuff today but that's how we started out and it must have been okay because we're still together.

"There is really only one thing I don't like about being married." Jackie thought about it for a minute, then continued. "I don't like being separated. My husband was in the Marines and we went through many years of separation, not by choice but because of his job. I just hated being apart from him. Nowadays women might get upset if they're away from their husbands two days or maybe a week but I had to go for nine or ten months sometimes. I didn't like it then and I don't like it now. After he retired from the Marines he got a job with the Internal Affairs Division of the police department and there are times when duty calls and I guess I'm jealous of that. I was jealous of that when he was a Marine and I'm jealous of that now. I'm jealous of the fact that sometimes duty comes first. I love him and I hate the fact that I have to take a backseat to his career. I always make every effort to put him first and I'd like it if he could do the same for me, but most times that's not possible.

"It seems like his career has always been first but that's probably why he's been so successful. He's a military-oriented guy. He always felt like, 'Hey I've got to put food on the table and take care of my family and the way I do that is by complying and doing everything that they tell me to do,' so the Marines was number one and I was number two. He excelled in his career, everybody loved him, and he was a great officer. He went through the ranks pretty fast and that was good, but still I hated the fact that I felt like I came second.

"Sometimes out of loneliness I would feel tempted, but I never pursued it so there was never another man. The thoughts were there but I didn't act on them." Jackie laughed. "I'm glad I didn't because things wouldn't be as good as they are now. We plan to grow old together. I asked him that just last night. I said, 'Are we going to grow old together?' And he said, 'Of course, baby.' I asked, 'Is there anyone else you'd want to grow old with?' And he said, 'No, you're the only one.'

"So, we will continue to build our lives together as we always have, buy a few things here and there, and work in the garden. I love to use fresh vegetables when I prepare meals. My husband is a homebody and I couldn't have stayed with him for so long if I wasn't a homebody as well. He loves being around family so that's basically what we do, hang out with the family, work in the garden, and do stuff around the house.

"When we finally retire we probably won't do anything different. We might take a vacation here or there but we're not big travelers. I'd like to travel more but I can't get my husband to go anywhere. By the time he got out of the Marines he'd already seen the world so as far as travel is concerned, he's been fulfilled. One of the hardest lessons you learn in a marriage if you plan on staying together is that somebody's got to bend, so I guess I'm the one who's always done the bending.

"Communication is what makes our marriage work," Jackie stated decisively. "We talk a lot. He talks and I talk and a lot of times if we don't have anything to do we'll just go for a little ride and our conversation is so good. It's like we both unwind and we just talk about what's on our mind or what's going on with our kids or at the restaurant. We talk about how cool it would be to live in a farmhouse and stuff like that but I think communication is what keeps us together.

"I learned a long time ago that I want my husband to know exactly how I feel about things so I make sure I break it down to where he understands *every* element of what I'm trying to say. Then I ask him, 'Do you know what I mean, baby, do you understand? Do you feel like that?'

"The one thing I think I could do to make our marriage even better is to add more romance. My husband isn't a very affectionate person but I can get it out of him when I really want it. But I'd like for him to be more affectionate without my having to initiate it. We don't have to be kissing in public and rubbing on each other's behinds, but just like you have quality time, I think having quality affection time is important too. Maybe something as simple as making sure that we make love often or just doing something that makes you realize that you're still connected. Just setting aside some special time to rub each other's feet or back could make things more romantic.

"Even after twenty-eight years the sex is still great but yes, the urge declines. We don't have sex all the time like we used to but it's not so stagnant that I have to sit down and look at a calendar to remember the last time. He doesn't seem to have the urge as often and neither do I, so it works. It seems like we're on the same page as far as how much we both want to make love.

"Everybody wants to be touched. Everybody wants to be loved. We're not a couple that goes around kissing each other all the time but I would like more affection. I bought four oversized chairs for my family room and they have worked wonders for us. It's nice to be able to sit close to one another when we're watching a movie or something. I think being able to be close is good. Just having a smaller space to sit in instead of a big, long sofa where you can both stretch out on separate ends is nice. I bought those oversized chairs with the intention of getting some quality snuggling time and they're working so far."

JESSICA, THIRTY-SOMETHING

Jessica is about five feet eight inches tall and still very athletic. She's a personal trainer and has thighs to die for. We interviewed her on the patio of her home in Dallas/South Oak Cliff. She told us that the house was more than twenty years old. From the outside it wasn't anything spectacular but once inside, it was amazing. Original artwork adorned the walls and the focal point of the house was the great room with walls painted a vivid red. The furniture was dark mahogany wood and the various sofas, chairs, and love seats were black leather and covered with pillows that were ruby red, sapphire blue, amber yellow, and emerald green.

The patio and backyard resembled an oasis and included a pool and swim-up bar with a separate bar and grill at one end of the patio. The patio floor was inlaid with Mexican tile and oversized clay pots held reddish purple caladiums and bloodred geraniums. We sat beneath slow-moving ceiling fans in some of the oversized chairs covered with zebra-print pillows. Small cast-iron tables were stationed between each of the chairs and the tabletops were made of thick Mexican glass with the shape of Texas in iron beneath.

Jessica had always been a wonderful hostess and today was no exception. She'd prepared a large pitcher of cold sangria and two beautiful snack trays. One tray held smoked Gouda, thinly sliced turkey, roast beef, ham, and club crackers and the other fresh strawberries, watermelon, kiwi, and cantaloupe.

I took a sip of the ice-cold sangria and relished the sweet taste that flowed past my lips and over my tongue. I carefully placed the glass on the Mexican glass tabletop because I'm known to be heavy-handed. We began by asking Jessica how she felt about marriage.

"Well, I've been married twelve years now and I think marriage is great *but*"—and she made a point of emphasizing the word—"you have to make sure you're ready for it. I don't think it's something you should jump into without a second thought because there's a lot of work involved and if I knew then what I know now I probably would've waited even longer.

"One thing I can say is that I like having a partner. A lot of my single friends say they're lonely. At least I have someone I can talk to but that's only when I'm in the mood to talk," she said, laughing. "It's nice to have somebody to help with life's challenges in general.

"Sadly, it doesn't take much thought and concentration to let you in on what I dislike. Sometimes I need my own private space and I don't want to be bothered. It would be nice to be able to say to my husband, 'Can you go take a trip for about a month?' and not worry about hurting his feelings.

"All marriages have their ups and downs, you just have to work through them. Couples should share in the responsibilities but it's almost as if when we said 'I do' my husband said, 'I don't do that anymore.' A good example of this is when his sisters' birthdays come around. It became, 'Okay, make sure you get them a gift and a card,' and I don't feel I should have to do that just because I'm his wife. Small things like that add up.

"Also, it seems like my husband is under the impression that it's my responsibility to do all the cleaning. I don't think he's ever dusted or cleaned the bathroom and I work full-time just like he does. He's never said he expects for me to do it but he doesn't help so to me that means he expects for me to take care of it.

"He does do the things that men typically do like empty the trash and has the nerve to tell me that if I want him to do some of those other things around the house, just ask him. I constantly tell him, 'Why do I have to ask you? You live here too; you walked over that spot on the floor, why can't you wipe it up?' He says, 'I didn't even see that spot,' which I don't understand because if you bend over and pick up something and there's a spot right next to whatever it is you're picking up, how do you not see that? Is that a problem that only men have?" Jessica raised her brows in question. "Something like that frustrates the hell out of me.

"I don't know what the future holds for us, who's to say what could happen. Sometimes you grow apart and sometimes you don't have the same interests or goals that you used to. If he walked out tomorrow I can't say that I would be surprised but I also can't say that I would sit on the couch and whine and cry either. I might be sad but I'd have to move on. I think of it like this: if he walked out of here tomorrow, what would I have to do to make this household run? The answer to that question, sadly enough, is that I'd have to roll that trash out to the end of the driveway, that's about it.

"I'd have to learn how to use the riding lawn mower or change the filter in the air conditioner and I'm sure I could hire some-body to do that. But things like maintenance for my car? I take care of it anyway. If he walked out tomorrow, the twins would cry and be sad but all I'd say is, 'Don't cry, you'll see him every other weekend, don't worry about it.' Nothing would change in my household or my schedule except that he currently picks the kids up from school, so all I'd have to do is swing by the school myself, no problem.

"I can honestly say that I know I do my part around here. He's the one who needs to work at trying to do more. If the tables were turned, I would make myself more responsible and accountable for things in the household to such an extent that I'm needed. But he acts as if he doesn't care; he's just too comfortable.

"I've heard all that talk about not starting what you can't finish"— Jessica curled her lips—"but when we first started out he did more. I worked long hours and he would get off at a set time every day and by the time I got home he would've at least cooked or washed a load of clothes. I can't say he ever cleaned, but the other things were a trade-off so I didn't mind doing that part. Then he got a job where he worked longer hours, but it was still just the two of us so in my free time, when I was at home and he was working, I didn't have anything else to do but clean and then sit around and read a book or something.

"Once we had the twins, it seemed like I took on all the extra responsibility that comes with having children and he didn't take on any so the relationship changed. I didn't start out doing everything I just think it was a result of normal lifestyle changes, which adds to your responsibilities. However, I took on those added responsibilities while he didn't.

"I believe the only reason our marriage works is because I have a lot of tolerance. I used to have much more than I do now though because now I just get tired and start issuing ultimatums. I'm like, 'Look, you have to help do something around here.'" Jessica slapped the glass tabletop with her palm. Apparently she wasn't afraid of breaking the top. "'I shouldn't have to ask you every time I need something done, that's like having another child.' I have to ask, 'Did you mop the floor, did you throw a load of clothes into the washer when you came home before you started playing on the computer? It's not really that hard, honey, the machine's doing the washing, not you.' I'm afraid that one day I'll get to a point where I'll say, 'You know what? I'm tired, I'd probably get more rest and have more energy if we were apart and you had the kids every other weekend because at least then I'd have some free time to myself.'" Jessica sighed and poured herself another glass of sangria.

"Sometimes I resent the way he acts and I think we might be better off in two separate households. I could see him when I needed to see him, if you know what I mean.

"I talked to my gynecologist the other day and she told me, 'Okay, you need to make a list. Put on your list the things you can change, the things you can modify, and the things you can't change. The things you can modify, try to modify. Let's say for example your husband throws his dirty socks on the floor every day. You're probably thinking, "Why can't he take the socks to the laundry room and put them in the hamper?" You need to have a hamper close by the area where he currently throws his socks, and you tell him, "Here's your hamper. You put your socks in here and make sure that it gets put in the laundry room or else your socks just don't get washed," so you're modifying it and he knows that if he doesn't do that he'll have to wash his own socks.'

"She said, 'You'd think as a doctor I would be stressed because I could have four women in labor; two in one hospital and two in another but you know what, I figure that I can only do so much because I'm only one person. So I take a deep breath and take it as it comes. You have to learn to prioritize. You need to assign different people responsibilities and tell them that it's up to them to make sure those things get done. You're probably afraid that you'll hurt people's feelings but if the only way things are going to get better is for you to tell them, then so be it. And whatever you say you need, you're going to have to stick to it, and not waiver, or you'll just go back to the way things used to be. Once you say what you have to say, that's it, just move on.'

"I thought about it and it made sense so I took her advice and it's even working a little bit. It was like she'd been reading my mind because just that morning I'd told my husband about leaving his clothes on the floor. He takes his clothes off in the evening and puts them in a pile on the floor right next to his closet. Then, in the morning he gets up, goes to start the coffee, comes back to take a shower, goes back to the kitchen to pour himself a cup of coffee, comes back to the room to finish getting dressed, then back to the kitchen to pack his lunch.

"That's *three* times he's been close enough to the laundry room and the last time he comes in here, if he has a towel or something from the bathroom, he drops it off at that same pile, goes to the kitchen to pick up his lunch, and walks out the door.

"I am not kidding you. I swear to God." Jessica held up her right hand. "I swear. I swear. I swear," Jessica said seriously. "I swear to you and it's not like I've said anything just once, twice, or three times, I've said things four times because it happens all the time. He would let the hamper overflow at the apartment we lived in before we bought this house instead of just taking the hamper to the laundry room so this is nothing new. I even tried the tactic of just taking my dirty clothes and leaving his, and his clothes would lay on that floor for a week until I finally had to say, 'Every night you help me make sure that our kids take their dirty clothes to the laundry room and you can't put yours in there? You act like something is wrong with you.'

"My other complaint is that he's very selfish. He believes that people should do things for him but he doesn't feel that he should have to return the favor. If my dirty clothes were lying on the floor with his and I asked him to carry the dirty clothes to the laundry room, he would sort through the clothes, pick out his, and leave mine lying there, I kid you not.

"Or I'll have a glass of water on the nightstand and I'll have left it there for two days. You know I'm not going to drink that water right? His cup will be right next to it and he'll get his cup and put it in the dishwasher but do you think he picks up my glass? Hell no, he acts like he can only see out of one eye and that's the one he sees his cup with.

"I try to rationalize it by telling myself that he acts that way because he's the youngest child in his family and he was used to his sisters taking care of him but that wears thin too. If I ask him to do something, he'll do it but he'll do it with an attitude and I don't want him to do it if he's going to have an attitude, which is probably fine with him.

"We can be sitting at the table, finished eating dinner, and here's my plate and here are the children's plates"—Jessica motions to the table—"and he'll get up from the table and take his plate and leave the children's plates like he doesn't even see them. He'll leave them there for me to pick up and it just pisses me off.

"If we go somewhere as a family, he gets up in just enough time just to get himself ready, so if we have to be there at 10:00 A.M., then I'm getting up at 7:30 A.M. or 8:00 A.M. so I can get the twins ready, and he's getting up at 9:15 A.M. Shit like that causes resentment and in so many words I've told him that.

"I'm like, 'You do shit like this and then you want to have sex with me? I'm not even feeling you so don't expect me to roll over. Here I have to take care of you like I have to take care of my children but I don't sleep with my children. So that's why I say if he had somebody else down the street and he packed up his shit and left I'd say, 'Bye.'" Jessica smacked her palms together, then waved. "Kick mud but don't forget to come get your kids next weekend.

"He used to say when we first got married, 'I bet if we divorced you'd act a fool.' I probably would've then but now"—Jessica slowly pulled a napkin toward her—'Baby, you slide that paper over here and see how fast I sign it.' I could be a nag or I could be a bitch but I choose not to be because that's not my nature; I don't have time to yell and scream and fight. I told my doctor, 'You know what? My husband is lucky to be alive this morning because I almost threw a frying pan right at his head.' But what good would that do? I might have broken my window and upset my kids.

"I don't think that there is anything else I could do to make the marriage better." Jessica let out a deep breath and tilted her head sideways. "I think I'm doing enough. I'm doing more than enough and I'm not adding another thing to my list. The only thing I could do different is stand up in the middle of the bed butt naked and dance, but what is that going to do to help make my marriage better? It might bring satisfaction just for the moment but then what?

"Now, if I thought that I could give sex to get other things done around here it would be different, but I'm not doing that because if I give all this sex then he's going to expect it and I want a return on my investment so why bargain with sex? My heart wouldn't even be in it. I'm not going to bargain with sex so he'll vacuum. Uh-uh. . . . I just don't see it.

"My husband just needs to step up to the plate. When the oil needs to be changed in my car, change my damn oil. Don't give me no excuse like, 'Well, you in it.' Come get it from the parking lot at my job or take it on Saturday. You make an appointment to go get your hair cut, make an appointment to go change my oil. My children even know what the oil-changing place looks like because I have to drag them along with me and the same thing goes for the car wash. I don't even ask him to wash my car because I don't want to hear his excuses. I go and pay somebody else twenty dollars, which is a damn shame, but I'm tired of asking.

"One day I got a serious attitude. I said to myself, 'You know what. I ought to find me a nigga who will keep my car clean and the oil changed and my husband bet' not ask me shit about my damn car. But then he wouldn't be able to get no coochie either 'cause the "fix-it man" would be getting it, and then I really couldn't live with him.' "

SADIE, FIFTY-SOMETHING

"Young folk don't take marriage as seriously as they should. I've been married quite a few years and it hasn't all been roses. Young people don't put enough effort into making a marriage work; to them marriage is more of a sex thing than anything else. They feel like all they got to do is work their ass just right in bed, do this and that and holler, 'What's my name,' and that will make the marriage work. That's not what marriage is. It's a give and take and you have to do a lot of giving to make it work.

"It's not going to be all fun and games or a party every night. Marriage is not like that. To have a strong marriage you have to be willing to give, you have to be willing to listen, and you have to be able to talk. You need to understand that your significant other is an individual as well and everybody needs space so don't smother one another.

"I think part of the problem is there has been too much free loving and living together, and divorce and welfare, and children see all of this and think that's the normal way of life. I think we should get back to the old way where if you get married, you marry to stay. Now if that man starts beating on you or something like that, then you need to do something else but if it's just a little infidelity or if he stays out real late or drinks a little too much you should be able to work through that, that is no reason to get a divorce," Sadie repeated firmly.

"If a person is out there in the streets every day and not coming home and not taking care of you and the family, and by taking care of I mean financially, then it's time to go. Most of the time you don't even know for sure that he's been unfaithful. It's usually from what somebody told you, or what you think, or you smell a woman's perfume on him or something like that. And if you do know for certain that the other person is cheating, I think you should work a little bit harder to find out why. What's lacking at home to make that person feel they need to go with someone else? And don't say there's nothing lacking because ninety percent of the time there is and you need to work on that instead of just going and filing for divorce 'cause it's entirely too easy to get a divorce these days.

"Some of the toughest times in my marriage were when I had to deal with my husband's infidelity, him not being there when I needed him and not being able to talk about our problems. There was always an argument but I dealt with that. Today a woman would say, 'Why don't you just kiss my ass then,' and she'd keep on stepping but I've had times where he was gone and I mean gone for days. We weren't separated, he'd just be out doing his thing and I wouldn't know where he was but when you have children you think okay, what's worse? Starting all over again and bringing in a brand-new man over my children or staying with my husband because I know what he *will* do. I don't know what that next one will do but I know what this one will do. The next one may beat me up or give all his money to other women so you have to think about what's best for everybody, not just you. I'm glad I stayed because it worked out and that's my whole point, you have to work through the hard times in a marriage if you want to make it work.

"There are men who have affairs, there are men who can't talk so they argue, and there are men who don't want a woman to speak her mind or know too much. Some men have problems with a woman making more money than they do. All of these things can cause problems in marriage and you have to realize and just deal with it.

"If he's doing something you don't like, you don't have to put up with it. You need to put a stop to it right at the beginning and make your needs and expectations known. Even if you have to go and join some organizations and be away from home sometimes yourself that's okay. See most of the time when a man is doing his thing, it's because the wife is sitting at home, nursing the babies, looking all ugly, cooking and cleaning and not taking care of herself. Start doing things for yourself. You don't have to go out and find no man to make yourself feel good, just do some of the things that you enjoyed before you got married because you are still an individual.

"I'm not saying that's always the reason men have affairs, some of them are just assholes," Sadie said, looking serious. "You can be the prettiest thing he's seen in his life and he'll still screw around on you, if that's what he wants to do. Haven't you ever seen a man married to a pretty woman go out and have an affair with a woman not half as pretty? That's because men have a one-track mind. They really don't care how the woman looks, they just want more, they want different. And that's another thing, you have to do different things to keep your marriage interesting, you can't get in a rut. I don't care if it's sex or whatever, the same thing you did to get that man is what you need to keep on doing but most wives won't.

"She'll say, 'Well, I got him now. My hair can be all over my head, I can put on my makeup every other day instead of every day,' that kind of thing. But no, he liked what he got and you have to keep it like that, you have to keep it going. You can't start off having sex every day when you're dating and then get married and say, 'I'm tired, I got to go in here and cook and I been working all day so don't be looking for nothing else when I'm ready to go to bed.' You were working every day when you met him, so that's just an excuse. I'll tell any young woman, don't start something you can't finish.

"I think when women become mothers they get a whole new set of priorities and sex is no longer one of them. Men don't understand that *but* women need to remember that they had that man before they had those kids. Love your children and take care of them but remember that they have a place and the husband has a place. Even if you have to say, 'Baby, I'm tied up with the kids right now, but if you'll help me get them to bed a little early the rest of the night is yours.' That man is going to stay there because he's got something to look forward to.

"You can't keep saying, 'Leave me alone, I've been dealing with these kids all day and I'm tired so don't *touch* me.'" Sadie frowned and shook her head.

"He'll say, 'Oh, to hell with this,' and you best believe that there's going to be somebody else out there shaking that thang as usual saying, 'I'll do whatever you want me to do, baby.'

"I've been married to the same man for a little over thirty years and we never separated. I don't believe in that. I left home one time when I was in my twenties and I was gone for about four hours and he came and begged me back. I went back but I told him, 'Now, I'm coming back this time but if I *ever* leave again, if I *ever* spend a night away from you, I will never come back.'

"I meant that. I don't make threats and he knows that even today. If I ever have to stay away from home all night he'd better look out because I know me, I'm gonna be out there poppin' that thang 'cause I know how to do it pretty good." Sadie laughed as she snapped her fingers. "I'm pretty good at that and he knows it, so I've never had to leave again.

"Come to think of it, I can't even remember what made me leave that one time. I think it was because he went out and stayed out all night long and spent all of the money and that was a problem 'cause I like money.

"I didn't have a problem with him partying but don't come home broke; don't leave that check out there because when you do that, you're giving whoever you were with more than you gave me, and then I'm pissed because I think he went to bed with her *and* he gave her our money, and that's not going to work.

"That's right, I said *our* money," Sadie repeated. "When you start feeling like that you need to explain it to him in a way that he will understand so that it doesn't happen again.

"If it does, you need to shock him. You can't let him try you over and over and all you do is keep saying, 'You bet' not do this or you bet' not do that or I'm going to leave.' You keep saying that and they know you're not going to *leave* so don't threaten him. Just tell him, 'Look, one day you're gonna say or do the wrong thing and when you do you'll know it 'cause you'll be by yourself.' When you put it that way he don't know when that one day might be, it could be tomorrow depending on what he does.

"Another thing I think is very important and that is that one person shouldn't have to do all the giving, never. But you will always find one person giving more than the other because you are going to find that one person is stronger than the other. In my marriage I feel I'm stronger.

"Now there are times when I feel like, 'I wish I wasn't married.' Sometimes you say to yourself, 'Boy, if I wasn't married the things I could do' and then you think again, 'Being by myself all the time could be pretty lonesome.' Marriage is pretty nice because you know you have someone there with you, someone who you feel is in your corner, someone who can help you, and of course, someone to make love with if you want to. Even if he really can't make love like he used to, his just being there means a lot.

"Sure, there are women who'd prefer to just have a boyfriend but you're never sure of a boyfriend. There's no commitment at all. So sometimes it works and sometimes it doesn't. I like that little piece of paper and even though it may be easy to get, I feel like we *need* that little piece of paper because it gives us a tie to each other and that means a lot. Now that other piece of paper, the one that breaks up a family and breaks people's hearts, that one should be harder to get.

"Really, I love marriage. I still have my freedom and I'm my own woman so I think it's beautiful. If I had my whole life to do over, I would still get married and probably marry the same man. I've seen a lot over the years and judging from everything I've seen, there isn't anything I like any better so I really can't say marriage is a bad thing for me.

"Things aren't exactly the same way they were when we first married because after a certain age, love is different. You're used to being treated a certain way and if you get with someone else later on in life, he may have his own idea of how he thinks you should be treated. So if I ever lose my husband, I don't think I'd get married again.

"We're winding down now, we're getting older. We're going to move into a smaller place where we can be more comfortable and enjoy life because at a certain age you realize that there are a lot of things you don't need anymore. You come to realize that a lot of things you felt were important aren't so important anymore. You wake up one morning and say, 'You know, honey, we don't need this big old house now, we don't need to be mowing this huge yard anymore.'

"What we really need to do is focus on making our marriage wonderful just like it was when we were younger but in a different style. You can do the same types of things and still enjoy one another but that's hard if you're obsessed about keeping up the house, keeping up the yard, or worrying about money. Let it go. Wind down and get into something that you can enjoy for the rest of your life together and hope we have thirty or forty more good years.

"With age comes wisdom so I think we've learned to stay in love with each other even through the tough times. I've also found that I'm a good giver, I accept a lot. I'm from a large family and we had to give and take a lot because of the size of the family, we had to. We had to give up our beds for the older ones or give up this or give up that. We had to accept things that people from smaller families didn't have to so I've had experience with giving in to things all my life.

"I've also learned to keep people out of our business. Never tell friends anything too personal. You may have one good friend that you're able to talk to about certain things but you'd be surprised at the friends who may be jealous of you and then they're going to tell another friend and before you know it all of your business is out.

"One thing I've always done, and still do even now at my age, is I never allowed a friend or associate to come to *my* house if I wasn't at home or just to drop in without giving me a call first.

"They'll say, 'Girl, you must really love your man.' But it's not even about that. If you want to come to see me that's fine, but I don't want no one coming around without calling me. Don't come to my house when I'm not expecting you because my husband might open the door in his shorts or something and then what?

"I've tried to do things that would make my marriage better, but frankly, my husband could do more. He doesn't try to understand me. He feels that women should just accept what men say or do but he should try to start doing some of the things that I enjoy doing. He doesn't go to church and it would make me feel better and make our relationship a lot stronger if he would. He was raised up in the church but he stopped going to church when he was seventeen and went into the service. When he came back he didn't want to go anymore. He doesn't try to stop me from going but when you and your husband go to church together, you can discuss things together. For example, I'm Episcopalian and when I talk about Father this or

Father that he'll make a joke. He'll say something like, 'So what did your papa preach about today?' And I don't feel like I can honestly discuss it with him because he doesn't take it serious.

"When we first got married I joined his church which was Baptist thinking he would come back. After he still wouldn't come back and I discovered that it really wasn't a church I liked very much anyway, I moved to a different church and brought my children up Episcopalian so we have different religions. He has not been to church since we've been married except for a funeral and maybe one wedding. He just won't go.

"He realizes it's important to me but if it's not important to him then it really doesn't matter. I hear a lot of men say, 'She don't want to do what I like to do,' but they don't want to do what you like to do either, it's a two-way street.

"For instance, my husband doesn't like to socialize, he doesn't really even like for friends to come to the house, but I'm just the opposite. I want to have fun and do stuff but he doesn't like that. For years I would have an annual Labor Day party and every year he would resent it but I still had it anyway because it made me happy. I told him the same thing then that I tell him now, 'I have to keep doing what makes me happy because if I stop, I die. I'm not going to let you or anyone smother me where I can't do anything. If you don't like it, I'm sorry.' "

VICKY, FORTY-SOMETHING

"I think marriage is great, my marriage wasn't horrible the entire time, I was happily married for a while, and I think if you're happily married that it's wonderful. Unfortunately, I don't think everybody is happily married and I don't think people try hard enough to stay happily married. That's just my opinion but I see that all the time. I see people married to each other who should never have been married and they got married for the wrong reasons. For instance, they're in love with someone else but because they happened to get into a situation that's hard to get out of, they married the wrong person. That's not a good idea and down through the years, it becomes obvious.

"I was in love with my husband when I married him. We dated two years before getting married, but it wasn't love at first sight. We were married twelve years and the first ten years were happy, so it wasn't so bad.

"What I liked most about the marriage was the companionship; having someone to share my life with, someone to reach my goals with, and someone to share life's ups and downs with. Sex was wonderful with my husband and of course I enjoyed it but marriage can't be based on sex alone.

"One of the downsides of the marriage was that there wasn't a balance between what I did and what he did. I did more, not that he was a slouch or anything; he just thought that his work was the most important thing." She held up two fingers and ticked each one off as she spoke. "It was work and then his family. I did admire the fact that he was devoted to his job, he made good money, and he supported us. However, he would work eighty hours a week and we never saw him.

"When we first moved here, I don't think my neighbors met him until after three or four months had passed. In fact, the neighbors who lived next door asked me once, 'Are you sure you're married?' because he was never around. My son was only a year old when we moved here and in the mornings if he would wake up crying or whatever, my husband would go into the room and my son would scream. It was like he didn't even know him.

"Even though he wasn't at home it wasn't always like he was always at work either. He was in sales so he did a lot of things with the customers which might cause him to be at the office until 6:00 P.M., then he'd call and say, 'Oh, I got to meet so and so at whatever place,' and then he'd be out with the guys till midnight, one or two in the morning. He'd come home drunk, get up and leave the house about 5:30 A.M., and start again.

"I worked a lot too at first, but we didn't have kids so it was okay. We were married for five years before we had our first child. After that, I still worked, but when it was time to go, I left. I got up, went and got my baby, and went home. He was there for me more with the first child than he was with the second one, but I've pretty much had to raise them both by myself. I'd cook, clean, raise the children, and spend time with them all while working full-time, so it was almost like I was single.

"Sometimes I would tell him, 'We need to go out and spend some time together as a couple and not as Mom and Dad.' I would get a babysitter, make dinner reservations, and plan to go to a movie or whatever, but he would never come home.

"I know . . . it was awful," she responded when she caught me shaking my head. "I'd have to pay the babysitter and send her home, and he'd finally come home drunk and tired and just go to bed. It didn't happen all the time but after it happens a couple of times, you come to expect it. I still loved him but at that point I wasn't happy.

"That's not even the reason we divorced. That happened because he thought he could have a girlfriend and a wife but we differed on that small matter. Bottom line is, he had an affair and I found out. I caught him on the phone with his girlfriend when he thought I was in the shower. I heard them talking and I was shocked because I never, ever would have thought that he'd have an affair; I never thought he would do that.

"He came from a very religious family and he was always talking about how his father had done that to his mother and how he would never do it, but never say never.

"What happened was, he thought I was in the shower because I had the water running. He was supposed to be keeping an eye on our oldest child. The other baby was still sleeping. Well, my oldest came running into the bathroom with something in his hand and said, 'My bug.' I was just getting ready to get in the shower, but instead I threw on my bathrobe and started chasing after him because by the time I got my robe on he'd run out of my bathroom, still saying he had a bug in his hand. I ran out into the living room, caught him, and found that he was in fact holding a bug so I took the bug away, then went to find my husband so I could get in the shower. I wanted to make sure he was keeping an eye on him because this child was always into something and that's when I heard him on the phone. I heard him say, 'Honey,' and I'm thinking, 'Who is he talking to?' So I just quietly got closer and stood against the wall, right around the corner from where he was, and I could hear him clearly.

"He was calling me names saying stuff like, 'I never want to wake up next to that bitch again,' and I was stunned. I let him talk for about ten more seconds before I walked into the kitchen and demanded, 'Who are you talking to?' He just hung up the phone.

"I said, 'Get your ass out of my house.' He put his shoes on and as he started walking out he had to come past me and when he got right in front of me, I punched him in the face. He fell down and then he had the nerve to say, 'I can't believe you actually hit me.' I didn't even give him time to get up before I told him again, 'Get the hell out,' but once he got to the front door he turned around and said, 'I'm not leaving. This is my house, I'm not leaving.'

"I said, 'I'll give you a choice, either you go or me and the children go. I'm getting in the shower, then I'm going to go to the grocery store, and when I get back either your clothes are packed or I pack mine, so you decide.'

"So, I took a shower." Vicky's tone of voice reflected her own disbelief. "I went grocery shopping, and I went home. The feeling was surreal, it just doesn't hit you right away because you have all this stuff to process. I'm thinking, 'Okay, if I leave I won't have a job because if I leave, I'm going back to New Jersey to live with my sisters and it will take time to find a job so what do I do?'

"Well, he didn't leave that night . . . he would not leave so I just sat up all night. He went to sleep, got up the next day, and told me that he wanted me to stay. I said, 'I don't know, I don't know if I can do that,' and he went to work like nothing had ever happened.

"All I could think about was how was I gonna raise these small children by myself? I didn't make a lot of money so I couldn't keep the house. But I stayed and we went to a marriage counselor, which by the way was a waste of money because he lied throughout the counseling sessions.

"He lied and said that he had just met this other woman, they'd only been together one time, but I came to find out that he'd been having an affair with her for over a year.

"Then I caught him with her again, this time he was in Hawaii with her but he'd told me he was on business. I called the hotel he was staying at and had them ring his room at 3:00 A.M. in the morning. There was no answer so I just kept calling. I finally called the front desk and said, 'This is an emergency, this is his wife calling and there is a family emergency, would you please go to his room and get him because he's not answering the phone,' so they said, 'Oh, sure, sure.' Then the man at the hotel desk finally comes back to the phone and says, 'Ma'am? I'm sorry but there's nobody in that room.'

"I said, 'Okay then ring another room. Do you have a Ms. Melissa whatever-her-last-name-was registered?' I knew the woman's name. I said, 'Is she in the hotel?' And he said, 'Yes.' So I told him to ring her room. So he rang her room and when she answered, sleepily because I had awakened her, I said, 'Where is Alex?' She said, 'I don't know.' And I said, 'Sure you don't know. But you can tell him that I know his sorry ass is lying right there and that when he gets back home, his key won't work.' Then I just hung up.

"When he returned, three days later, the locks had been changed but I ended up letting him come back anyway. I decided I would try again after he begged and begged, but after a couple more unexplained absences I just couldn't do it anymore. Then I found out he had his own apartment. He made the mistake of putting the canceled rent check in the bathroom trash can and I saw it before he had a chance to take the trash out. See, once you find out about an affair you start looking for signs, any kind of signs, so my eyes and ears were always open, looking and listening.

"He kept denying that anything was going on and I finally said, 'You know what, forget it. This isn't worth it, you need to get out,' and he finally said that he would. I took the kids and went back to New Jersey for a visit and while we were gone he called me and said, 'I don't want to get a divorce, we're gonna get through this.' I think what finally hit him was what the financial impact of the divorce would be for him.

"I said, 'Look, I'm on vacation, I'll talk to you when I get home. I'm here with the kids and my sisters to have a good time and to get away from all that; I'll talk to you later.'

"Then one night during the week that we were away he stayed out all night and I know he was out all night because I kept calling the house. I kept calling because I didn't trust him anymore. When I finally caught up with him he said, 'I was at Dan's house and I drank too much so I didn't want to drive back home,' which I knew was a lie. I said, 'You know what, in the situation you're in right now you shouldn't have been out with Dan or anyone else, you should've been home.'

"We tried again or I should say I tried to make things work for about ten months. Finally I decided I could not live that way forever. If I had to live in a little apartment, I didn't care, I didn't want my children to grow up knowing that their mother put up with such bullshit, I wouldn't want them to put up with that. So I found a lawyer and filed for divorce, and he was shocked. He could not believe it.

"To this day he still says, 'I do not understand how you could divorce me.' Even during the divorce I might have still been in love with him, but I saw a side of him that I didn't like. I had no respect for him and I still don't. We get along fine now and I realize how much happier I am now than I was when I was going through all that mess with him.

"I didn't tell all of my sisters about the divorce, I told my oldest sister because we're really close but not my two younger sisters. I didn't want to have to explain what happened and then having them tell everybody, so I only told my older sister then made her promise not to tell anybody else.

"She kept it secret, so nobody knew. My mother didn't even know and we'd been divorced for a while. I just didn't want to upset her because I knew she'd gone through the same thing with my father, and even though she was miserable she stayed with him anyway. I didn't want my life to be like that so I'm glad I divorced him.

"If I had to do it over again, I'd wait longer before I got married. I was twenty-six and we dated a year but you need to know somebody really well before you marry them. I would insist that we spend time as a couple and if we had children I would make sure we did things together as a family as well. People forget that before they became parents they were a couple.

"Someday I would like to remarry. I like the idea of growing old with someone instead of by myself. I like to think that I can still fall in love with someone, and stay in love and not go through something like that again.

"I know things don't always work out in marriages but if you're thinking about having an affair because you're not sure you want to be with your spouse forever, and you want to sleep with other people, then talk to him about it. Go get counseling and if it doesn't work get a divorce. Then be intimate with as many people as you want to."

LADY, FORTY-SOMETHING

"I think marriage is good, it's a wonderful thing," Lady said with a slight sigh. "I think everybody needs somebody and I think you need marriage because you need that commitment, that's very important. There are some women who don't but in my opinion it seems like more men than women don't want to commit. I don't know how young women can deal with that lack of commitment so easily. They're like, 'Well, we don't have to have no paper but we can still just live together, whatever,' and maybe I feel this way because I talk to more men who are single than I do women. To me, you need some kind of commitment because if we're going to live in the same house, and we're going to put our money together and pay bills and all this, then I don't need to be sitting here worried about him walking off and leaving me tomorrow. If we're married, he can't do that without having to pay a price for it, but if we're just living together, he can do whatever the hell he wants to and I can't say shit.

"So I think marriage is good and I think it's good for our society. I think it's good for the African American family to have a husband and wife raising their children together and instilling good values in them. Marriage has its drawbacks but for the most part I think it's a good thing.

"I've been married twelve years and I like the fact that I have somebody I can talk to about almost anything. I like the fact that even though we've had our ups and downs and we've had our hard times, I know that if I got sick or something and couldn't take care of myself, he'd be right there. He's already proven that. I like knowing I have that person there for me and I like the fact that you can do more when there are two of you.

"Now, what I dislike in the marriage is that I give more than he does. I put way more into our marriage than he does," Lady stated matter-of-factly. "He's a hard worker and I'm sure he'd disagree with me, but I don't think that he realizes all I do. Not only do I work, I'm also taking care of the house and I'm taking care of the bills, I'm making sure we have groceries in the house, I'm taking care of the kids, I'm making sure that all these things are done and I have to stay on top of it every single day. A lot of it's my fault because when I first got married I thought I was supposed to do everything. I thought it was the woman's responsibility to do all those things, because my mom did it but then my mom didn't work so it was a lot easier for her to do all that. Sure, I'm good with handling the money, I'm good with making sure that things get taken care of, and I believe in handling your business, but damn, it just wears me out sometimes.

"Another thing is that my husband acts like he doesn't care whether or not I'm still attracted to him physically. Just because you've been married to a person a long time and you're both getting older, does that mean you just let yourself go? I don't think so. I can't let myself go and if I did he'd probably be out there looking at somebody younger than me who was looking damn good and taking care of herself, so I think he ought to give me the same respect. I take care of my body and keep myself up because I want to look good and feel good. Even if he doesn't expect me to, I do it for myself. But it's like he doesn't put any pressure on me to look good all the time so he doesn't think I should put any pressure on him either.

"Sometimes I wake up in the morning and look over there at him and I say, 'Damn. Is this what I've got to look forward to for the rest of my life? Shit, I don't know about this.' He needs to keep up his appearance, he knows what I like and what I don't like, so that should not be an issue. He should do it for himself anyway, regardless of what I think. I feel like he doesn't care about himself, and if that's the case, how can he care about me?

"Then, last but not least, I hate the fact that he wants me to acknowledge everything he does. He's always like, 'Come look at this, come look at that, I fixed this, I fixed that, and you didn't say nothing about it.' 'Well, I'm not your mama. I paid the bills but did I come and show them to you and say, "See how I moved this money and robbed Peter to pay Paul over here? Did I come and show you that?"' I don't want to have to say thanks every time he does something. That's so childish and immature. Hell, I'm grown and he's grown, I'm not his mama, and I don't feel like babying him. A man should handle his business because that's what he's supposed to do.

Whether he gets kudos or praise for it or not shouldn't matter. It's a real turnoff to me when a man acts that way, but he acts like a spoiled little boy if I don't pat him on the back, and it's gotten real old.

"Hopefully we'll stay married, I don't have any plans to divorce him or leave him or anything like that, and there's nobody else I'd want to marry anyway. I know we love each other, so hopefully we'll be able to retire and get things back to the way they were in the beginning. When you get married and have children, and go about the business of living and working, you just lose that fire you used to have. So, I hope that once they're out of the house we can focus on each other more because otherwise, there will be no reason for us to stay together, and I don't want that.

"I'm sure my marriage would be better if I wasn't having an affair because I could use all that energy to make it better. But for some reason, I'm just tired of being the one to try to make things happen. I feel like I have three children instead of two sometimes, and that's part of the reason I ended up in this situation in the first place. I'm not making excuses, but everyone needs space, and time, and peace of mind. When everybody is calling your name and needing you to do this or that, you just feel like you're falling apart, and that's how I rationalize what I'm doing outside home, even though I know it's wrong.

"I guess if I would compliment my husband more, and make him feel needed and wanted, my marriage could be better. But some of what he needs, he has to get for himself. I can't work magic and if he's not happy with himself, that's not my problem. I've talked to several ladies who have been married for a long time, and some of them say the secret to getting your husband to do whatever, whenever you want him to, is to boost his ego and make him feel like he's the most important thing in the world in your eyes. But you know what, that's too much damn work and I just don't have that kind of energy anymore. One of my friends told me, 'When he cuts the grass and he wants you to come look at it and tell him how beautiful it is, do it if that's what it takes for him to go out and do it again next week.' But I got a problem with that too because I don't ask him to come look at the bathroom every time I clean it. I don't need his praise all the time.

"Maybe if he needs that encouragement and stroking all the time, I should give it to him, but I'd prefer that he just grow up and stop acting like I'm his mama. That would make things better for both of us."

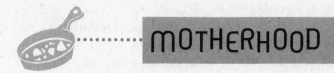

MOTHERHOOD

ALICIA, FORTY-SOMETHING

"I have one daughter who's almost thirty and I helped my third husband raise his three children. The reason I wanted a child was because I came from a large, close-knit family and the way I grew up, the natural order of things was to get married and have children, nothing else. Not grow up, go to college, and get yourself a career. Not grow up and join the military, it was nothing like that. The goal in my family was to get married and start your own family. I've always loved being around children and when I was growing up there were *always* a lot of kids around, be it brothers, sisters, cousins, nieces, nephews, whatever, there was never a time that I can remember when a child wasn't somewhere underfoot.

"I started babysitting before I was ten years old and I always wanted a baby, so I got married at seventeen, which is way too young in this day and age. By the time I was nineteen years old, I had my daughter. I enjoyed being pregnant. I loved it. There is nothing like the soft flutter of your baby's kick or the feel of your baby turning and doing somersaults inside. There is nothing like it and to top it all off, she was a good baby. She wasn't a whiny baby, she slept through the night almost immediately, she wasn't a finicky eater, and she never met a stranger. Everybody fell in love with her because she was such a sweet baby.

"I have never regretted becoming a mother, not one time. Being a mother is one of the most fulfilling things in this world; it's one of the most satisfying things that I've ever done. And no matter what anybody tells you, you know all the warnings that come your way when you first get pregnant like you better get all the sleep you can, or have all of the fun you can now because when that baby gets here you can forget about having any fun for a real long time? Well, no matter what people tell you and no matter how hard you think being a mother is going to be, you still end up wishing that it *was* that easy. Loss of sleep or not getting to go out and dance is the least of your worries as a mother and I've found that it only gets harder as they get older.

"My daughter was a perfect baby and a very easygoing child. She wasn't a horror as a teenager either, as a matter of fact; we remained good friends throughout the so-called rebellious teenaged years. We became even closer when she became an adult and had children of her own. We'd talk on the phone almost every day and then one day she literally dropped a bombshell at my front door. Her children are ages two and four and she brought them by my house and said that she no longer wanted to have the responsibility of being a mother. She'd decided that she was going to leave her children with me.

"I was like, 'Fine, you want to leave the children with me for the weekend so you can get yourself together, right?' And she said, 'No, I want you to have them permanently.' She said she was close to having a nervous breakdown and she thought it would be best if I took the children." Alicia paused and took a deep breath before going any further.

"Now here I am in this new relationship with this loving man in what should be the prime of our lives, and my daughter is dropping off her two small children for me to take care of indefinitely.

"Any other man would've run the other way so fast it would've made your head swim, but he hasn't done that. I even gave him the opportunity. I said, 'Look, I know you didn't sign up for this, the situation has changed so if you want to go on about your business and come back when all of this is over, then I will understand,' but he said, 'No, I'm here for you.' How can you not love a man like that?" Alicia asked.

"I tried to talk my daughter out of it. I said, 'Why don't you just leave the kids with me for the weekend and get yourself together, go check into a hotel room and have some time to yourself.' She said, 'No, I can't take this anymore and maybe that's why God has placed a special man in your life; maybe He did that because He knew you would need some help with the kids.' To say I was flabbergasted didn't even begin to describe what I felt," Alicia said.

"It never ceases to amaze me how selfish children can be when it comes to their parents, it's like everything is all about them and that your only reason for being is to serve them.

"At first I was just shocked that she would even do such a thing and then I started to become angry. She left those kids with me and didn't look back. She didn't even call for the first three or four days so I put out a missing person report on her because I was worried. Well, they finally caught up with her at a hotel, right here in this area and she called me and asked, 'How can I get these people to stop pestering me, I'm fine.' I said, 'The only way they will stop pestering you is if you check in with me every day to let me know what's going on and how you're doing, if you don't do that I'm going to send them after you again.'

"I don't know what happened to her." Alicia shook her head in bemusement. "When she was married to her first husband she was like a little Sunday school teacher. She didn't drink, she didn't smoke, she didn't curse, nothing. Then she meets the loser she's currently married to and he is the worst thing that could've happened to her. He doesn't want to work, half the time she doesn't know where he is, he sells drugs, and he's abusive. So what else could I do except take the children, where else were they supposed to go?

Here it is six weeks later and at my age I'm raising two young children and I'm still in shock that this has happened.

"As a mother I guess you have to be ready for anything with your children but nobody could've ever told me to expect this. There are no guarantees, you can raise them right and teach them but sometimes no matter what you do, all of your hard work and dreams for your children can sometimes just go right down the tubes. The only thing I can do for her now is take care of her children, be here for her when she needs to talk, and be a soft place for her to fall, if she does. That's all I can do.

"I'd always instilled faith, trust, love, and honesty in my daughter. I always wanted her to be the best person she could possibly be. She didn't have to be perfect, I just wanted her to do her best and I know for a fact that she isn't doing the best she can right now by being with that man. It's awful to say, but I wish something would just come and take him out of her life. He's involved with drugs and I think he's gotten her involved as well and my heart breaks knowing that there is nothing I can do to control this. I've had to let go of her in my heart and turn it over to God.

"When she was younger the only thing I wished for was for her to be happy. I wanted her to have a safe and comfortable life. Now I just want her to be able to survive and get out of the terrible lifestyle she's currently living. I still want her to be happy, but most importantly I want her whole and at peace."

KAT, THIRTY-SOMETHING

"If you want a story about a sister who's got a dysfunctional relationship with her mama, you should just go ahead and use this one," Kat said. "Maybe somebody else will read it and get some help because I sure as hell can't seem to make sense of it. I know I've bitched and moaned about it before, but I just don't know what I can do to make my mama happy.

"As you know, we used to be more friends than mother and

daughter until I got serious with Tim and married him. He treats me like a princess, and she can't stand that. The other day while she was at our apartment, I asked him to get me a drink of water and she made this face, looked me up and down, and said, 'Lazy, lazy girl. Why can't you get your ass up and get your own water?' Like I don't deserve to be treated nice by my own husband. I just can't do anything right in her eyes, but I'm sorry if she lost her best friend when I got married. I guess I can't be her best friend and her daughter, too. It just doesn't work. And I shouldn't have to choose between her and my husband anyway."

Kat reached for her purse and pulled out several lipstick samples and placed them on the table. Kat was regal and had full, sexy lips like her mother, and she was always trying on some new shade of lipstick, trying to bring even more attention to them.

She had been upset when she called me earlier that day, almost in tears, and asked if we could meet at the local coffeehouse after work. I didn't really feel like doing anything except going home and relaxing with some hot chocolate and a good book because it was an ugly, cold, rainy day. But she needed to vent because her mother had pissed her off again, and she didn't want to discuss it with her husband because she didn't want him to know how she really felt about her mother. You know how it is—there are some things you don't tell your husband because later, he might wash your face with it.

I agreed to be her sounding board, and she agreed that she'd let me bring my recorder so I could take some notes for the book. Once I was there, I was happy I'd come. It was such a nice place to sit and talk because the atmosphere was so calming. It smelled of fresh coffee and baked goodies, and they always kept a fire burning in the big fireplace during the winter, which made it feel really cozy. We chose a spot close by where we could feel the heat of the fire without getting too hot. Since they had open mike scheduled for 8:00 P.M., most of the crowd wouldn't start showing up for at least another two hours. I figured maybe Kat would be okay by then.

Kat's mother, who's from Jamaica, raised Kat and her three

sisters alone after their half-French, half-black father walked out on them. Kat was only seven at the time, but she was the oldest. Her mother came to depend on her more than she should have, and continued to do so even after Kat was married and trying her best to change their relationship into a healthy one.

Even though her mother had no formal education, she always pressed Kat to go to college and get a degree so she could ensure herself a stable financial future. But lately, she seemed to be more concerned about her own future than she was about Kat's, and it made Kat angry because her mother had always been so domineering that she was afraid to confront her. I'd tried several times to get her to tell her mother how she felt, but she said the mere thought of that made her shudder.

So, knowing all that in advance, I was basically there to listen because I knew that's what she needed.

"Okay, girlfriend, here's your coffee," I said, eyeballing the lipstick spread out all over the table. "And I don't know how you plan to try on lipstick, drink coffee, and eat tea cakes all at the same time." She just looked at me like she didn't even hear what I was saying and started talking again, while trying on the first new shade and looking in her hand mirror.

"You know, I was the only girl in my building to finish high school without getting pregnant. I finished college like Mama wanted me to, and now I'm working on my master's degree. When I tell her that I'm getting mostly A's and B's she says, 'Well, the courses must not be that difficult,' like I'm not smart enough to make those kinds of grades.

"That's not the end of it either. I used to give her a hundred dollars a pay period just to help her out. But last week I didn't have it because I had some bills I had to pay and you know what she said? 'Well, I'll just loan you what you usually give me, and you can pay me back later.' Here I am putting my relationship with my husband in jeopardy because I'm giving her money behind his back, and she's acting like I actually *have* to give it to her.

"My three sisters don't give her shit, and the youngest one has done everything she was big enough to do, but still, she's my mama's favorite. She's had two kids out of wedlock, has never been married, dates married men, and talks to Mama any way she wants to. But you know what Mama told me and my other sisters? She said she's leaving everything to my baby sister because she needs all the help she can get.

"Here I am running over to her house every Sunday afternoon to balance her checkbook, and going to the grocery store for her every Wednesday. One of my other sisters cooks for her, but she doesn't give her any money. And the other one cleans the house, but she's leaving everything to the one person who won't do shit for her." Kat looked like she was fed up.

"But that's okay because I'm learning. Sometimes when the phone rings and I see her name on my caller ID, I don't even answer it because I don't feel like hearing her shit. My two other sisters won't do that. She has them on a guilt trip. They'll see that it's her calling, take a deep breath, and answer the phone, knowing that whatever it is she has to say might leave them in tears, but I'm not doing that shit no more. I finally decided that I'm not dealing with her unless I want to. My sisters say I shouldn't do that because it could be an emergency. But if it is, she needs to call 911 anyway because there's nothing I can do. Hell, I'm not a doctor.

"Just last month, she accused me of being part of something I had nothing to do with. Mama and the sister right under me are co-owners of a house. Well, this same sister and her husband are in the middle of a divorce, but she was going to let him rent the house so they wouldn't have to worry about finding another tenant. My baby sister happened to drive by there and sees this strange woman with a moving van in front of the house, so she immediately went running to Mama, swearing that my sister's ex-husband was letting a woman move in there with him.

"The other woman just happened to be his sister, and not a girlfriend at all, but Mama wants to kick him out of the house anyway, just to be mean. My sister doesn't want him to have to move because it makes this whole divorce thing easier on their son, who's going to stay with his father. When Mama found out that my sister discussed it with me, she got mad and said I'm the one behind all this shit when I didn't even have anything to do with it. So, I decided to go over to her house and talk to her about it, and she cursed me out.

"I didn't even try to defend myself, I just walked off and went outside where my baby sister was standing, looking like a damn fool with a fake-ass weave down to her shoulders, picking at her too-long, fake nails. I told her silly ass off for starting this whole mess, but I couldn't say everything I wanted to say because I ended up crying.

"Well, weeks went by and my mama didn't even pick up the phone to call me. I finally got my nerve up to go over to the house to check on her, but when I opened the door with my key and walked on in, she jumped when she saw me, like she was startled. I know she was just faking because that woman can hear a rat piss on cotton. After she got through acting all surprised, she peered over her glasses at me and said, 'Oh, it's you. You finally decided to come on by and check on me, huh?'

"She didn't even offer an apology for cursing me out. But come to think of it, I've never heard her apologize to anybody after she's been mean to them. Then she said, 'Well, I need you to balance my checkbook and pick up a few groceries for me,' as if all this shit had never happened.

"My mother never was an affectionate woman because she didn't receive any affection when she was a child. Her own mother died during childbirth, then she was raped when she was a young girl and raised by her grandmother, so she never received any affection and doesn't know how to show any. She often says, 'I've seen y'all hug other people, but y'all never hug me,' and I feel bad because I do hug other people all the time. But we hardly touched each other in my house when I was growing up, so I can't bring myself to hug my own mama.

"It may sound mean for me to say this, but if there's anyone I don't want to be like, it's her. And I hope I don't treat my children that way when and if I have any because this is the kind of shit that screws people up.

"I've decided that I'm not going to dwell on this situation with her anymore. I'm not even going to visit her unless I feel like it. I'll call her once or twice a week, and if she calls me and asks why I haven't been over, I'll just tell her I've been busy or something. I know that's not the whole truth, and maybe not the solution to the problem, but I do have my own life. I have a husband, a career, and other things to do besides run to her house and get my feelings hurt. So, I'm not doing it anymore. If she doesn't care about me any more than that, I'll have to care about myself."

AYOKA, THIRTY-SOMETHING

"My children are my life. Even after the marriage and separation when people have asked me if I could have done something differently what would I have done I'd say, 'You'd have to erase my children from my memory or I would do the same thing. I'd go through all the shit with my husband knowing I would've had my children.'

"He had me believing I was a bad mother and that no judge would ever let me have my kids because of my job. He would tell me, 'You can go but you can't take the kids, even if you tried to take these kids no judge is going to let you have them. You don't even know where you might have to travel this month or next month.' And I would sit back and think, 'He's right. I travel a lot.' In hindsight I see that all I would've had to do was hire a live-in nanny and pay her $500 a month and she would cook, clean, and everything else but I didn't know that. He had me believing that if I tried to take the kids I wouldn't stand a chance.

"Even when we went to mediation his attorney would come back to my lawyer and me with something he'd said like, 'Well, she was never a good mother. While I was at home raising those kids she was out whoring around and she don't deserve to have nothing.' Even though I know all that's not true and I really shouldn't receive it, it just kills me to know that he can say those things about me. As I sat there with tears running down my face, my lawyer said, 'He is so in your head, he just has you so wound up. The first thing you need to do is get him out of your head and the second thing you need to do is figure out what you want out of this divorce.' That's when I finally realized that when all is said and done, a divorce is basically a business transaction. Tina Turner recorded a song a little while back and now I finally know what that song means. Love ain't got a damn thing to do with nothing when it comes down do it.

"He talked about me so bad that I was to the point of saying, 'Okay, you can have the lake house, the rental property, and everything else because I was such a bad mother.' My lawyer said, 'He's playing you, he's in your head,' and I didn't even realize that until after I had gotten out of the marriage and thank God that I did get out because he was making me as crazy as he was.

"What finally made me file was when he put me out of the house and I do mean he literally picked me up and took me outside and ran back and closed the door in my face. He'd put me out at least two times before and here I am in the middle of the night, knocking at the door of my own house, whining, 'Please let me back in, please don't do this.' The last time he'd done that I'd made up my mind that if he ever put me out again I was going to keep going. I didn't know where I'd go or how but I knew I'd keep going.

"I couldn't believe it when my oldest child asked me six months later, 'Mom, how could you just leave us when you knew how crazy Daddy was?' I said, 'I've never left you, I've always been only a phone call away. I just didn't know what to do and I'd made up my mind that I wasn't going to go back.' I said, 'I didn't leave you, your father put me out in the middle of the night and threw my clothes out behind me. I had no immediate family here, no cousins, not even a distant cousin, all I had around me were the people I work with so how and why would I just leave? I know it may look like I left and I'm sure your father made it seem that way but the truth is he put me out while you all were asleep, and I was so tired and worn down that I decided I wasn't going back. I just couldn't do it anymore.

" 'And since you're old enough to know, let me just be frank and tell you the whole truth. The first time your dad put me out you were just three weeks old, I'll never forget it. I was still wearing maternity clothes. He'd told me, "If we move back home, my grandmother can help with the baby while you work." I agreed with him and we'd only been living in that house a week when he put me out the first time. I remember sitting on the curb because I had nowhere to go and it was cool that night. I didn't even have shoes on, just a maternity dress and nothing else.

" 'He didn't give me my keys so I couldn't take my car and he wouldn't open the door after I stood there for what seems like forever knocking and saying, "Please let me back in the house." He wouldn't open the door so I'm sitting out on the curb, after just having moved here. I was about twenty-three years old and you were inside that house, where was I going to go? He knew I wasn't going to leave and that's exactly why he did that. We'd had a disagreement about something and he put me out with his crazy ass.

" 'I kept asking myself, "What have you done to your life, you had a normal life. You had a good life, you had a lot of friends and a lot of people around you, what have you done to your life?" I kept asking myself that over and over again because I just couldn't believe I'd allowed myself to end up in this situation.'

"You know, being a mother can be hard, sometimes it even hurts. Like now, since they're older, my kids can talk to me about their feelings and our family life and it's always so emotional when they do. My oldest child told me, 'I spent my entire freshman and sophomore years in my room and you and Dad never noticed. I used to come home from school, go in my room and close the door and only come out when you would say it was time for dinner. Then I would eat and go back in my room and you and Dad never asked me why I spent so much time in my room by myself. I was really lonely and I never felt that anybody in that house even realized it.'

"Then my youngest child said, 'How come you never ate dinner with us when we were little? You always cooked when you were home but then you'd disappear when we ate. How come?' I explained to him that I used that time as quiet time because I'd always rush in and try to hurry up and cook to keep from making their dad angry, so when they ate I'd go in my room and try to relax for a few minutes. That was the only time I had for myself.

"In the midst of all of that, I don't remember my daughter not talking to me which makes me sad because maybe I was away too much. I hung out with her on the weekends and we ran our errands until she got to the age where she was able to drive herself around. I remember her not talking to me sometimes but I thought it was because she was a teenager and that's how teenagers act sometimes, they prefer to be with their own friends and not their family.

"Now that we're past all of that mess, my fear for my youngest is belonging. I'm scared he'll get involved in gangs but somebody told me that if it doesn't happen by the seventh or eighth grade, you're pretty safe. I'm hoping that he's already passed that peer pressure age where they try to get you into that kind of stuff.

"For my oldest I worry that she might end up with a man like her father. She even tells me, 'I'm probably going to marry somebody just like Dad.' Isn't it pathetic when you *don't* want your daughter to marry a man like her father?" Ayoka had this puzzled look on her face. "It should be the other way around.

"I tell people in bad marriages, especially my boyfriend, that you really aren't helping your kids when you stay. Parents try to rationalize that it's better for the kids if they stay together and not separate but those kids don't want to see their parents yelling at each other and fighting every day, they'd be much better off not witnessing shit like that. The best thing you can do if you have a relationship like that is to live separately because all you're doing is fucking your child up mentally. How can they know what a loving relationship should look like if they grew up in a house where love never existed?

"I pray all the time that God will put somebody in my daughter's life who had a loving family background, a man who can show her what a good relationship can be like. I am so afraid that she'll be attracted to some guy who sits on her and beats her up and tells her she's not worth shit and she'll think, 'This is the way it's supposed to be,' when she deserves more than that. Even now when I tell her to never let anyone put her down and make her feel bad about herself, her response is, 'Well, I don't know . . . you put up with a lot of mess.' And what can I say to something like that because she's right, I did put up with a lot of shit."

JACKIE, FORTY-SOMETHING

"Because my husband was always gone I didn't feel married sometimes. I really couldn't go out with my girlfriends anymore because they were still single and doing the nightclub thing. My husband and I had been married for about a year and a half before we talked about having a baby. I said, 'Hey, I need a baby, I need something to keep me occupied because when you're away, I get lonely. I want you and I feel like if I had a little you with me it would be great.' So we talked about it and the next thing you know we were trying to get pregnant.

"My family lived in a huge house so when the baby was born we moved into the family house. We had our own room and I had a good support system. I had my mom, dad, my little sister, an older sister and her husband and her kids so there were eight to ten people living in this one house at any given time. I could just up and say, 'I'm going to the store,' and somebody would take care of the baby, it wasn't a problem. It was like everyone was there for my baby and me. They knew my husband was gone and they wanted to help out so it was a perfect fit.

"I found that once you have children, your perspective on kids change. When you see kids that belong to somebody else and you don't have any you're like, 'Oh, they're cute,' and you go on about your business. When you have kids of your own, you see what it's all about. You start nurturing them, kissing on them, playing with them, and loving them, and they make you laugh. They make you happy and that lasts for a good while especially when they're infants because all they can do is just lay there and sleep while you just look at them and adore them and say, 'This is my baby. My husband and I made this baby and it's just a beautiful thing.'

"Then as they get older and they're able to walk and stuff you start admiring their accomplishments. They learn to crawl and then walk and before you know it he's reaching out for stuff. Later on they become teenagers and you realize that they're really becoming a part of society, saying yes and no and I want to do this or I want to do that. You start admiring their personalities and their character and seeing how all of that is developing. I got a kick out of it. When they became teenagers, I liked the idea that they had girlfriends and wanted to bring them over and that they were involved in sports. Then later on, they get married and then you've got to deal with the daughter-in-law, which is a *totally* new area for me." Jackie made a face.

"I didn't tell my sons that if a girl acts a certain way then you should steer clear of her. I just didn't do a lot of that because I thought that by watching me and my lifestyle they would see how a woman should act. I didn't put much thought into telling them what to look for in a woman but now, in hindsight, I can say that I wish I had because it's important to have similar backgrounds. If you come from a two-parent background then you should try to find a mate that comes from a two-parent background.

"I've learned from experience that people with different backgrounds clash. Somebody who's been raised by a single parent or a parent who has had a lot of husbands or boyfriends has put a lot of baggage on their child. That would be difficult for a child who comes from a two-parent household to deal with because he's working from a different perspective, they just don't have the same type of issues. When your son or daughter goes out and marries somebody from a different background and I'm talking socially and financially, they've got to learn to deal with problems that they never had to deal with before and I can't really give them advice because I didn't come from that type of background either. So it's like you got to work through all of that stuff and sometimes it can be a big task. You should stress to your children how important it is to be involved with men or women who come from similar backgrounds. It just makes life a little easier.

"After you teach them that, you really can't control it but at least you will know that you tried to give them the help they needed. I didn't give that kind of advice to my children but I wish I had. Another thing I wish I would've told them is, 'Don't marry anybody who's not as smart as you, please don't marry no damn dummy.'

"Sure they go and do what they want to do and you can't control who they fall in love with, but at least you told them. So I think that's a responsibility that parents should strive for. Tell your kids everything you can, whether they want to hear it or not, just give it to them so that at least they know.

"I guess I wasn't as concerned with things like what kind of person they should marry. I spent more time trying to teach them to be honest, hardworking, and enthusiastic. I can't stand a lazy person," Jackie said. "Get interested in something—I don't care what it is. Be alive about something. I don't admire a child who never cleans up his room and I don't admire a child who never wants to help out. When a child is slow to get up and do stuff when you ask them to do something, that's what I mean by lazy.

"That was one of the two things I worried about, because you can't be successful if you're lazy. I also worried that they would marry the wrong women," Jackie said, slapping her hands on her thighs for emphasis. "I want so much for my kids . . ." She paused and gathered her thoughts and I could see that she was struggling to contain her outburst but it came out anyway with her next sentence. "See this is what I'm saying, you can raise them right, teach them good manners, send them to college, you can do all these things, and then they go out and marry the wrong woman, which just ruins everything. You know what I'm saying? I just can't . . . ugh. I have no words for it. That just bothers me but you have no control over it. They're gonna do what they want to do. They fall in love with whoever it is they want to fall in love with, but I wish I could help them pick, I wish I could have a little input.

"Remember when we were kids our elders always asked, 'Who are your people? Where do they work, what do they do for a living?' They asked that because they wanted to make sure the backgrounds were similar. One of my sons is married and he's married to someone below his level financially and socially. His wife is not ambitious at all and could care less about having some of the finer things in life. She never had it; she doesn't expect it so she's not missing it.

"Even when they were eighteen, I tried to tell them all this stuff but it was really over already, the raising is over once they reach a certain age. Now they've got to show you that they're making some good decisions and using the knowledge that you gave them.

"You never stop worrying, and that's why I say that everybody should take their time before they have children. I think the right age to have children is twenty-five. The reason I say twenty-five is because if you get married at twenty you can spend five years together getting to know each other and then you'll be able to determine if you want to go further and have a family, so to me, that's the magic age for having children. I think you should be at least twenty before getting married even though I was only eighteen.

"I know now that I was too young and a lot of people can't believe I'm still married because I got married so young. Everybody said, 'You're too young to get married, you don't know what's out there, you don't know what's gonna happen, you don't know what life holds for you. What do you want to get married for?' But I was so in love that I thought I'd just die if I couldn't be with him twenty-four/seven.

"I try to caution my boys about getting married too young even though one of them already did. I just want them to be happy and successful in life, which to me means being able to supply your basic needs, have a roof over your head, being able to feed your family, and have a little extra money left over. It doesn't mean having all these extravagant things. If you can get all that stuff, that's fine, but if you're just able to sustain your own livelihood and your family and don't have to be on welfare, I would classify that as being a success."

VALEKA, FIFTY-SOMETHING

"I definitely wanted children, but I was in the eleventh grade when I got pregnant with my first child. I'd met a guy who came over with my sister's boyfriend one day, and he was gorgeous. He was half French, had beautiful hair, was very good-looking, and drove a big, black, shiny Buick convertible that blew my mind. When he asked my parents if he could come see me, because in those days you had to ask for permission to come see a girl, they said yes, and I couldn't stop grinning. My mother fell in love with him right away but he turned out to be nothing but a liar.

"One night he said he was going to take me to meet his auntie who was coming in from out of town. He and I went to a motel room, but I was so ignorant that I didn't even know it was a motel, I thought we were just sitting in a room waiting for her to arrive. He tore my clothes off and forced me to have sex with him, and I was so afraid of him that I didn't want to make him angry. Afterward, he took me to my older sister's house and told her that some girls had jumped me and torn my clothes, and that's how I ended up pregnant.

"I found out later on that this man was not only married, but he also had six children. He was almost fifteen years older than me and I didn't know that, because he looked so young. I learned not to trust men after that, and I was still pretty skeptical of men when I met and married my first husband two years later.

"Within thirteen months of that marriage, I had a child, and two years later I had another one." Valeka grimaced. "Still young and naive. I love my children very much, but I didn't want to have them that close together. If it had been left up to me, I would have done other things with my life before having children, but things don't always fall into place the way we want them to.

"A lot of my dreams got lost along the way while I was raising my children, but I still feel they're the best things that happened to me. Because of them, I had to stay positive. They gave me a reason to keep going when I really wanted to quit sometimes, and they've reached many of the goals I never reached, so it makes me happy to have them in my life.

"Children are very, very special, and being a mother is a wonderful experience. Each child is unique and you have to recognize that and treat each one accordingly. I see some of me in my children, I see some of their father in them, but I also see their grandparents' personalities in them as well, so they're beautiful to me because they're part of all of us.

"I feel special to be a mother because every woman cannot be a mother. There are women who call themselves that, but I know from the bottom of my heart that I have been a true mother to my children. I did the very best that I could for them, and I always worked more than one job when they were growing up because I wanted them to have the better things in life. I'm grateful that I was blessed with them, and I think they are the most special human beings in the whole world."

TAMIA, THIRTY-SOMETHING

"I never really thought about having children. As a matter of fact, I didn't even like to baby-sit, that was just one chore I could do without. Children always seemed to be so needy to me and that made me uncomfortable, I don't know why. I always enjoyed sitting somewhere in peace and quiet and reading a good book, so maybe that has something to do with it.

"I remember that one time I had to baby-sit this little boy who wore cloth diapers, and when I had to change him I thought that was the grossest thing I'd ever had to do up to that point in my life, and I must've been about thirteen or fourteen years old. When I got home, his mother called and complained that I'd just dumped the whole diaper into the toilet, and said the next time I should rinse it out and put it in the diaper pail, but I told my mother that there wouldn't be a next time because I didn't ever want to baby-sit again, so she didn't make me go back.

"I probably would have been fine without children of my own, but I always knew that my husband wanted children because he came from a large family. He was comfortable with taking care of all his nieces and nephews, and he'd always told me that he loved kids and wanted a family so that's the major reason I had children. I hadn't really planned on having four, but since we have two boys and two girls, it's a good fit and we have a lot of fun.

"Now that I have them, I wouldn't trade anything for them. Even though it takes a lot of work to raise good kids these days, I can truthfully say that I feel we've done a wonderful job. They don't talk back, they usually listen to what we have to say whether they want to or not, and they only had to get a couple of whippings when they were younger to learn that we meant what we said. We know they're good children because their grandparents, their teachers, and complete strangers often tell us they are. On more than one occasion when we were eating out, another patron came to our table and complimented us on how well behaved our children are.

"When my oldest son first learned to drive, a neighbor complimented us on how mature he was because he didn't go racing up and down the street like a bat out of hell the way some of the other teenagers on the street did. It feels good to get compliments like that because it lets you know that you've done a good job. I'm sure they'll raise their children the same way, because if we go somewhere and they see a child falling out and acting a fool, they'll just look at us and shake their heads and say, 'If that was my child, I'd spank his butt, that doesn't make any sense.' They do not like bad, unruly children and I think that's a good sign that they will bring their children up to have manners and respect themselves and the people around them.

"Being able to teach your children that they're special is what's important to me as a mother. I always tell them they should never let anyone talk down to them, and that they should look people in the eye when they talk. I can't stand to see a child hold his head down and talk to the ground when somebody asks him a question. To me that demonstrates master/slave mentality which is not acceptable. I always tell my children that when you're talking to somebody you look them in the eye, don't look down at the ground. They know that they're just as intelligent as anyone else and that they can do and have whatever they want in this world as long as they're willing to work hard, so they have no reason to ever feel as if anyone is better than they are.

"I've also taught them to think highly of themselves and of their bodies, the boys as well as the girls, because a boy's body is just as precious as a girl's. He shouldn't be out there sleeping around with any and every female just because he's a male and society acts like it's okay. He needs to respect himself and his body just as much as a female should.

"The only thing I could say I dislike about being a mother was that I didn't know what to expect when I had my first baby. I tried to breastfeed and I was a mess at that, so it lasted all of six weeks. I didn't know that your milk leaked, and once when I was at the mall with my mother and the baby, I happened to catch my reflection in the mirror and the whole front of my dress was wet with milk and I was horrified. I even had those pads on but the milk just soaked through them. After that, I was afraid to go anywhere with my baby because I didn't know what might happen. I was afraid that his diaper might need to be changed while we were out, or that he might get hungry and start screaming. Plus, you have to lug all of that extra stuff like the baby bag, the stroller, and the car seat, so it was truly a learning experience for me.

"It was hard to give up my quiet time because as you know, it's always about the child once you have one, and I really wasn't prepared for that. My husband and I were married for almost four years before we had our first child, and I was used to having quality time with him and quiet time for myself. I was not prepared to have to give up so much of my time, but that's part of being a mother.

"On the other hand, I enjoy watching them as they grow and become intelligent individuals with minds of their own. My children are very secure in themselves and they don't give in to peer pressure. They have never been followers and I think that's because they have high self-esteem. We instilled that in them by telling them how much they mean to us, how smart they are, and how beautiful they are. We also let them know from an early age that they were going to college. There has never been any doubt in any of their minds as to what they are going to do after they graduate from high school. There is no 'I think I'm gonna get a job,' or 'I think I'll join the military,' they know that they're going to college because that's all they've ever been told. You have to give your children high expectations when they're very young if you want them to have them when they're on their own.

"I know they're not perfect, none of us are, but in my mind they're pretty close to it." Tamia smiled. "We always tell them to pick their friends carefully. We say, 'If you're around bad people then bad things can happen and you don't want to be caught up in being in the wrong place at the wrong time,' so basically they're pretty particular about the friends they choose.

"I talk to them about what to look for when they grow up and start dating too. One time a girl who was just a friend of our oldest son came to our house, and she had the nerve to go in his room and sprawl across his bed. I wanted to yank her up and tell her about herself, but in order to be polite, I called my son to my room and told him, 'Look, I've been married to your dad for over twenty years and I have never gone over to your grandmother's house and laid across her bed like that. A lady doesn't do things like that.' I tell them those kinds of things because I don't want them to end up with just anybody, and they need to realize that everybody is not raised the same way they are, so they need to watch for things like that.

"I even used that popular young athlete as an example. I told them that I'm sure his parents raised him right. He's traveled all over the world, he's well spoken, has a great career, and is very intelligent, but that one mistake, whether the woman is lying about being raped or not, may ruin his whole life because he was in the wrong place at the wrong time. I tell them that they have to be careful and think about the choices they make.

"All I want is for them to be happy, and successful in life. I want them to find spouses who are equal to them in their desires and dreams and who have been raised with high standards and good morals, just like we've tried to raise them. That's the bottom line."

JEWELL, SIXTY-SOMETHING

"I wanted more than one child because I love children. Being from a large family that was just the normal thing to do because everyone in my family has children. I'd been married like five or six years before I had my son and I would've had more than one but I had problems with that pregnancy so the doctor recommended that I not have any more or wait at least ten or twelve years. By that time I was in the career field that I wanted to be in so I couldn't afford to quit and back then if you got pregnant they would just about fire you. I grew up in that era. They didn't appreciate you getting pregnant. They wanted people who were already through having babies or people who didn't want children so I had this one child and that was that. By the time I was ready to have another child, my son was like seven or eight and when a child gets that old really it's hard to start all over again.

"I always wanted boys because girls seem to always be in some sort of power struggle with their mother and I didn't want that.

"Even though my son is grown, I'll see little things he's doing and I'll be like, 'Baby, you don't need to be . . .'

"And he's like, 'Mama, I don't want to hear that.'

"I'll say, 'Well, you're going to hear it.'

"And he'll come back with, 'Mama, I didn't come over here for that.'

"So I say, 'Well, you're going to hear it anyway.'" Jewell laughed.

"He'll be walking away from me the whole time but I'm right behind him talking, talking, talking. Then he'll tell me, 'You need to go sit your little self down,' but that's my job.

"Even though he may not want to hear what I have to say, I still say it because I've been there and done just about everything he thinks he can do. What kind of mother would I be if I didn't try to help my child? Back to having children though, if a person is healthy and has a healthy marriage I think they should have at *least* two or three children. I really do. Don't ever stop at one unless there's a medical problem because children need companionship while they're growing up.

"The other reason I wanted children is because I like feeling needed and being a mother you feel like you're needed all of the time. You always have someone to love and there is always someone out there who will need you and love you for the rest of your life. It's unconditional love.

"A child is not like a husband, a husband could walk away. You might *want* your child to walk away, but they always come back. It's a wonderful feeling that I can't even explain—you have to have a child to understand it.

"People who don't have children just can't relate. They don't know how it feels because there are both heartaches and sweetness in having children. You'll go through your heartaches and you're going to cry a lot of nights but I wouldn't want to change that. I wouldn't want to go through life without my child.

"You worry about them when they're small and you think you'll be glad when they grow up but that's just when you get started. You worry about them every night, even after they are married and away from home, you *still* worry about them. You never stop worrying, that's the truth. Don't think that just because they go off to college or get married and have babies and all that your worrying days are over, no, because they may still have problems and their problems are your problems. That's your baby and if your baby is not happy, you're not happy, so it never stops. That's your baby until you die. But I still think motherhood is just wonderful and I think every mature woman should experience it. Notice that I said mature. That's the key word. Every woman is not a mother and having a uterus, a vagina, and breasts don't make you mother material. It takes honesty, maturity, love, and compassion—four qualities that I hope I've instilled in my son. I've tried to give him everything that I had and things that I wished I had. I think I have given him everything he needs to succeed in life if he listened and paid attention but that's not the way it works sometimes. Children blow you off because they think you're old and that you don't know what's going on. Regardless of what they think, you still have the responsibility of telling them the things they'll need to know in order to succeed in life. That's a never-ending battle for a mother.

"I guess I'm probably a little too big on giving him advice because since he is my only child there is an unbelievable fear, unbelievable. Every day of my life I'm scared that something's going to happen to him. *Every day of my life.* I'm serious. He's all I've got. If anything happened to him I'd have nothing else to live for and that's the truth and I've told him that, I've said, 'Please live your life a little bit for me. Don't take a lot of chances, don't do a lot of the things that I know young people do because you are my whole life. When you go out there acting a fool and do something crazy, you're killing me because if anything happens to you, you have no more worries. I'm the one who would have to live with that and I couldn't live without you.' That's just how I feel.

"I'm sure it hurts even if you have twenty kids, to lose just one of them. But when you have just one, you have *nobody* else to love if something happens. All of that love goes into the ground with that child and you're left just hollow.

"For me there would be nothing else to live for and I can honestly say I don't think I could live without him, I wouldn't want to live, I'd have nothing to live for." Jewell shrugged her shoulders decisively.

"When you have more than one child you have to get yourself together because you've got to be strong for that other child. I know you've seen it happen before where most of the time, when an only child dies, the husband and wife fall apart because they take it out on each other because they're looking for something. They're trying to heal themselves but all they're doing is tearing each other down even more. To lose my child would be devastating. There's not a day that passes that I don't think . . . 'I hope he drives carefully today; I wonder how he's doing.'

"When he was young I had to force myself to let him spend the night away from home and then when he started driving I thought I'd go crazy. Most of the time I would stay up all night until I heard him pull up in the driveway and then I'd go to bed and pretend to be asleep. But I have to admit he was pretty good about coming home on time or calling when he was going to be late. He could never know how much I appreciated that.

"I want him to have a good life but the thing I want most is for him to be happy. I would love for my baby to marry someone who loves him back and be happy, no matter what. I look at him and say all the time, 'You know I had other things in mind for you, but they didn't work out. Everything is not picture perfect. I wanted you to go to college and get your degree and you didn't want to do that. I wanted you to go and pursue other careers but you didn't want to do that. I hoped that you would marry someone and ya'll would love each other and I'd have grandbabies but that hasn't happened yet. But what I want most of all is for *you* to be happy. If you never have a wife, if you never have children, I can live with that, I just want you to be happy.'

"When I asked him what would make him happy he said, 'I would love to find a wife that would take care of me like you took care of Daddy when he had the heart attack.' That just melted my heart.

"He tells me a lot but he won't tell his dad anything. I let him be as free as he wants to be, no matter what he says and even if it's not nice. Everybody needs somebody they can talk to, somebody that won't judge them. I guess I'm his sister, and mother, and everything but that's fine with me. If that means I've done such a good job of raising him that he feels that close to me then I've accomplished what I was supposed to as a mother."

VICKY, FORTY-SOMETHING

"You know, I never really thought about why I wanted children," Vicky said, sipping her margarita. "I guess I felt that once I got married, having babies would complete my family. I was happily married, so I wanted to have children to watch them grow up and add to that happiness, that's just the way I felt it was supposed to be. Now that I have them, I realize it's more than just a notion. It's important that my children grow up to be good people. I mean, I want them to do good things, not just be financially successful. It is very important to me that I instill in them that being happy and being a good, honest person is the most important thing in life, no matter what profession they choose or how much money they make, because when they're happy I'm happy too. And oh, don't let me forget the other wonderful things that I get as a bonus for having children; all those hugs and kisses, those chubby little arms around my neck, just seeing them do good things that make them and others around them happy is a feeling I can't explain. I love the feeling of being proud of them when they do something good, because all the hard work of raising children is worth it when they do something they can be proud of. It just does something to your heart when they feel good about themselves.

"The downside of that, if there is one, is that I'm so worried that they'll come home with tattoos and body piercings all over the place like kids do these days, and I do not like that. I see other boys with their ears pierced and that's okay but I don't know that I'll let mine do it. One of my daughter's friends who is only eight years old and in third grade already has her eyebrow pierced. Now, you know her parents had to let her do that and paid for it too. That's crazy for a child that young. What will she want to do when she's fourteen or fifteen?

"I'm just afraid they're going to get into the wrong lifestyle, you know, drugs and alcohol and stuff like that. I know that all I can do is talk to them about those things, and I do that, but I hope that I've talked to them enough so that they don't think those things are cool and get involved anyway. I want them to know that what's really cool is that they finish school and go to college and have a good job and become successful.

"The drawback, though I hate to admit this, is that since I'm the only parent in my house, I can't do what I want to, when I want to. When your kids are young like mine, you still need a baby-sitter, and that's a pain in the butt. I can't have my boyfriend sleep over at night unless he leaves early in the morning before the kids wake up, because I think it's disrespectful to my children. And I can't have wild, passionate, loud sex if they're at home, so even though I'm single, I'm still somewhat limited as to what I can do, I have to put their best interests first.

"Really, being a mother is a wonderful thing but you need to be mature and unselfish. Yes, there are many sacrifices you have to make. Many times you have to give up what you want in order for them to get what they need, but there should never be a time when a mother feels like she's 'missing out' because of her children. They didn't ask to be born, so even if you didn't plan them, once you've played the big girl game, you have to pay the big girl price, and believe me, it costs a pretty penny in more ways than one. Still, if I had to do it all over again, I wouldn't trade my children for anything in the world."

JESSICA, THIRTY-SOMETHING

"I've always wanted more than one child and surprisingly we had twins the first time so I'm through. There's nothing like receiving news like that when you're expecting only one child. I grew up just like an only child myself and that's why I like having my space. My only sibling, a brother, is thirteen years older than me so I don't even remember him living with us. By the time I was five he'd already left for college. I look back now and realize that I don't have anyone to share memories of growing up with and if my parents died tomorrow it would just be me so I didn't want it to be like that for my children. I wanted my children to have someone else to share memories with so I always wanted at least two or three, and I wanted them to be close in age.

"What I love most about being a mother are the hugs and kisses every day. There's nothing I dislike, absolutely nothing. Yes it's a big responsibility but you expect that if you've ever been around anyone who has children. Responsibility is a given but the rewards you get for all the work is worth it.

"I want my children to be independent, loyal, and have leadership qualities so they won't be followers and it's my responsibility to instill those things in them. I want them to have a sense of responsibility and ownership, and I want them to be successful individuals, and I want them to be happy and have loving families. But like all mothers, I do have my worries and fears. I think my biggest fear for them is that they would have to grow up without me. I worry that if I get sick or something I won't be here for them but I can't do anything about that except take better care of myself.

"The other thing I worry about is that I will try to give them too much and spoil them." Jessica rubbed her hands along her thighs as she spoke. "See, my parents gave me whatever I wanted. I had my first job when I graduated from high school and I was fortunate enough to work in my uncle's business so I brought home about $300 a week. My parents made me put my money in the bank because whatever I wanted, they would buy for me. I just saved my money. When it came time to go to college I was thinking, 'Oh, this is nice, I'm going to college and I got money in the bank.'" Jessica shook her shoulders from side to side like she was dancing. "I wasn't thinking that I would have to spend that money, I thought I'd be able to keep it in the bank because my parents were always giving me money.

"Well, to my amazement and surprise, they made me pay for our plane tickets when it came time for me to get moved in for college and I was shocked. When we got to the town that I was going to attend college in, my parents and I opened up a checking account. The bank gave me this cute little checkbook but I still didn't understand the concept. I'd put some money in the bank, then turn around and take it right back out so it was like why even bother putting it in a checking account when I'm going to have to write a check and use it. I might as well keep the money and buy what I want.

"I was spending the money too fast and by now my parents had the responsibility of paying my college tuition so they didn't have as much 'free money,' as I call it, to splurge. I was calling home for an extra $100 when I had just gotten $300 and my mom was like, 'No, you need to get a job' and I was like, 'Get a job? For what?' Well, I got a job and started paying for the things I wanted but it still didn't hit home until I graduated from college and I had to pay rent and a car note. I got my own car on my own credit and I had to budget so I could make that car note because if I didn't have a car I couldn't get to work. I'd never had to do these things before, so I didn't have all that 'free money' to buy clothes.

"Every day I used to go shopping and bring something home.

I was used to it because that's what I did when I was living with my parents, and I never realized it until I came home and my room-mates said, 'Every time you come home you have a bag.' It wouldn't be any big thing, maybe something like a bra, panties, whatever, but every day I did have a bag.

"Because of my personal experience with money, I've learned to make my children think they're using their own allowance when they want something, then I'll pocket their money and save it for them. I once heard the comedian Jamie Fox say that his grand-mother raised him and when he got a job every time he got paid she'd make him give her his check. Well of course he got mad at her and called her all kinds of names under his breath, but when he was working his way up the ladder on his way to becoming a comedian, he got in a tight and he needed some money so he called his grand-mother to help him out. She told him, 'I have some money for you; it's your money. I've been keeping your money all these years,' and he appreciated that.

"So I think I'll do something like that with my children. I want to instill in them that they're using their money when they want to buy something and if they don't have enough to buy whatever and want to borrow from me I'll keep a little notepad and let them bor-row. Maybe that way they won't feel like I just give them or buy them whatever they want."

LADY, FORTY-SOMETHING

"Children just do something for you. They make your life worth living. You want to see them successful and happy, and you want to see good things happen for them, and when it works out that way, it makes you feel proud. The most important thing about being a mother is that you need to be ready when you have children. I don't know how you get ready, but you need to realize that you don't come first anymore, those children come first. Whatever you've got to do to make sure they have what they need, that's what you need to do and that means you cannot be a selfish person.

"I try to raise my children to have good values; I hope I've instilled self-respect and self-love in them, because if a person can't love themselves, they can't love anybody else. Children need to understand that they're important, and that they have something to contribute to society, and I tell them that as often as possible. I try to say positive things all the time, because children believe what you tell them. I also tell them they should always put God first, read the Bible, and talk to God every day because you can't have a relationship with God unless you spend time with Him—just like you can't have a relationship with a person unless you spend time with them. If the time ever comes when they can't get Mama, Daddy, or anybody else on the phone, they know how to get on their knees, and they know God will be right there with the answer they're looking for.

"I want them to be honest, open-minded, and positive about life, especially since they're young. There's so much opportunity out there for them that they don't even know it. I tell them, 'The only limitations you have are the ones you set for yourself. Right now is the best time in your life and you don't have any commitments to anyone but yourself, and everything you're doing right now is for your future, not mine.' When I send letters or cards to my daughter in college, I find myself telling her to get a little bit of everything life has to offer. I say, 'You're a young, beautiful black woman, and you're getting a college degree so that you can have more choices in life. Your future is out there just waiting for you, but you have to go and get it, and it may not always be easy. However, with an education, the possibilities are endless.

"It's nice to have a boyfriend and all that, but if you ever find yourself in a situation with a person who is negative and has no dreams, or goals in life, you need to let him move on to the next girl, he's not for you. If he doesn't make you happy, don't be bothered with his ass, do not waste your time because you don't have to. As a matter of fact, don't waste your time being around any negative people who are always depressed and talking about the white man is holding them back. Yeah, he might have his foot right smack in the middle of your back but that's no excuse for not trying. If you get that college degree, somebody's got to move their foot sooner or later.

"I try to make sure they have high self-esteem because I feel that's really important for girls. If they don't think highly of themselves, they grow up with very low expectations of how others should treat them, and that's not good. Once a month me and my girls will go to a play, a musical, or a museum, and then we'll have lunch or dinner at a nice restaurant, because I want them to have those types of experiences. And every now and then I talk my husband into taking them out on a date, just because I want them to know how a lady should be treated. I think that's very important.

"It's important that boys have high self-esteem too, but girls just seem like they get walked on so much more in life if they don't. They're not only going to get walked on by men, they're going to get walked on in the workplace or wherever they go if they can't speak up for themselves. If they don't have enough faith in themselves, they become very negative and once that happens, they're not going to get anywhere in life and they end up with all this baggage that nobody wants to deal with. Since my girls are so softhearted and affectionate, I worry about their self-esteem all the time.

"When I look at them, and see that innocence in their eyes, and when I hug them and feel the softness of their skin, those are special moments for me. I often look at them and think, 'Those are my babies, they're part of me.' They're part of my heart and if something happened to one of them, a part of my heart would just die, so I'm always praying for their safety.

"There are many other sweet things I could say about being a mother, but I think it's also important to say that sometimes no matter what you do, they don't always please you. They're human, and they're not perfect, so there are times when they do things that are disappointing. For instance, I have heart-to-heart talks with my oldest about young men and relationships. I want her to know how she should be treated, so that she won't put up with a whole bunch of shit, but sometimes she still doesn't make the choices I'd like her to make. There have been a few times when I had to ask myself, 'Did I do a good job? Or did I miss the mark and mess something up?' It's funny how we as mothers always feel that it's partly our fault when a child makes bad choices.

"Another thing that I need to say is that when you are involved in too much outside your home, it takes away from what you need to be giving to your children. Whether it be your job, going back to school, or a relationship with someone, you are shortchanging your children when you spend too much time away from them to pursue your own interests. I'm not saying women shouldn't go back to school and try to get a degree, or that they shouldn't have any interests outside of home, but if you want to go back to school and it means you have to go at night, when your elementary school-aged child needs help with homework, then maybe you need to put that off until that child is a little older and doesn't require so much help. They're only children once, and if you miss the opportunity to nurture them when they need it most, you can never get it back.

"I know that there were instances when I could've been spending quality time with my oldest daughter after my divorce, but I was dating some fool who didn't even deserve the time of day. I learned the hard way that you should never let anything or anyone take quality time away from your children, because when you get old and gray, if nobody else is willing to take care of you, hopefully your children will. All those other things and other people don't mean a damn thing when you really come down to it.

"Sure, having children means you have to temporarily put your life on hold, but as adults, we need to remember it was our decision to have children. They didn't ask to be born, so we shouldn't put them on a guilt trip about how we've had to do without in order for them to have things, that's a very selfish thing for any mother to do. I'm not saying I've never felt that way, but once I decided to have children, I knew it was a big decision, and I've never regretted my choice. If I had it to do all over again, I'd still have them, even though I have my moments when I want to be selfish.

"It's all about them and it seems like the more you give the more they want, or the more they require. It's not easy being a parent, not being a good parent anyway. But it's a choice that you make and you need to remember that.

"My biggest fear for my girls is that they'll marry somebody they have to take care of because both of them are very quiet and easygoing. They're mama's girls, and even though I've tried to enlighten them about boys, I've also sheltered them, probably too much. My hope is that they both will marry somebody who will treat them special. Even though they both plan on getting a college degree, I want them to be able to stay home with their children if that's what they desire. But if they marry some slouch who can't even keep a job, that's not going to happen and guess who ends up helping to raise the grandchildren? You guessed it, me, and I'm not even trying to do that."

SHRIMP C'EST BON

3 pounds unpeeled
large fresh shrimp

1 (16-ounce) loaf
French bread, cut in
half lengthwise

1 cup butter

2 onions, chopped

1½ teaspoons minced
garlic

1 teaspoon Creole sea-
soning

Peel shrimp, and devein, if desired. Set aside.

Place french bread halves on a baking sheet, cut
side up. Bake at 350 degrees for 5 minutes or until bread is lightly browned. Cut each bread half
into 3 pieces and set aside.

Melt butter in a dutch oven. Add onion, garlic,
and seasoning. Cook over medium heat until onion
is tender. Add shrimp.

Cover and cook 8 minutes or until shrimp turn
pink. Serve over bread. *Yield: 6 servings.*

········· ## FRIENDSHIP

MISS DELORES, FIFTY-SOMETHING

"I had a friend who was very dear to me. We'd known each other since first grade. She called me one day and said her husband had left her, and she needed me to cosign a note to help her get a loan. It wasn't a big deal for me, especially since I knew it would help her out, because I knew she'd help me if I needed it.

"I signed that note and ended up having to go to court and pay *cash* for whatever it was she'd bought with that money because she never made one damn payment.

"I paid an attorney to locate her, but he wasn't able to find her because all he had was her social security number and she was never one to work. I just couldn't believe she'd do me that way because she was my lifelong friend.

"I haven't heard from her since. She just took the money and left. I don't even know if the story she told me about her husband leaving her was true. She could have gone off with him for all I know. That's low, isn't it? Really low. And I thought we were tight. So, since that happened, I don't sign for anyone, no matter who they are."

GIOVANNI, FORTY-SOMETHING

"My best friend is a really sweet guy who I used to be very much in love with. I still love him. I mean, we still love each other, but we're both married. So after three years of meeting at every Motel 6 in town, we decided that we should do the right thing and leave the sex out of our relationship because we were becoming very possessive of each other. Besides that, I got tired of asking for a room in the back.

"The reason I can truly say he's my best friend is because he's been there for me through thick and thin. We can talk about God, marriage, children, sex, money, politics, and even though we may not agree on everything, we respect each other's opinions.

"I remember one time we got into a heated discussion about religion. I was looking for a church to join and he suggested I visit his church with my family. Well, that didn't sit well with me because I'm not trying to be friends with his wife, and his pastor is a straight-up ho and everybody in town knows it. You talk about the blind leading the blind. I don't even know why they're following the man and paying their tithes at that church because most of it's probably being used to take care of all his women.

"I tried to get my friend to understand that I know we don't worship the pastor and that I'm not perfect, myself. I even agree that what the pastor does is his business, as long as I'm doing what I'm supposed to be doing. But I wouldn't be up in the church trying to lead somebody else if I was living foul, so I can't follow someone else who is. How can you follow someone you don't respect, and how can you respect a man with a wife on the front row, a girlfriend in the choir, and one on the usher board at the same time? That's just insane to me.

"Anyway, my friend and I got into a big argument over this and didn't call each other for three months, but I thought about him every day. But since he'd hung up on me, I felt he should make the first move to apologize. I was really hurt that he might let something like this come between us after all we'd been through. But then one day he beeped me, and when I called him back he was like, 'Hey, Giovanni, how ya doing? Um, did you page me a while ago?' I paused—you know I had to savor the moment. Then I said, 'No, sweetie. I didn't page you, and you know it, so stop trying to play like you got a page from somebody you don't know. You'd know if I'd paged you 'cause I would have put in my number, so there would have been no doubt in your mind it was me. Where have you been?'

"We both cracked up laughing then, happy that we'd been able to make fun of the situation. But since that time we don't discuss church too much. When we do, we keep it light so we don't offend one another.

"It's really nice to have someone to discuss my husband and children with who I know I can trust. If my husband pisses me off, I can call my friend and tell him what's going on, and he'll calm me down and get me to think about things before I jump to conclusions and make decisions that I'll regret later. I do the same thing for him. When he complains that his wife ain't giving him none, I ask him has he given her a reason to want to give him some. I've explained to him that women don't just turn their emotions off when they lay down like men do, and I think that has helped him to be more patient and understanding with her.

"One of the best things about our relationship is that I don't ever have to worry about him repeating anything I say to anyone else. Hell, both of us have too much to lose to be running off at the mouth. That's one of the things that has kept us together for so long. I often tell him that if I had it to do all over again, I'd find him and marry him. Then he could be my best friend, my lover, and my husband."

MARCELLA, FORTY-SOMETHING

"As far as friends go, let me tell you a little story about what friends will do for you. About fifteen years ago, there was a girl I used to call my best friend, until I found out she'd had sex with my husband in my driveway, in my car." Marcella lit some incense and blew out the match.

"I guess I should have known 'cause she was always hanging around my house and was up in his face a lot more than she should have been. Always grinning and smiling and shit when he came around—that should have been a clue right there, but I was naive I never thought she'd do something like that. I was always taught not to get involved with another woman's boyfriend or husband, so I guess I thought everybody else was taught the same thing. Back on the islands, the whole community would look down on you for doing such a thing. But in this country, things are different.

"To make matters worse, about two weeks before I found out they'd had sex, this same girl had asked me to charge some furniture for her, and I did it, like a fool, because I felt sorry for her. She was a single woman with five little children, and the children were all sleeping in one queen-sized bed and using one dresser, so I thought I'd help her out.

"Well, one evening when I was getting my mail, my next-door neighbor, a nosey old lady who was always at home watching everything that went on, stopped me and said, 'Sugar, I hate to tell you, but that little Tonya, who you call your friend, ain't your friend at all. I been wanting to tell you but every time I saw you, I saw her too, so I couldn't get to you. That little slut has been sliding across the street in them little short dresses she always wears for the past two weeks, coming over to your house late at night as soon as your husand gets off work. He's been meeting her out in the driveway, and they always get in the car, but the car don't never go nowhere. I reckon he figured you'd wake up if he started the motor, so they just sit out in the driveway and do their business at about two in the morning. Most of the time you can see him sittin' up in the seat, but you can't see her at all with her little nasty self. That's why she got all them damn babies by different men. She always been a ho, and her mama, God rest her soul, was the same way. It's just a damn shame.'

"I was floored. Here I thought he was up watching TV when he said he couldn't sleep, while instead he'd been screwing my friend, outside in my driveway. I was fit to be tied.

"I went over to her house and confronted her and she laughed, looked me straight in the eyes, and said, 'Marcella, girl, I know you don't believe that crazy old lady. That old bitch ain't got nothing better to do than make up shit on me just because she never liked my mama and she's never liked me.'

"But the look on her face told me she was lying, and I told her I was going to kick her narrow, natural ass if I found out it was really true. She rushed me off, saying she had to go and would be over later to straighten it all out, but she never came over that evening, which was a Thursday, and when I got home from work on Friday, she had moved out of that house with her kids and the furniture I'd bought. She just moved with all this shit I'd charged without saying a word.

"She wasn't working at the time and she'd been talking about moving in with some family down in Austin, Texas, so I figured that's where she'd gone. But what was I going to do—get the police to find her and make her bring my shit back? And my marriage was already on its way to being over anyway, so I knew that sorry husband of mine wouldn't confess, so there was no point in asking him.

"Well, about six months ago, I had to call the worker's compensation commission, and guess who I ended up talking to? Oh, she didn't know it was me, but I always take the name of the person helping me so I asked for her name. When she said 'Tonya,' I almost passed out. I asked her if she'd ever lived in the Dallas/Fort Worth metroplex area and she told me yes, trying to sound all proper and shit with her little country ass.

"Well, I let her finish giving me all the information I needed, then I asked her if she remembered a girl named Marcella who she used to be friends with, and after she beat around the bush for a minute, she told me that my accent sounded familiar. I told her who I was, and I know she almost dropped the phone. She started talking all fast and shit, asking me how I'd been, and lying about how happy she was to hear my voice. I just sat there and didn't say nothing because there was nothing to say. After she finished fumbling over her own words, the bitch had the nerve to invite me to come and see her if I was ever in Austin.

"As proper as I could, I told her ass off. I told her if I ever saw her black ass again, I was going to get a stick and beat the shit out of her for screwing my sorry-ass husband while her little crumb snatchers were sleeping on beds that I'd bought. I told her if I never see her bald-headed, no-man-having, green contact—wearing, ho ass again, that would be too soon and she'd better never come up this way to visit anybody and run into me because if she did, she'd regret the very day she met me. Then I just hung up the phone.

"Now I'm satisfied because even though she was known for having a quick tongue, for once in her sorry life, she didn't get a chance to say anything.

"To this day, the closest I get to friends is a close acquaintance. But I'll never have a best friend again."

KIANA, FORTY-SOMETHING

"When I was twenty-one, there was a girl who was about nineteen who was engaged to my brother, and we'd gotten as close as sisters. In fact, I treated her better than I treated my sister. She had a daughter who was around the same age as my daughter, and we were both single parents; so we decided to move in together to share expenses.

"We had a small apartment and a wall divided our two bedrooms. My bedroom was on the far side and in order to get to the kitchen I had to go through her room. Well, I was walking through her room to the kitchen to get my coffee started before I got dressed for work and I was wearing nothing but my bra and panties, and there she was straddling some nigga, riding him for all he was worth. I was trying not to look because at first I figured it must be my brother, right?

But when I came back through to go back to my room, she was sitting up in the bed looking like a fool and the guy in the bed with her was definitely not my brother.

"I just kept on walking, finished getting dressed, and went on to work. It really made me mad because I felt like, number one, she disrespected me, and number two, if she was gonna fool around while messing with my brother, she could have at least waited until I was at work.

"So, when I got to work I called her and told her we needed to talk. That evening, after we'd discussed it, I packed my stuff and moved out because I didn't want to be in the middle of no mess like that. I liked her, but I loved my brother and I couldn't keep nothing like that from him. So I moved back home, and of course, I had to tell my brother what had happened.

"When I was talking to her, she acted like she didn't understand why I was so upset. She thought we were so close that she could trust me with something like that, but like I told her, blood is thicker than water. You don't take advantage of my friendship just because your ass got hot in the middle of the night.

"She said they would have gone to a motel, but she really didn't think he would still be there when I woke up, so she just let him spend the night. How dumb. I mean we were tight, really tight, and I was hurt. I couldn't even talk to her for a while after that happened.

"After I finally calmed down, I called her and told her it wasn't the fact that she was messing around on my brother that hurt me so much because people do stuff like that all the time. It was the fact that she didn't respect me. She didn't care how I'd feel about seeing her in that position, and by doing that she walked all over me and my brother, like she really didn't care about either one of us.

"She asked me to please forgive her, but I was never able to and I'll never forget that. My brother was heartbroken, and I've always resented her for that. So, I don't have too many women friends. You just can't trust them."

VERONICA, THIRTY-SOMETHING

"Now you know I have a lot of acquaintances," Veronica began. "But I can honestly say I'd much rather have male rather than female friends, and let me tell you why.

"I met this girl when I was in the military and we became best friends. Even when our assignments were up in Germany and we went to different bases, we kept in touch. I remained close to her for the next two years or so, speaking by phone, writing letters, and sending cards because we were both so busy. Then she finally decided to come for a visit without her husband, and that's when I realized why her first husband had divorced her.

"This child had lost her real mind. I knew she'd been saved and was calling herself an evangelist, and I had no problem with that. But I also knew something was wrong with her making long-distance phone calls to her senior pastor every morning while she was at my house. I'd try to give her some privacy when she was on the phone, but the calls lasted so long that I just couldn't stay in my room and wait for her to clear the line. Hell, she was in my damn house. Why was I tiptoeing around like I didn't want to offend her? And the way she was whispering and giggling, there ain't no way in hell they could have been talking about God. It was very obvious that the two of them had been touching and agreeing, but not on nothing in the Bible, and she was acting as if I was blind, deaf, and dumb.

"Well, she'd planned to stay with us for two weeks, which was too damn long for me in the first place, but after that first five days, I'd had enough of her getting up and going through my refrigerator and fixing breakfast for me and my husband without so much as asking me if I minded. So, I decided I was gonna make up some lie that we planned to visit family in another town for the weekend to get her to leave, but she still didn't get the hint. At least she didn't act like she did.

"Just when I figured there was no other way out except to tell her that she had overstayed her visit, wore out her welcome, whatever the hell I needed to say to get her to pack up her shit and leave, she made it easy for me. I walked in on her late one night while she was on the phone in my living room, and she didn't even know I was standing there because she had the lights out.

"'Hey, boo,' she said in a voice so sweet it sounded like somebody else. 'Yeah, I miss you too. I been playing with myself every night thinking about you . . . No . . . I can't come home yet 'cause he might not think I'm serious about leaving him if I come back too soon . . . Yeah, it's nice out here, but my friend is a trip. I told her I call you every day so we can pray together and she's so dumb, she believes it. She living in this nice house and all, telling me her husband is so good to her, but I'll bet if she left me here with him for about forty-five minutes, and I gave him some of this poonany, he'd tell her to pack her shit and leave. You know how I do it.' Then she laughed a deep and what she apparently thought was a sexy laugh, while still trying to be quiet, but it was too late.

"I turned the lights on her ass and said, 'Bitch, if you don't get your hands out of your little funky coochie and get off my damn phone right now, you gonna be speaking in tongues, wishing your pastor could come save you while my foot is in your ass. How dare you come into my house and take my kindness for granted, when you don't even deserve it. You got ten minutes to get that little raggedy shit that you brought in that raggedy-ass suitcase you had to borrow from somebody, and get out of my house. Ten minutes, you hear me? And don't say shit because if you do, I'm calling your husband to tell him what's really going on. In the meantime I'm going to get my gun, just in case you think I'm playing games with your stupid ass. Now you and your pastor pray about that.'

"Honey, her eyes got all big and she hurried up and got her stuff together while I stood at the door and watched her. I didn't even give her time to change clothes or call a cab or nothing. I just pushed her ass out the front door and slammed it right in her face. How's that for a friend?"

REGINA, FORTY-SOMETHING

"One of the best things my friend Caroline did for me was introduce me to the man destined to be my husband and to this day I love her for it.

"Caroline and I met while attending Southern University in Baton Rouge and have remained friends ever since. I'd met her mom and a couple of her sisters whenever they came to Baton Rouge to visit but I'd never had the chance to visit her in her hometown. After college I moved to Texas but even though Caroline moved back home to Opelousas and found a good job, she'd been right there for me throughout all of my failed relationships and I'd done the same for her.

"She knew that the type of man I liked had to be well-educated, career-oriented, at home in tailor-made suits, enjoy dining at fine restaurants, able to identify fine wines, and comfortable going to plays or to the opera. Caroline knew this but she would always tell me I was too boogie for my own good and that I was blocking my blessings.

"For the past five years she'd talked about this guy she'd wanted me to meet but I was always involved with the man of my dreams, or so I thought at the time. The guy was a good friend of her boyfriend's, and just like her boyfriend he wasn't well-educated but he had a good paying job with the city, he was a country boy who raised cows and traveled the rodeo circuit. Caroline told me, 'He might not know the difference between a Chardonnay or Merlot but he damn sure knows how to treat a woman and that should be all that matters.' I always tuned her out because frankly I like men who enjoy the finer things in life and a black cowboy didn't fit the bill.

"I didn't like homebodies, or so I thought. I liked men who weren't afraid to do different things and who didn't mind spending money on me. If I care for a man I don't mind spending money on him but I also expect the favor to be returned. I can't stand a cheap man but sometimes you don't find out a man is cheap until you get to know him. One guy I dated started out real nice, he fit all of my qualifications, but by the time our third date rolled around I was able to see his true colors. One night we were supposed to go to dinner and a movie, but when he got to my house he told me he'd already eaten so he really didn't want to go out to dinner and if it was okay with me could we just go to the movies. I said fine and figured I'd just get a snack at the movies because there was this one movie I was dying to see.

"When homeboy got the movie section of the newspaper, spread it out on my counter, and had the nerve to call out to me what was showing at the dollar theater, girl I was too through. First of all, the movie that I wanted to see was a new release and wouldn't be at the dollar theater for a while, and secondly, what made him think I wanted to go to a dollar movie anyway? I mean damn, it was bad enough that he didn't want to go out to dinner, now all my company was worth was one dollar? It wasn't like he didn't have the money to spend. I'd seen his home and his car and I knew he had a well-paying job. It wasn't like I was stingy with him either, because on our second date I'd invited him over to my place for filet mignon and all the trimmings prepared with my own hands and now here he was on a third date talking about a dollar movie? I don't think so.

"Anyway, Caroline would always invite me to this big zydeco festival every year but the man I'd been seeing would be like, 'Zydeco? Baby please. I'll take you to a play or something but I there ain't no way I'm going to go to no country ass town to no country ass party.'

"Even though Caroline and I are total opposites in most ways, we still enjoy some of the same things. I'm a pampered city girl and she's a down to earth country girl. She hates to shop, I love it; she knows how to ride horses and I've never been within touching distance of one, but it always intrigued me when I would hear her speak in casual conversation about her horses and the property her father owned in the country. I never even realized that black people rode horses, I'd never even thought about it until I met Caroline.

"All of my life I'd read romance novels and the stories would always describe these white women with a white male hero and both could ride horses but never, ever in any of the hundreds of books I read was any mention made of black people riding horses. Now you got to remember that when I was growing up and reading these romance novels all of the characters were white. There were no romance novels that I was aware of that featured black heroes and heroines.

"Well, the last time Caroline called me and asked me to come to this zydeco festival I surprised her and said yes. I'd broken up with my boyfriend of five years and was still going through the grieving process even though the breakup had been more than ten months ago because I'm the kind of woman who loves hard so it's tough for me to let go of something even when I know it's the best thing for me.

"Caroline tells me, 'I'm glad I didn't give up on your tired, always got to have man in your life ass. It's a shame that it took you and what's-his-face to break up to get you out here to a festival. I hope you remember how to zydeco.' Caroline had taught me some of the basic steps while we were in college but all of that was long since forgotten.

"She was a single woman then but is now happily married to the man she'd been dating off and on since they were childhood friends. Her family is large, she has six sisters and no brothers, and as soon as she picked me up from the airport that Friday afternoon we dropped my bags off at her house and headed over to her parents' to dine on some of her father's famous smoked catfish. I had never in my life eaten any fish that tasted so good, and to this day, I've never had any that was better than that.

"Her daddy used some secret spices to season the fish, wrapped the fish in foil, and smoked it on the grill. Even when I begged and pleaded to know what kind of seasoning he'd used he refused to share the recipe, but he did give me a jar full of his secret spice to take home with me. Caroline told me that no one in the family knew exactly what kind of spice he used. Her sister had made some fresh rolls to go with the fish and her mother added boiled corn and a green salad so we were good to go.

"Caroline had told me to bring comfortable clothes because you had to be comfortable when you danced the zydeco. You couldn't walk around trying to be cute and shit. She told me, 'Girl leave all of that fancy shit at home and just pack some jeans, comfortable shoes, and shirts because we going to a zydeco and when you dance the zydeco, you get the workout of your life.'

"The party was held on a small ranch owned by a man they called Little Paul and we were told that we would see a sign pointing the location out to us. Sure enough, after we'd gone down this long dirt road that had no street lights to speak of, Caroline's car lights caught this hand-lettered wooden sign that actually read 'Lil Paul's Place' with a crooked arrow pointing out which way to turn. When we pulled up onto the property I noticed that the parking lot was filled with full-sized trucks and everybody was heading into this metal building, actually it was a huge barn. Inside were black cowboys and cowgirls mingling, laughing, dancing, and drinking. In my whole life, I'd never read about anything remotely resembling this, but it was wonderful.

"Everyone wore starched, snug fitting, black, khaki, or blue jeans, and starched button-down shirts. These were some of the most neatly dressed people I'd ever seen. Some of the men wore huge belt buckles. Caroline told me that they'd won them in rodeo contests. The men and women wore cowboy boots or ropers and I had done like Caroline told me and brought my jeans, but they were nothing like the jeans these people wore, which along with my shoes labeled me an outsider—but they never made me feel that way.

"The barn contained two huge rooms. The first room held a wall-to-wall bar where you could buy setups, consisting of ice and cups, and you could also buy beer and wine coolers. This room also held several booths for people to sit and mingle when they got tired of dancing. Since this was a B.Y.O.B. (bring your own bottle) party, most of the tables in the second room circling the dance floor held all kinds of liquor, from rum to gin to vodka.

"There was a live six-member zydeco band on the homemade stage and they were magnificent. One band member had this metal washboard-looking thing hooked over his shoulders that covered his chest, and he was playing this instrument with silverware, which made for some exciting music, and the words of the songs reminded you of the music your parents used to listen to, except it was much faster.

"I sat back and watched Caroline twirl around on the floor with her boyfriend and they moved so gracefully, it was as if they'd been dancing together forever. All of the couples moved in tandem and I noticed that this was a dance where you actually touched your partner, be it around the waist, on the shoulder, or holding hands.

"I soon realized that the steps I'd learned from Caroline were elementary compared to some of the stuff those people were doing and on about the fourth or fifth song this tall, fine brother, wearing tight-fitting blue jeans, a starched white shirt, black hat, and black cowboy boots, moved in on Caroline and her partner. Her boyfriend grinned, obviously thankful for the break, and moved off the dance floor looking for something to quench his thirst.

"When I tell you I couldn't take my eyes off her new partner, believe me, I literally. Could. Not. Take. My. Eyes. Off that man. The word 'fine' couldn't even begin to describe him. He was big and fine, pretty and fine, just fine with a capital F. Watching him dance with Caroline I found myself wishing I knew how to zydeco, because that would give me an excuse to put my hands on those broad shoulders of his. When he twirled Caroline around and smiled and caught my eye, I almost forgot to breathe. He had every single woman in the room staring at him, and even some who weren't so single.

"The song came to an end and Caroline, with her I-love-to-dance ass, finally left the floor with this good-looking man trailing behind her, and they walked directly up to me. I closed my mouth and tried to act like I hadn't been staring so hard. 'Hey girl,' Caroline said. 'This is the guy I've been wanting to introduce you to for the past few years. Now that you've finally torn yourself away from that big city of yours and decided to grace us with your presence, I'd like you to meet Tyler.'

"I stammered out a hello and he flashed that smile again, and all the while I was thinking, 'Damn, if I knew the brother was this fine, I would've been down here a looong time ago.' But I just smiled and shook his hand.

"My friend Caroline continued to rattle on and she said, 'Remember all of those times I told you there was this guy I wanted you to meet? Well, this is the guy. He's heard me talk about you, he's seen pictures of you, and I always told him what a nice lady you are, so he wanted to meet you.'

"He held his hand out to me and said, 'This must be my lucky day.' The next song that came on had him pulling me out to the dance floor. I thanked God it was a slow one. We danced and talked for the rest of the night, he taught me how to zydeco, and here it is four years later, and we're married and very happy. We go out dancing at least twice a month and believe it or not, he's even taught me how to ride a horse.

"My friend Caroline proved to be a true friend when she said I was blocking my blessings, and I'm glad that I finally listened to her. I found out that knowing how to choose the right wine or how well you wear a suit does not make the man, it's all about what's inside."

LADY, FORTY-SOMETHING

"When my boyfriend of two years graduated from college and accepted a job offer with a company in New York, he asked me to marry him. I was crazy about him so of course I said yes, and we decided that I would transfer to a college in New York to finish getting my degree, before we set a wedding date.

"I spent the next two months checking on colleges and sending out résumés, and even though I was extremely busy, I was happier than I had ever been. We had an engagement party and invited our family and friends and told them about our plans, and then we flew to New York to spend a week looking for an apartment.

"I'd never been to a place like New York, and it was awesome. We stayed at the W Hotel in Manhattan because that's where the company he would work for was located, but we looked for apartments all over New York. We took the subway, the train, the bus, and a taxi all in one day, going from Harlem, to Brooklyn, to New Jersey and everywhere else we thought we could find a nice place to live. And it's not that nice places to live in New York are in short supply, it's just that coming from Oklahoma, everything seemed so expensive.

"The week was coming to an end and we were almost out of time because we actually spent more time sightseeing than we should have. We finally settled on a small apartment in a newly remodeled brownstone located in Harlem, and believe me when I say it was small, I do mean it was small. The kitchen, dining, and living areas were all in one room, and the bedroom and bathroom were on the other side of the wall. It was nice and clean, and my fiancé was relieved to have found something we could afford.

"When we got back to Oklahoma my best friend, Randi, picked us up from the airport. She said she couldn't wait to hear about all we'd seen and done, but when we walked into the terminal, she had the funniest look on her face, almost like she wanted to cry. Something was wrong. At first I thought she was getting sentimental about my moving so far away, but the look in her eyes told me not to ask her anything just then.

"After we dropped Reggie off at his place, Randi suggested we go have lunch so we could talk, and I agreed. We went to get barbecue at a place in the neighborhood where they have the best hot link baskets in the world, and sat outside at one of the picnic tables to eat.

"She asked how New York was, so I told her about Central Park, the doormen on Park Avenue, the subway, Grand Central Station,

Battery Park, and the Statue of Liberty. But as I talked I could tell she wasn't listening to me. Her mind was obviously in another place, so I stopped in mid-sentence and asked her what was wrong and why did she have that strange look on her face.

"She goes, 'Oh girl, ignore me. I'm happy for you, but I'm also sad that my best friend is going to be moving so far away. What will I do without you?'

"I told her that my being in New York wouldn't change our friendship. We'd still be best friends, only now she'd have a reason to come out East to visit, and have a place to stay, for free. Then I told her that I sensed that something else was up. So I said to her, 'Be honest with me, is something else wrong?'

"She said, 'Well, I don't know how to say this, so let me just put it out there. You know that Reggie's old girlfriend Tammi is pregnant. Well I heard that the baby could be his. The guy who told me knows her real well, and she's telling him that it might be Reggie's baby.'

"The world just stopped for me at that point in time because I don't think I heard anything else after she said, 'The baby could be his.' I'd heard that she was pregnant and had even asked Reggie if he knew anything about it, but he became angry at me for even bringing her name up. He said he hadn't seen her, didn't want to see her, and didn't want to talk about her. He said that relationship was over before he and I started dating because she wanted to see other people. Yes, he'd been in love with her and had even proposed marriage a few times, but she wasn't ready to settle down, so he finally had to let go and move on.

"All I could think about was the way Reggie had turned his back to me when I brought Tammi's name up. I remember feeling like he was hiding something, but I didn't want to push, so I'd dropped it, and I had no intention of bringing it up again, no matter what Randi said.

"I said, 'I heard that same rumor and that Reggie and I had already discussed it. He said he doesn't know anything about whether

Tammi is pregnant or not, but he hasn't seen her or talked to her, and didn't even want me to mention her name. The bitch didn't want him two years ago because she wanted to see other guys, so I don't know why she would start a rumor like that. That's a horrible thing to do to anybody. I can't stand her, I never could, and now I know why. She has always been a troublemaker, going around acting like she so sweet and innocent with her high-yellow ass. I don't even know how he could fall in love with somebody like her in the first place. And I can't believe you even brought it up; you know Reggie better than that.'

"My friend said, 'I'm sorry Lady, all I'm trying to do is help my best friend out. If you heard something like that about my man you'd do the same thing, so don't get mad at me. If Reggie told you there's nothing to the rumor, then I'm through with it. Forgive me for even saying anything.'

"We finished our lunch in silence, except for a little small talk about when I'd be leaving for good and what school I'd decided to enroll in. When she dropped me off at my apartment, we hugged and said we'd talk later, but deep down inside I was pissed off at her for planting that seed of doubt in my mind. Nevertheless, I decided to just let it go. Surely Reggie wouldn't lie about something so serious. If Tammi really was pregnant, and if the baby was Reggie's, then that would mean I've been a blind fool, and that was not possible. Nobody could be so in love that they'd be that blind.

"Reggie and I moved to New York and settled in. He was working for *Essence* magazine as a junior editor and loving it. I was working part-time as a receptionist for a hotel and would start going back to school in about two weeks. Everything was moving forward nicely until I went to his office to surprise him for lunch. The receptionist said she'd page Reggie to come up front, but I told her that I'd rather surprise him, so she showed me a little map of the office and told me where his cubicle was. As I came around the corner, approaching him from the back, I saw an eight by ten photo of a cute little baby boy on his desk. At first I thought he must be sitting at someone else's desk, but no, his name was there on top of the cubicle plain as day, and when he turned around and saw me, his eyes said it all.

"He was on the phone discussing the layout for the magazine, and he began stammering and stuttering so badly that he didn't even make sense. As I stood there with my mouth open, looking back and forth from him to the picture, I literally felt my knees get weak. I didn't know whether to run, slap him, or scream, so I just stood there. When he finally managed to get off the phone, he had that *Oh no, I think I just shit and stepped in it* look on his face. I asked, 'Whose picture is that on your desk Reggie?'

"He tells me, 'Listen, don't come up here on my job making no scene. I was going to discuss this whole situation with you when the time was right, but I knew you wouldn't understand so that's why I haven't said anything yet.' He looks down at his watch and said, 'It's eleven o'clock anyway so let me tell the receptionist I'm leaving for lunch and we can go somewhere and talk. This is not the time or the place but I guess I have no choice since you've snuck up on me at work.'

"I could not believe what I was hearing, and he didn't need to say anything else. That baby looked just like his ass with those big eyes, and his ears sticking out from that little round head. There was nothing to say. And what the fuck did he mean by saying I snuck up on him? I guess I'm wrong for trying to surprise my husband with an unannounced lunch date, right?

"He grabbed his jacket and almost pushed me out of the office, but I swear my legs felt like concrete pillars, and that's the only thing that kept me from putting my size seven and a half foot up his narrow ass. When we got outside and made it about three blocks away from his building, I just stopped, dead smack in the middle of the sidewalk, with New Yorkers bustling by me like I wasn't even there. He looked at me like I was the one who'd done something wrong, and I looked at him like I still couldn't believe this was happening, and even though I tried as hard as I could to hold them back, the tears came. I was so humiliated that words cannot even begin to explain it, but at that point I felt I had nothing to lose anyway so I screamed as loud as I could, 'How could you do this to me you selfish bastard? You had me leave my family and friends and move all the way out here knowing that your *ex*-girlfriend was pregnant with your baby, and when I asked you about it you acted like you didn't even know what I was talking about. I left everything that I know, everything that was safe, and this is what I get? This is what you do to somebody you love Reggie? Well if you can lie to me about something that serious, and still lay up between my legs at night like it doesn't matter, then you're a pitiful man. As a matter of fact, you ain't even a man; I don't know what you are. But don't worry about it, just give me a few hours and you won't have to worry about lying anymore because I'm out of here.'

"He said something about, 'Please don't leave me—I love you— We can work this out—I'm sorry,' but I'd already turned around and was strutting down Broadway in my three-inch heels, crossing the street even though the DO NOT WALK sign was all lit up like a true New Yorker, and was on my way back to Oklahoma. I pulled out my cell phone so I could call home, then it hit me that I couldn't call my mom because she'd get too upset, and I didn't want to go through all the details with my sisters, so what was I going to do? Then as if that wasn't enough, I remembered that because I wasn't working at first, I'd used all of my savings to help Reggie out with bills when we first moved, so I didn't even have the money to buy an airline ticket to get back home. I was stuck. So I just stood there for a moment, crying my eyes out, too delirious to think straight, when Randi's sweet face popped into my head.

"I called her at work, but was told she was out with the flu. So, reluctantly, I called her at home. As soon as I heard her voice, I lost it. I tried to calm down enough to tell her that I just needed to get home but all I could get out was, Reggie and his ex-girlfriend have a baby together and I can't stay here another minute.

"My friend Randi, as sick as she was that day, calmed me down and told me that I didn't have to explain anything. Thank God I'd saved some of the boxes we used to move because she had a wonderful plan, but I'd have to work fast.

"She told me to calm down and listen. She said, 'Go to the apartment and pack the largest suitcase you have with whatever you'll need for the next few days. Then put some of those boxes together and pack whatever else you can in those. Call UPS and tell them you have some boxes that need to be picked up within the next two hours, use my address for the delivery, and tell them you want to send them C.O.D. and I'll pay for them when they get here if you need me to. In the meantime, I'm going to make you a tentative reservation on American Airlines for a flight that leaves tonight, but I won't pay for it until you call me back and let me know if you can make it there in time. There are flights leaving LaGuardia every other hour going to Dallas/Fort Worth International, and from there you can get a commuter flight to Oklahoma City. You'll be home before morning girlfriend, I got your back.'

"I rushed home and threw everything I could into that suitcase and those boxes, crying and cussing the entire time. But when it was all said and done, and I was sitting in my seat waiting for take-off, I knew I'd be okay, eventually.

"Randi paid for my airline ticket, paid for my clothes when they arrived, let me stay at her place for three months while I got back on my feet, and never once said, 'I tried to tell you but you wouldn't listen.' She didn't even bring the ex-girlfriend's baby situation up until I did, and even then she didn't criticize me for being naive or stupid, she just listened and said, 'Lady, a woman in love is sometimes blind, and you are not the first. You'll get over this and you'll be a better woman because of it, and I'll always be here for you if you need me, even if you were to get into the same situation again. You're my girl. But if my man does something like that to me, you'd better have plenty of money to come bail me out, because I promise you, I'll do a lot more than just cry.'

"When I did get married a few years later, Randi was my maid of honor, and even though I have sisters, she is the godmother to my first child. True friends like her are hard to come by; they are few and far between. So I never let her birthday or anniversary or any occasion that she likes to celebrate go by without letting her know how much I appreciate her. She is and always will be my very best friend."

PORSCHE, THIRTY-SOMETHING

"When I was a sophomore in college and it was getting close to Christmas break, I found myself wondering what I would do. My aunt and uncle had already told me they'd be spending the holidays with their daughter who was never really crazy about me, so I didn't want to go there, and my 'real' family was still as loony as all get out, so I didn't want to go there either. I finally decided I'd just stay on campus during the holidays and pick up some extra hours at my part-time job, so that the people with families could take time off. I figured that it would be better to keep busy so I wouldn't have time to think about what I was missing out on and get depressed.

"My roommate, Chazz, was a really sweet sister from Atlanta. We'd become close during our freshman year, and as we discussed our plans for the upcoming holidays she started telling me about all the fun, traditional stuff her family always did. Stuff like eating at five different houses on Christmas Eve and ending up at her grandmother's large, old, house where they'd munch on all of these fabulous desserts while drinking homemade eggnog which her uncles would spike, and laughing and singing Christmas songs all night, and then waking up on Christmas morning and holding hands in front of the fireplace to have prayer before opening any gifts.

"After listening to her talk and watching the expressions on her face, I could tell that she and her family were really close, and even though I tried not to let it show, I became really sad at the thought that I'd never had such a wonderful Christmas with my folks.

"When she asked me what me and my family were going to do,

I explained my aunt and uncle's plans, then burst into tears. I didn't want her to feel sorry for me, but being the friend she was, she hugged me and cried with me anyway, telling me how sorry she was that I'd be alone for Christmas. She asked if I wanted her to stay with me, but after hearing about everything her family had planned, I couldn't ask her to do that.

"Two weeks later as she was packing for her trip home, she asked me again if I wanted her to stay with me, but I declined. Lord knows it would have been nice to have some company and maybe do something special on Christmas day, but I couldn't be that selfish. The next day I took her to the airport and told her to call me as soon as she got to Atlanta, so I wouldn't be worried. She promised that she would, and then told me she hadn't had time to go shopping so she'd be sending my gift in the mail. Of course, I got all sad again and we both started crying, but by the time she was ready to board the plane, we'd started people watching, laughing and making fun of just about everybody there, so we were smiling before she left and that made things better for both of us.

"For the first week of the holiday break, I worked twelve hours every day because the store was so busy, and by the time I got to the dorm at night all I could do was shower and go to bed. But on Saturday morning, I got the surprise of my life. The front desk clerk called my room and said I had a package that had just been delivered by UPS, so I hurried to put on my robe and ran downstairs, thinking it was the gifts my aunt and uncle said they'd mailed. When I got down there and saw this little envelope, all I could say way, 'Shit. I ran all the way down here for a letter? Who the hell could this be from, got ya'll waking me up all early in the morning.'

"'Stop bitching and open it so I can see what it is,' ordered Yolanda, the country little desk clerk who never seemed to have a day off. Ya'll know how Sha-na-nay on *Martin* looks? I swear, Yolanda looked just like that, red lipstick, long fingernails, mustache, and all. 'It ain't got no return address, so whatever it is, I guess yo ass won't be sending it back,' she said and laughed out loud.

"As I was opening the envelope, the phone rang and old nosey butt had to turn away to answer it, so I started for the elevator, just in case this was something I didn't want her to see, but she stopped me, yelling out, 'Wait a minute, Miss Thang. This phone call is for you. She wants to know if you got an envelope this morning, but she won't give me her name.'

" 'What the hell is going on,' I said, ripping the envelope all the way open and finding a round-trip ticket to Atlanta inside with a short note. 'Oh my goodness, no she didn't,' was all I could say. 'Tell me that's not Chazz Davis on the other end of that phone Yolanda. Is that her? Is that Chazz?'

" 'Is this Chazz?' Yolanda said, smacking on her Juicy Fruit gum. ''Cause this don't sound like Chazz, unless you trying to disguise your voice or something. What you say? Forget you heffa, I knew it was you anyway. Here Porsche, it's Chaaaaaaz trying to sound like somebody else with her crazy self.'

" 'Chazz, girl what in the world are you doing sending me a ticket? I know you can't afford this and you should be spending your hard-earned money on gifts for your family. I can't come to Atlanta, I've already picked up hours for people at work, what am I—'

"Chazz cut me off. 'Porsche, stop talking and look at the ticket, girl. Christmas is two weeks away, and your flight doesn't leave until December 24 at 5:30 in the morning. Surely you haven't committed to picking up hours all the way through Christmas and New Year's too? Work all you want to for the next two weeks and tell those people you're going to Hotlanta for Christmas! That ticket is my gift to you and my family is looking forward to having you spend the holidays with us, so what now?'

"I couldn't help it, I was already crying because I was so overwhelmed, 'Chazz, you are such a wonderful person. I can't believe you would go out of your way and spend your money to have me with you and your family, just so that I won't be alone on Christmas. I don't even know what to say.'

" 'Don't say shit except that you'll be on that plane on Christmas

Eve, 'cause that ticket is non-refundable, non-changeable, and will self-destruct if you don't use it. You coming or what?'

" 'I'll be there, Chazz, with bells on. And tell your family I said thank you so much for allowing you to do this, I can't wait to meet them.'

" 'Okay, okay, stop snotting the phone up before Yolanda gets pissed. I know she's right there looking all up in your face with her disinfectant wipes ready. You know she thinks she runs that office, don't you? I'll bet she's got her face all made up and has on that ugly red lipstick she buys from the dollar store, like somebody's coming up on campus to see her or something, don't she?'

"I was laughing and crying at the same time, because Yolanda was doing exactly what Chazz said she was doing, except that while she was holding a disinfectant wipe between the thumb and index finger of one hand, she was tapping those long nails of her other hand on the desk, staring at me with her mouth all pushed out like she was waiting for a kiss.

" 'Ooh girl, you are so crazy. I still can't believe this but okay, I'll be there. I gotta run so I can get ready for work. I'll call you to see what the weather is like in Hotlanta before I start packing. I can't wait to get there.'

"I left for Atlanta at 5:30 A.M. on Christmas Eve, and after meeting Chazz's immediate family and eating a large, Southern breakfast which included biscuits made from scratch with butter and homemade molasses, yellow grits, and fried fish, I looked at pictures of Chazz growing up, and walked around her old neighborhood where she introduced me to some of her high school friends. Later that evening as we were in her room getting dressed for the festivities, I hugged her again and told her that I would never forget the wonderful gift she had given me.

" 'Porsche,' she said, 'don't you know that's what friends are for? It makes me feel good just to see you happy and enjoying my family for the holidays. What kind of friend would I be if I'd left you at school all alone with nothing to do but work? When we started this friendship we said we'd always be there for each other, and that's what I'm doing, being there for you when you need me. You don't have to thank me, just enjoy yourself and that will be enough for me.'

"I did enjoy myself, more than I imagined I would. I enjoyed her family, their food, their Southern hospitality, the spiked eggnog, singing Christmas carols, everything. The next morning when we gathered around the fireplace, we held hands to have prayer before opening gifts, as was their tradition every Christmas. I asked if I could say a short prayer of my own after her grandfather was finished. Well, Chazz and her cousins had warned me that Big Daddy, as they called him, didn't really say too much most of the time because he was saving it up for his prayer on Christmas morning, and would drag it out until Big Mama cleared her throat, indicating that he'd prayed too long.

"They weren't lying. Ten minutes into the prayer, me and Chazz's hands started sweating, and then she started to giggle, and so did I, and so did her cousins, before her mother nudged her. Big Mama cleared her throat after what seemed like an eternity, and it was my turn. I quickly thanked God for the opportunity to meet such a special person with such a unique family, who had allowed me to come into their homes and make me feel as if I was one of their own. I prayed that this family would be greatly blessed for opening their hearts to me, and I also prayed for those who were spending Christmas alone. And finally, I prayed that next year Big Daddy would drink a little more eggnog on Christmas Eve so he wouldn't have the energy to pray so long, and with that everybody burst into laughter and said a big 'AMEN.' "

FRANCIS, SIXTY-SOMETHING

"When I graduated from high school in the late sixties, I found a job as a receptionist in a law office. It was boring because basically, I just answered the phone and made sure that the coffee pot stayed full, but still it was better than the job my best friend had found working at a dry cleaners. Pearl and I had been friends since elementary school, but just before our senior year, her father got a job with some factory in the South and they had to move. We stayed in touch by writing to one another on a weekly basis.

"The two of us had always talked about getting jobs that would allow us to travel, but I knew for sure that no travel was in my future with this job, and damn sure none for her working at the dry cleaners.

"That fall after we'd graduated, she called me up with the most fantastic news. I'll never forget how excited she was when I picked up the phone. She didn't even say hello first, she said, 'Guess what girl?' And I knew it had to be big news because not only was she calling me long distance, she was calling me before the rates dropped for the evening. Usually, if she had anything to tell me she'd just drop me a line. I asked her what was going on and she yelled into my ear, 'I got a job working for the airlines!' I was like, 'What, you going to be a stewardess?' She says, 'Now girl you and I both know that the airlines ain't gonna' hire no sister with hips and a big ass like mine, you know how teeny tiny those stewardesses are. I got a job working in reservations. I start next week. And you do remember how we always said we wanted to travel? Well you need to go and apply and get on so we can travel together. If you work for the airlines, you can fly to any city the airline travels to for free. Please, please, please . . . you know how we always talked about traveling together. You need to get busy on this tomorrow.'

"Of course her phone call got me to thinking and by the time we'd said our goodbyes, I was just as excited at the prospect of working for the airlines as she was. I hadn't even applied yet but I knew for a fact that somehow I would get the opportunity to travel anywhere I wanted to, especially if it was free.

"The very next week I gave my boss a two-week notice before quitting my job. When my co-workers asked me if I had something else lined up I said, 'Yes, I work for the airlines.' I didn't have the job yet, hadn't even applied, but that was how sure I was about it.

"My mom was very supportive, she'd always been one to say you got to go after what you wanted in this life and fortunately I still lived at home, had a small savings and didn't have any bills to speak of.

"I took out the phone book, looked under the listing for airlines and set about applying to each and every airline listed in the phone-book from the letter A to Z. After three or four weeks had gone by and I hadn't received any response on my applications I started to become dejected. My girlfriend would keep in touch and tell me to just stay positive, she reminded me that it hadn't happened for her overnight either and said not to forget that a lot of companies were looking to hire black people due to the Affirmative Action program.

"By the time six weeks had gone by I was ready to go and look for another job because I had to do something, I knew I couldn't just lay around day after day living off my mom. Then finally, the phone call came that I'd been waiting for. I was lying in my bed, in the middle of the afternoon, cramping like crazy on the first day of my period. It was cold, dreary, and raining outside, and I was just lying there feeling sorry for myself, listening to some sad music that was playing as a background to my own personal drama. I heard the phone ring on the table in the hallway but didn't have the energy to go out and pick it up. I knew it wouldn't be for me anyway because my boyfriend and I had broken up several weeks ago, and my other friends were either at work or going to school that time of day.

"My mom picked up the phone and answered it. Her voice was muffled because I had my door closed and the music turned up kind of loud. She knocked on my door a couple of times before opening it and stood there holding the receiver in one hand and the phone in the other with the long phone cord trailing behind her from the hallway. She said, 'It's for you, it's a woman from the airline,' and she was smiling from ear to ear. I grabbed the phone, cramps all but forgotten and my heart beating a mile a minute. The lady on the other end of the phone told me that my application had been received and asked if I could I come in to take some tests. The company had several positions in reservations that needed to be filled immediately. She told me that the test would be given the following week and after telling me the location and time she hung up.

"The next week I showed up to take my test an hour earlier than scheduled; there was no way I was going to miss this opportunity. It was pouring down rain and I had to take two different subways to get downtown to the test location, but as far as I was concerned the sun could've been shining because my spirits were that high and I was determined that I was going to get this job.

"The test was a written one and pretty difficult, but the woman giving the test was kind enough to explain things clearly and precisely, and she answered my questions whenever I became confused. Not once did she get impatient with me or make me feel like any of the questions I asked her were stupid.

"In my heart and to this day I know, if it hadn't been for that woman helping me out when I was taking that test I never would've passed. Afterward she took my paper and sat there and graded it right in front of me and she was as happy as I was to see that I had received a passing score. She asked me when I could start and I said, 'I can start today.' She laughed and said that wouldn't be necessary but to come back in a couple of days and I could begin my orientation and training.

"That was over thirty years ago and now I'm planning to retire from American Airlines. My best friend and I were able to travel to all the places we'd dreamed of. Can you imagine being nineteen years old, single, and having the opportunity to travel to a place like Chicago? Oh honey, in the late sixties Chicago was the place to be. It was a serious party town and it was fun to be in that city as a young, single woman. Me and my best friend would go out to dine in nice restaurants, and then we would go to a club and dance until the wee hours of the morning with all of the good-looking and even some not so good-looking men, until the club closed. Afterward we might go to breakfast or go to another club to listen to a live band. We had the time of our life and to this very day, I still thank my friend Pearl for encouraging me to follow my dream. Because of her, I've had the opportunity to see the world and it's been an experience I will never forget."

SEX

SEX (seks) noun
The sexual urge or instinct as it manifests itself
in behavior. Sexual intercourse.

Sex is an emotion in motion.—MAE WEST

Men would always rather be made love to than
talked at.—DOROTHY M. RICHARDSON

Aren't women prudes if they don't and prostitutes
if they do?—KATE MILLETT

Whether a pretty woman grants or withholds her favors, she always likes to be asked for them. —*IBID*

You mustn't force sex to do the work of love or love to do the work of sex.—MARY MCCARTHY

I don't know what I am, darling, I've tried several varieties of sex. The conventional position makes me claustrophobic, and the others give me either a stiff neck or lockjaw.—TALLULAH BANKHEAD

FIRST TIME

MISS DELORES, FIFTY-SOMETHING

Looks are deceiving. At least that was my first thought when this lady I've known most of my life started talking to me about her sexual experiences. I didn't really think interviewing Miss Delores would be any fun because she was my best friend's mother, and seeing how she'd been so strict on her when we were teenagers, I just knew she didn't have sex, let alone talk about it. When I walked in, she greeted me with her usual peck on the cheek, and then stood back and looked at me. "My Lord, it's been years since I saw you, girl" she said. "And you're cute as you want to be."

"Thank you, Miss Delores, but you're the one who looks good. You haven't aged a bit. You still look just like you did when we were in high school."

"Child, stop lying. You know I've got that grandbaby now. If I'm not aging it must be because he makes me move around and use muscles I didn't even know I had. That boy is a mess, just like his mama. By the way she's working on another one, did you know that? I told her she'd better slow down but I guess she does need to go on and get it out of the way before she gets too old. These babies nowadays can run circles around the parents. What's this book going to be about anyway?" she asked.

After I explained all the details to Miss Delores, she was too happy to talk. She was still a pretty woman, even after all these years. Her hair hung past her shoulders, but she always had it pinned up, and she still wore those horn-rimmed glasses. I'd often wondered if she ever really "let her hair down" and after we got into the interview, I was shocked when she began to talk so freely.

"When I first had sex I was nineteen," she began. "I waited what seemed to be a hundred years and was dumb as anything because parents didn't explain things back then. They'd say, 'Don't get pregnant,' which was fine, but they didn't tell us how to prevent it. My mother didn't discuss sex with me because she was too embarrassed. I can still remember when her younger sister got pregnant out of wedlock. Everybody was whispering, 'She was messing with those boys.' I was like, 'Messing with boys? What does that mean?' I'd kissed boys and nothing had happened to me, so something must've been wrong with her sister.

"Just to give you an example of how dumb I really was: when I was a girl you didn't have to participate in gym if you were on your period. You got to sit out on the bench. I hadn't started having periods yet, but every week when one of my girlfriends would be sitting on the bench, I'd sit there with her. I'd sit on the bench with a different friend every week. They finally said, 'Girl, you need to go and get checked out because you're bleeding every week.' I knew why they were sitting on the bench, and I wanted to sit there with them because they were my friends. But I didn't realize you only had a period once a month because mine hadn't started yet. I thought I was really fooling that gym teacher.

"When it did start, I was eighteen and so ignorant, I ran all the way home thinking, 'My mom is going to kill me. She's just going to kill me because she's going to say I was messing with those boys.' I was scared to death because I didn't know what was going on.

"In school they used to separate the girls from the boys while they talked about the menstrual cycle, and I used to slip out of class because I thought only fast girls menstruated. The boys would be out on the playground, and I'd go out there with them because I didn't feel I needed to learn about menstruating since I hadn't started yet. Even when I was married and got pregnant, I didn't really know I was pregnant because my periods never came regularly, and my stupid doctor said I probably couldn't conceive because I was so irregular. You know doctors weren't as knowledgeable back in the fifties and sixties as they are now. My period would come for two months, and then I might not see anything for four months. Then it might come for four months and on the fifth month, nothing. Well, one time I hadn't seen my period for June, July, August, or September, and when I went to the doctor with this bad cold in October he said I was pregnant.

"He asked, 'When is the last time you had a period?'

" 'I don't know. I think the month before last.' I couldn't even remember because it hadn't been important. 'I don't mark the calendar because it never comes regularly.'

" 'Well'—he paused, looking at me real crazy—'You're pregnant.'

" 'Oh, no. My doctor back at home said I couldn't conceive. I don't want to hear that garbage.'

" 'Well, you might not want to hear it, but you are pregnant.'

" 'Well, I'll tell you what. My husband and I just ordered a new Cadillac, so I can't be pregnant because that's what I'm going to spend my money on.'

" 'You know what? You can cancel your order and that Cadillac can go back but there's only one way out for this baby.'

"We went back and forth, and I kept telling him he was wrong because he was young, and I didn't think he knew what he was talking about. I finally told him, 'Listen. You're young, and I think you're trying to experiment on me because I know I can't conceive.'

"He finally stood up, got right in my face, and said, 'Lady, you are pregnant. Now you might as well accept it and make an appointment to see your gynecologist because I'm not going to argue with you anymore.'

"I sat there for a moment, dazed, then finally gathered myself and walked out. I made an appointment to see the gynecologist that next week, and when he confirmed that I was indeed pregnant, I was ecstatic. I wasn't trying to get pregnant, but then I wasn't trying not to either.

"Nowadays, there's no excuse. When girls get pregnant, it's usually because they want to. I have a grandniece that just had her second baby at seventeen. I told her she needed to do something because there's no reason for that. Sex is wonderful, but you don't have to be stupid just because it's good."

KIANA, FORTY-SOMETHING

"My first sexual encounter was awful. I was seventeen and it was with this guy I'd met while playing tennis. We'd gone to a party together and left to go to the store to get some ice and beer. But first, he needed to go by his friend's house to pick him up and of course this friend wasn't home. Now, the sex wasn't forced because I was curious to find out what it was like, but I didn't think it would go as far as it did. He came before he completely entered me, and I was grossed out. I'd heard about sex, but I guess I hadn't heard everything because I thought his semen just felt nasty. I felt like I'd been drenched in slime and was mad at myself because I didn't even like him that much. I was really only with him because I thought he was cute. I really didn't intend to have sex with him.

"Since that time, I've been with about eleven men. I'm not ashamed of that because at one time in my life I was kind of wild. I used to think like a man. I was like, 'Hey, I'm out to have a good time. I ain't trying to date or marry you.' I'll have to admit, I used to be a dog. But once I had my fill of men and found that most of them were just about the same, I calmed down and changed my ways."

SADIE, FIFTY-SOMETHING

"The first time I had sex it was terrible, terrible, terrible," said Sadie. "Back in my day, you couldn't even go out with a young man unless his parents knew your parents and both sides agreed it was okay. This young man I was dating took me to the movies and when he brought me home, we decided we'd kiss in the car where no one could see us. That was nothing new. We'd always done serious petting and stuff, but this one time it got too hot and heavy, and he wouldn't stop. I guess you'd call it date rape nowadays but back then, you'd get accused of being a 'little fast wench' if you told anybody what happened, so I knew I couldn't tell anyone.

"After that I didn't like him anymore because I felt so hurt and violated. He literally tore my panties off and screwed me so hard I could hardly walk into the house. That's just not the way a girl should lose her virginity.

"If my daddy would've caught him with me in that car or found out about it later he would've killed him, so I never told anybody. I talked to him after that, but we never mentioned what had happened. As a matter of fact, this is the first time I've ever mentioned it to anybody."

JEWELL, SIXTY-SOMETHING

"I started masturbating when I was in the seventh grade. That's when I found out I had a vagina. By the time I was sixteen, I was ready to know what it was all about. I had been feeling around down there and I knew what made me feel good, so I started doing it on a regular basis. When I had sex for the first time, I was disappointed because he didn't make me feel the way I felt when I did it by myself. I was waiting for the whistles and streamers and firecrackers to go off, but when they didn't, I asked, 'Is that it?' "

MARCELLA, FORTY-SOMETHING

"My first sexual encounter was with my son's father," Marcella said, looking disappointed. "I was nineteen, going on twenty, and I was so scared because Mommy always told us that sex was bad; therefore, I didn't enjoy it. I didn't start enjoying it until I was about twenty-three or twenty-four years old. Really, because it had always been put in my head as something bad by my mommy as well as other women on the island where I lived. After we had sex I felt so guilty, I couldn't face nobody. I was very depressed because I'd been taught that good girls don't do that, and you go to hell if you do.

"I've had sex with a total of six men now and the last time was nine months ago, but that doesn't bother me. I'm not gonna ruin my life behind sex. I've had a lot of opportunities, but I'm not gonna have sex just to be doing something. I wouldn't do that. I don't want to be with somebody who already got somebody. I want to be with somebody who don't have nobody but me. Even if he has somebody but they're not together, I'd rather be alone, because I don't believe in sharing a man.

"I work, I go to aerobics, and when I come home I'm sewing, baking, or doing something else, so it don't bother me to be alone. On Saturdays, my girlfriend and me do a lot together. We either go out or we go to all the carnivals. Next weekend we're going to Houston for a carnival. We've been back to Trinidad together twice, and last month we went to Carnival in Miami.

"So, I really don't have time to be sitting around worrying about sex. Life has too much other stuff to offer for me to worry about that."

BIANCA, THIRTY-SOMETHING

"I just had my first orgasm with a man last year, and I'm in my early thirties. I thought something might be wrong with me, so I asked my mother. I can talk to her about everything. She told me, 'Bianca, baby, some women never reach an orgasm and some women don't reach them until they get older because it's not always easy to have an orgasm with a man. If his body isn't touching yours in exactly the right spot at exactly the right time, it just doesn't happen and most men don't even know when and where to touch you. That's why you have to tell them most of the time.'

"I was so disappointed to hear that because I think that's why some women don't want to have sex. The men are getting all the thrills. They do all this talking like they know so much about our bodies, but without instructions, most of them couldn't make a woman have an orgasm if you paid them.

"I even talked to my doctor about it and told her it was hard for me to have an orgasm during intercourse. She said that a lot of times, because women are doing so much these days, when they have sex their body is there but their mind isn't, so it's hard for them to relax enough to have an orgasm. She said a woman's clitoris is very much connected to her mind. If the two don't connect, and your man is not moving in the right spot, you're not going to get yours.

"Now that would be a good subject for a book. But you know men hate to ask for directions, so they probably wouldn't even read it."

CATFISH FRY

6 (¾–1 pound) farm-raised catfish fillets

1 cup buttermilk

1½ to 2 tablespoons salt

1 tablespoon pepper

1½ cups self-rising cornmeal

½ cup self-rising flour

1½ to 2 quarts peanut oil

Make shallow diagonal cuts 2 inches apart in thickest portion of sides of fish. Place in large shallow dish.

Combine buttermilk, salt, and pepper; pour over fish. Cover and marinate in refrigerator at least 8 hours, turning fish fillets occasionally.

Remove fish from marinade, discarding marinade.

Combine cornmeal and flour. Dredge fish in cornmeal mixture, coating fillets completely.

Pour peanut oil to depth of 1½ inches into a large deep skillet; heat oil. Fry fish, two at a time, about 6 minutes or until golden. Drain well on paper towels. Repeat procedure with remaining fish. Serve immediately. *Yield: 6 servings.*

MOST EROTIC

LADY, FORTY-SOMETHING

"My most erotic experience was with the man I dated just before I met my husband. I'd gone out of town on business for a week and we'd had a little disagreement before I left. Both of us were being stubborn, but he finally called me about three days before I was scheduled to come home, and after we talked and worked out our differences, he said he'd pick me up when I got back.

"The day I was to return home, the weather was bad so I had to take a later flight and that irritated me to no end. You know how it is when you're away from home and all you can think about is getting back to your own bed. When I called to tell him what had happened, he told me to calm down, be patient, get something to read, and he'd make things nice for me when I got home. I didn't put much thought into his comment about making things nice, I figured he was just going to pick me up and take me to a nice hotel so we could get busy without having to worry about my daughter interrupting.

"I got in at around 8:00 P.M., tired as hell, and all I wanted to do was go straight home but he insisted that we go to dinner so that he could at least feed me, and I was hungry so I agreed. We went to one of our favorite spots, The Cheesecake Factory, and I had the herb crusted filet of salmon which was delicious, and of course I had to order some dessert to go so I ordered the chocolate pecan turtle cheesecake.

"By the time we finished eating and having a few drinks, I was ready to go to bed but he said he had one more thing to show me. Since he'd been so sweet, I didn't want to ruin everything by complaining about how tired I was, but when he pulled up to the Westin hotel, I was like, 'What the hell?' He looked at me and smiled and said, 'Come on, baby, just work with me.'

"He already had the key so we went straight up to the room, and when he opened the door all I could see were rose petals and candles everywhere. It was beautiful and I was grinning from ear to ear. I walked in, put my purse down and kicked off my shoes, and before I could take another step or say a word he pulled me to him and kissed me. It was one of those deep, passionate kisses that make your knees weak and your panties wet, and I suddenly forgot all about being tired.

"He led me to the bed where the covers had already been turned down. There were rose petals all over the sheets and pillows, and the air was filled with the scent of roses and vanilla-scented candles. It was so lovely and touching that I wanted to cry but he pulled me down on the bed and started kissing me again while removing my clothing, and I just closed my eyes and gave in to him. I felt like I was in a dream, but then I realized he was getting up and my panties were still on. When I opened my eyes, he was standing there smiling at me and looking at me like he'd never seen me undressed before.

"Just when I thought he was going to take my panties off, he got up and told me to move up on the bed, and he placed all the pillows behind my back except one, which he placed under my butt. Then he went back to the foot of the bed and began to kiss my feet, my ankles, my calves, and as he laid himself down onto the bed, he gently pushed my legs apart, and licked and sucked the insides of my thighs, all the way up to my, crotch.

"My panties were so wet that I could feel the moisture on the pillow beneath me, so I attempted to pull them off but he said, 'Be still, baby, I don't want them off yet. You know how much I like it when your panties get wet, but just give me a few more minutes.' Before I could respond, he'd begun licking again, this time around the outline of my panties. Then he said, 'Damn, your pussy smells so good. Are you ready?'

"But once again, he didn't give me time to respond before he pushed my right leg up so that my foot was off the bed, grabbed the elastic on my panties and pulled them to the side, and slid his tongue and fingers inside me and started sucking and licking like a starved animal. I was moaning so loud that I thought for sure they'd put us out of the hotel, but I couldn't help it, and the more I moaned, the better he made it feel. I was holding on to the back of his head so tight that I thought he'd suffocate, but it didn't stop him at all.

"After he'd got me off, he flipped me over and put another pillow under my hips, and then entered me from the back. I got wet all over again, but he still didn't come until we'd made love for about two hours, fast and then slow, in every position he and I could think of. When we finished, we just lay there exhausted. Then he sat up and said, 'Oh, I have another little surprise for you.'

"He got up out of the bed and headed for the small refrigerator. When he pulled out a pint of Häagen-Dazs Vanilla Bean ice cream, I burst out laughing. He laughed too and said, 'I meant to feed you your dessert before I ate you for mine, but once I started kissing you and tasting you on my fingers I totally forgot.' Then this beautiful man, naked and as fine as he could be with his six-foot three-inch, muscular, bowlegged, chocolate black self, proceeded to feed

me that ice cream and used his tongue as my napkin to catch anything I missed.

"Now, for anyone who has never slept on one of those 'Heavenly
Beds' at the Westin, let me tell you that it is indeed heavenly and
you need to go experience it as soon as you possibly can. Lying in
that bed felt like what I imagine clouds would feel like if you could
sleep on them. As a matter of fact, I ordered a king-sized heavenly
mattress set for my bedroom that next day, and every time I climb
into it I remember that night. Ooooh, baby, what a way to be
treated. It was just wonderful."

PORSCHE, THIRTY-SOMETHING

"I've told my boyfriend so many things about me that I know he
wouldn't want to be with me on a permanent basis," said Porsche,
sipping on her wine. "I even told him about the time I pledged with
my sorority. Don't look at me like that. I know I'm not supposed to
reveal my sorority secrets but that was so long ago.

"One of the things we had to do to prove our sisterhood was
make love with another woman." I guess the shock was all over my
face because Porsche bucked her eyes at me mockingly, even though
she didn't appear to be embarrassed at all. "Yes, I've been with
women just like I've been with men and I'm not saying I enjoyed
the experience, but I've done it. They told us we were supposed to
love our line sisters the way we loved ourselves, but in hindsight I
think they were just being freaky because they knew they could get
away with it. I'm not a lesbian or anything; it was just part of hell
week. The whole line participated. It was one big female orgy.

"We all got high first, so there was no emotion involved, just
pure sex. I didn't touch anybody's coochie, but I saw others who
did. I remember kissing and massaging my roommate's breasts and
we both got a real rush from that, but that's as far as it went for me.
All I can say from that experience is that you shouldn't knock anything before you try it. When I did tell my boyfriend about it he

wasn't even shocked. All he said was, 'Damn, I wish I could've seen that. Maybe I should call your old roommate up and find out a few more ways to please you.'

"See, that's the reason I don't have time for no man under thirty. Think about it. Even if it's just a plain old physical relationship, most men between the age of twenty-one and thirty haven't realized that they're in it to please you. They're still in it to please themselves. You get a man who's about thirty-five or older, he's already learned that his dick don't get as hard as he'd like it to get, and when it does it don't stay that way all night, so he's in it to please you."

EBONI, FORTY-SOMETHING

"Me and a guy I was seeing were on our way home from a dance one night when all of a sudden it started to storm. Now, I don't know what it is, but for some reason thunder, lightning, and hard rain make me feel sexy." Eboni paused for emphasis and crossed her legs. "So, we drove to a secluded area, parked, and started to make love, but I felt like I just wasn't getting all of him like I wanted to. I said, 'Forget this. Let's get out of the car.'

"Honey, I came out of my dress, kicked off my heels, and we got out there in the rain, buck naked on the side of the road. My feet were muddy and my hair was soaking wet, but I had a fresh perm so I wasn't worried. I got on my knees and took care of business, then he put me on the hood of the car and we screwed for a while in all that rain. It passed through my mind that the police or anybody could catch us out there, but it was so good I didn't give a damn. That was the best come I ever had.

"I didn't get pneumonia, but I did catch a cold that had me coughing off and on for a week. I swear, every time I coughed it made me think about how good that brother was banging me on top of his hood and I got horny all over again."

GIOVANNI, FORTY-SOMETHING

"Growing up in a family that had lots of money, I always had to be the perfect little lady. I'm originally from Atlanta, and my grandfather owned the first and only chain of black bookstores in town, which he passed down to my father, so my family was well known. The only bad thing about that was I couldn't do anything without my parents finding out, sometimes before I even got home.

"If I wasn't at church I was in charm school or tap dance lessons—always something to do to keep me from doing what I wanted to do. But I also had the benefit of attending an all-black private school, and I received a two-seater Mercedes as a birthday gift when I turned seventeen. Now that I think back on it, I really couldn't complain. But you know how it is when you're young. You feel like you're being bored to death while the other girls you know are having fun because you're looking from the outside in. I didn't seem to be having much fun at all so I was constantly complaining.

"I guess my parents trusted me, but by the time my father got through lecturing me on my way out the door, I almost didn't want to go anywhere." Giovanni stood at attention. "To this day I can distinctly hear him saying, 'Giovanni, remember that when you walk out of this house you are representing your family. Don't go out there and do anything that would embarrass us or yourself because if you do people won't ever let you live it down.'

"I always felt like I was living in an aquarium or something, so I really didn't get to have much fun with boys when I was growing up. I vowed that when I left home I was going to do whatever I pleased to make up for all the fun I'd missed as a teenager.

"My first year in college, I decided not to go home for spring break. My girlfriend and me went to Jamaica instead. Hell, I had the money in my expense account and my parents thought I was going to Cancún with the rest of the college kids, so they didn't complain. Well, we were on the beach hanging out the first night there, and I met the most beautiful man I'd ever seen. He had dark green eyes, skin the color of a caramel apple, and I got hot just listening to him talk.

"So, I decided, that I would try to have sex with him sometime during the next week. This was my chance to do something I never had the opportunity to do: be promiscuous and enjoy it without worrying about someone telling my daddy.

"It turned out he was actually from Jamaica, but had left to attend college in New York, and was home only during spring break himself. His family lived about an hour away from the hotel, but his older brother lived and worked at the hotel, so he was staying with him for the week.

"We sat there on the beach and talked until it was pretty late, and then he asked me if I'd like to come to his brother's room for a drink. At first I was thinking, 'I do not know this man, and his brother might be up there waiting for him to bring some innocent girl up there so they can run a train or something. I don't have any business going to his room.' I asked him if he was sure his brother wouldn't mind, but it turned out his brother had just left for work and wouldn't be home until early the next morning. So I gave my girlfriend the room number. She was running her mouth with some guy she'd just met. Off we went to his room with me thinking I was all grown-up and that nothing would happen that I couldn't handle.

"By the time we got there, the crotch of my swimsuit was soaked. His brother actually had a suite, which was nice because we could go into the bedroom and close the door. He fixed me a drink, and we'd barely closed the door before he was all over me. He was working his way down my body but I'd been swimming in the ocean, so I didn't feel clean. So he said he'd wash me and we got into the shower and he washed me from head to toe with nothing but soap and his hands. I wanted to pass out because his hands on my body felt so good, especially when he moved them between my legs, but then I got scared because I was thinking, 'How could a girl like me be doing something like this? What if my parents found out? Hell, what if his brother walked in on us.'

"After he got through washing me and drying me off, he laid me on the bed and kissed me again. Then he looked right into my eyes and said, 'Relax, I won't do anything you don't want me to do, and I won't go anywhere you don't invite me. But I want you to know I intend to please you completely. If I'm too rough, I want you to stop me, and if I'm not rough enough I want you to tell me. If there's anything you would like me to do, let me know. I don't expect you to do anything other than open yourself up to me unless you absolutely want to. I'll do the rest.'

"All I could do was shake my big head up and down like a dog in a window, and before I could even think of a response he'd slipped on a condom and was already inside me. And I do mean inside me because the brother was filling every spot I had, even the ones I didn't know I had. Even though I should have been nervous, I wasn't because he was kissing me and touching me like he knew me.

"He told me everything I wanted to hear, kissed me everywhere I wanted to be kissed, sucked my fingers, my lips, my earlobes, and everything else I had that could be sucked. He must have stayed hard for at least two hours before he finally came. And when he did, he held me and kissed me and said my name, 'Umm, Giovanni . . . Giovanni . . . where did your mama get you from, girl?' Whew. I gotta stop. I'm getting horny just thinking about it.

"If I would've stayed with him I'd have a house full of babies by now. That man knew how to make love. He did it like it was something he'd studied. I mean, I haven't been with David for twenty-one years for nothing. He's a great lover. He just doesn't move like that man did. Lord have mercy, I don't know of any other man who moved like that. I wonder where he is now." Giovanni sighed deeply.

"I spent every day with him the rest of that week. There was no way he was going to make me feel that good and leave me hanging for five more days. That was the best sex I have ever had, seriously. We tried to stay in touch when we went back to school, but with me in Texas and him in New York, it was just too expensive. We probably wrote and called each other for about six months after we got back to school, but we both had busy schedules and too many other things going on. Somehow we just stopped communicating. I guess it just wasn't meant to be.

"Anyway, I started dating a guy about a week after I got back to school who was really nice and he was a good lover, too. He wasn't no Jamaican, but he was pretty good. Our relationship got pretty serious so I didn't dare go back to Jamaica for spring break that following year because I know I would've got turned out for real. Besides, I didn't need to go back to Jamaica a second time like Stella. I got my groove back the first time I went."

MACY, FIFTY-SOMETHING

"The most erotic sex I ever had was in a swimming pool at a hotel. Me and my boyfriend were spending the weekend at a little private resort in Palm Springs, and he wanted to go to the pool at about one in the morning when there was no one else around. Now, I'm fifty and he's thirty-eight so you must understand that his energy level is a little higher than mine. I thought we were in for the night after dancing for two hours straight, but he said he wanted to show me something, so I put on my little leopard-print swimsuit, the one I bought specially for this trip, and pranced out to the pool on his arm. Thank God the lights in the pool weren't on.

"When we got in the water, he put his hands underneath me as I floated, and he told me to relax. Then he said, 'Open your eyes and look up at the moon and those beautiful stars, and visualize that there's no one else in the world but you and me. Don't think about anything else but how peaceful and quiet it is out here.' Just listening to him talk while looking at the moon and stars was so soothing I almost went to sleep. He could've dipped my big ass under that water and drowned me I was so relaxed.

"Then, he pulled me toward him and whispered in my ear, 'I'm going to make you feel like you're up there on that moon. Just hold on to me.' I can't even begin to tell you the things he did to me in that pool, but, baby, let me tell you, I went to the moon that night and that's no lie."

KAT, THIRTY-SOMETHING

"My lover and I have this fantastic chemistry. We never even need foreplay, just hearing his voice on the phone telling me he wants to see me is foreplay enough and when we get together lip to lip, chest to chest, pelvis to pelvis, it's on. One of our most erotic experiences so far was in a park. It was the first of several times we made love outside.

"It had been raining all morning and it was just the beginning of spring and he called me and asked me to meet him at the park because we hadn't seen each other in a few days but we'd talked on the phone and we'd talked about the last time we made love and how good it was which is most likely what led up to this phone call. I wanted to see him too, so we set up a time and specific location in the park to meet.

"I took a quick shower, dried off, and lotioned my body, then spritzed on some musky-fragranced cologne that I knew he liked. I pulled on some black thong panties and a light cotton sundress that hit me just at midthigh. I slipped on some backless sandals, picked up my keys, and headed out the door, as sexy as I wanted to be.

"He was there when I arrived and smiled when he saw me pull up. The park was pretty secluded and being that it was a weekday and about one in the afternoon there weren't too many other people around. He was sitting atop the picnic table and after we stood there and kissed for a while, I sat down on the bench below him and asked him how everything had been going, you know just small talk and while we were talking he was stroking my arms and I was rubbing a hand along his thigh, he is so hairy, even the hair on his legs is sexy to me. I'm normally not one to make the first move but he was looking good to me and I noticed that he had a slight hard-on so I stroked my hand a little farther upward.

"The shorts he wore were made out of some jersey knit material so it was easy for me to maneuver my hand into the leg of his shorts and stroke his dick, and it was so hot to the touch. The more I stroked, the harder it got so I thought, 'Hmmm, I wonder how it would be to kiss it, just a little short peck, nothing more because after all, we were outside and even though there wasn't anyone that I could see you just never knew.' But the place that we had parked was pretty remote and if someone were to drive up we would see them coming a mile away so I thought to hell with it, I want to do this so I slowly bent my head to him and just tasted the tip with my tongue and his dick jumped. I thought, 'Hmm, nice, maybe I'll go a little bit farther and just put the head in my mouth,' and I did it but that only left me wanting more and evidently he did too because his dick was throbbing by now, the veins were just popping.

"He has a great deal of self-control. He doesn't do that thing a man usually does while receiving oral sex. You know how they grab you by the back of your head and just force your mouth down onto the dick and you automatically resist? Well, he never does that. He just sits back, relaxes, and lets things flow. He lets me take things at my own pace and is never in a hurry to come and that turns me on. I slipped the head of his dick into my mouth and then a little bit more and a little bit more and before I knew it I was making love to his dick like there was no tomorrow. I don't know how long I licked and sucked on his dick but I knew that I was getting so wet that he was going to practically drown once he got inside of me. I go into a zone when I make love with him so it was up to him to act as lookout but apparently he was just as much into it as I was because he opened his eyes just in time to see a stranger walk past. He grabbed my shoulders to get my attention and I stopped. When the stranger was out of sight, we couldn't get to his car fast enough. He sat down in the passenger seat and I straddled his lap and he pulled my thong to the side and because I was soaking wet he slipped into me easily. It was the ultimate finish to an erotic escapade.

"That stranger is probably still telling the story to his friends about how he walked upon a man getting a blow job in the park in the middle of the day. He didn't see anything but he certainly had a good idea as to what was going on."

CELESTE, FIFTY-SOMETHING

"I've lied so many times about the number of men I've slept with that I can't remember what the truth is. I'm pretty sure it's fourteen. I can say that I've always known their names and I've never had a one-night stand. I don't believe there's anybody out there fine enough to have a one-night stand with."

SADIE, FIFTY-SOMETHING

"Well, let me start by saying I admire a woman who waited until she got married to have sex, and has had sex only with that one man, but I'm not one of those. I learned a lot of things from the men I was with before I got married, and I'm not ashamed of that. I even tell my husband he married me because I'm a good bitch. He's been with me as long as he has because I'm good at what I do.

"He wasn't no virgin when I met him either, so what can he say? Shit, he's glad I know what to do. It's sad when a woman has been with only one man because women like that are very inexperienced about men and the things men tend to do. Those are the women who get hurt most of the time. Every now and then they might get lucky enough to get a good man who will stick with them and teach them a few things, but more than likely they end up with a man who takes for granted that they're so naive.

"I even had a man tell me one time, 'I know my wife. I'm the only man she's ever been with and she don't know what else is out there. She likes sex, but she won't even think about doing some of the things I want to do, and I like nasty sex every now and then. I know she'll always be there for me, but I keep me a woman on the side so I can get real freaky every now and then.'

"As a matter of fact, the experiences and relationships I had before I got married have helped me to stick with my husband this long. Otherwise, I would've been gone after the first little argument, thinking there might be something better out there. When you've been with a few men, you realize they're all the same in one way or another, and you just learn that they are the way they are and you deal with it. Basically, they all do just about the same thing. Some are rough, some are not rough enough, some are inexperienced, and some know exactly what to do. You just have to find the one you love, and tell him what you want.

"I think it's good to have somebody to compare to. A lot of times when a woman has had sex with only one man, she doesn't know the good from the bad and that's how she ends up accepting someone who can't please her. The problem is, if you get into a relationship where the sex is bad, it only gets worse as you get older. If it's just mediocre now, it's definitely going to get worse."

MISS NORA, SIXTY-SOMETHING

"I've had sex with a lot of men. I can't even count how many. But there were times when I had to close my eyes and grit my teeth because it was all about money and nice things that I needed for me and my children. It sometimes made me sick inside for a man to touch my body because I didn't care for some of them that way. They liked me and did all of these nice things for me, so sometimes I had to produce, but it still made me sick inside to have sex with someone I really didn't care for. Even though they didn't know how I felt, I knew."

MACY, FIFTY-SOMETHING

"Let me count. Okay, twelve, I think. I might have missed one, but if I did I guess he didn't leave an impression. Now, I'm not boasting or anything because I don't think that's anything to be proud of. I don't think women, or men for that matter, should be so promiscuous with all the shit out there nowadays. But most of the men I slept with, I slept with before I got married, before AIDS was an issue. I can't say I'm happy that I slept with that many, but at least I can say I had some variety and I know what I like and what it takes to turn me on. Some of them were sorry lovers who didn't know the first thing to do, and some were okay lovers who were just that—okay. I honestly can't say I had more than four out of that twelve who were really good lovers, and that's a shame. I guess the problem with the ones who weren't any good is that they were young and inexperienced. The men who were in their midthirties and up were the best lovers because they were patient and they actually made love to me or at least they made it feel that way.

"I remember one fool I was messing with, every time I'd get ready to come, he would raise up looking all crazy and say, 'No, uh-uh, not yet,' and move me into a different position. That shit used to piss me off because half the time I would never get back to the point of orgasm before he did, so I wouldn't get mine at all.

"Let me tell you, when you find a man you really care for and you're compatible in bed, stop looking because most of them don't even know what the hell they're doing. One guy even spit when he was going down on me because he got pubic hair in his mouth. He didn't wipe his mouth on the sheet or try to take the hair off his lip with his fingers. He actually spit. I hear him down there making this noise, but I didn't feel anything so I raised my head to see what he was doing, and the fool was spitting, like he had lint in his mouth or something. I tell you—that took the cake."

VERONICA, THIRTY-SOMETHING

"Veronica, girl, look at your plate. I thought you said you wanted to lose some weight? You got fried fish, fried potatoes, fried squash, and turnip greens—not to mention that big old piece of chocolate cake and Big Red soda you're gonna wash it all down with."

This was the same conversation we always had whenever I went to lunch with Veronica. She's always telling me to help her because she's worried that her husband might stray if she doesn't lose the sixty-five pounds she's gained since she married him five years ago and had a baby. Veronica wears beautiful, expensive clothes, but she recently had to start shopping at The Avenue, a shop for full-figured women, and she's been depressed ever since. I always tell her that beauty is skin deep, even though her face is getting so round that her eyes look squinty when she laughs. But she listens for a while, gets her self-esteem back, gets a new haircut, and starts exercising and dieting, only to fall off the wagon a week later and go on another binge.

"Ooh, you know you're being trifling. I have mirrors at home. I know I need to lose weight. I don't need nobody to tell me that. Besides, I'm not dieting today. I'm splurging because I deserve it."

"You deserve it? For what?" I asked. "Aren't you the one who said you needed someone to be accountable to? I'm just trying to help you, sister-girl. That's why we stopped coming here for lunch. Remember? All those vegetables they got and you want the fried stuff. Believe me, I know how hard it is. I need to lose some weight myself, but when I get serious, I'm not coming here anymore. I'm going to bring my lunch."

"Whatever. I didn't say I was giving up. I just said I was splurging today, that's all. I don't know if I'll ever have that figure I had when I was twenty-one anyway. My body hasn't been the same since I had the baby. Now let's get to this nosey question you asked me. If I wasn't so sure I could trust you, I wouldn't even answer. But I know quiet is kept with you, right?"

"You know I'm not trying to tell your business to everybody, girl," I assured her. "But I saw that picture you have on your desk. You know that one you keep to motivate yourself. You must have had all the guys drooling over you back then. Come on, how many men have you had? Reminisce a little and then maybe you won't want all that food on your plate."

"You heffa," she replied. "Well, I thought about it on the way here, and I think I've been with thirteen."

"Tell me about the one who you remember most."

"Let me see. One in particular stands out because he was by far the worst. When I was twenty-one, I had sex with this guy who was eighteen because he was just crazy about me, and I wanted to blow his mind. I used to really be like that. I liked to impress men, even if I didn't really want them. We'd met at college. He was a freshman living in the dorm, and I had my own apartment because I was a senior. To this day, I still remember getting ready for him to pick me up.

"I showered with Johnson's Baby Bath, put baby oil all over myself before drying off so that my skin would be especially soft, and then put on a cute little tangerine-colored sundress that came only to the top of my thighs. It was summertime so, of course, I didn't wear any panties, and the bra I had on was so sheer, all it did was offer some support and show off what I had to offer. When he got there, I sashayed in front of him while making him a drink, making sure he got a good view of my big pretty legs and the way that dress was hitting my butt, and, honey, by the time we got ready to go to dinner, he was ready to eat me instead. I must admit, I'd made myself horny by wearing that dress with no panties, but I had to make him wait, just to ensure my own pleasure.

"We went to dinner and then to a movie and he couldn't keep his hands off my legs. I'd let him get so far, but then I'd stop him. I knew I was driving him crazy, but that was the whole point. When the movie was almost over, I let him get his hand up far enough for him to realize I didn't have any panties on and when he felt the hair on my coochie, he almost jumped out of his seat. I threw my head back and let out a quiet, sexy little laugh, but I really wanted to laugh out loud. I was tickled. As soon as the first credit started to roll he had me by the hand, up and out the door, and on our way back to the car. 'Ooh wee,' I thought. 'This is going to be good.' An eighteen-year-old football player with all that energy, those fine thighs, and big fine hands. I couldn't wait to saddle him up and ride.

"Anyway, to make a long, long story short, we got back to my apartment and it was over in five minutes. Yes, that's what I said, five minutes. I was so pissed I could have slapped the shit out of him before he even got off me. My immediate thought was, 'What in the hell was that? You mean I did all that for this?' My mind went back to how he kept grinning while we were eating, and I guess I should have known right then that he was too damn excited to do anything for me. I mean, the boy was packing, but he just couldn't do shit, and I know he was embarrassed to come that fast at his age, but I didn't care about his feelings.

"I was like, 'You have to be at practice at seven in the morning, so I guess you'd better go.' And even though I tried my best to say it nice, I know it didn't sound nice because it was all over my face. Here I was thinking. 'I'm gonna show him something tonight,' and I guess if he'd known what he was doing I would've had a chance. But when he went soft after five minutes, the thrill was gone. I wanted to tell him, 'Get your no-screwing ass out of my apartment right now,' but I didn't want to make him feel worse than he already did.

"I learned my lesson that time. Rule of thumb: If a guy is fine as hell, big and strong-looking and says all the right things, but his teeth start chattering when you kiss him because he's nervous, leave him the hell alone because you're in for a big disappointment if it goes any further."

HAVING SEX VS. MAKING LOVE

MINA, FORTY-SOMETHING

I thought I'd never have a chance to interview Mina since she's so busy with her dance studio. We canceled at least three appointments because her schedule kept changing and I was just about ready to give up. When she called me on a Saturday night, saying her husband and son would be at the Dallas Mavericks game for at least four hours that next day, I figured it was now or never, so I canceled my own plans for the afternoon.

I met Mina about four years ago at the Women's Business Center where we were both taking a class on Women Entrepreneurs, and we instantly hit it off. She was one of the most friendly, positive, and upbeat women I'd ever met, and I really enjoyed talking to her about anything, so I knew interviewing her would be fun because she was just a nice person to be around.

When I arrived, she escorted me to the family room. It was nice and big, with a wall of windows that looked out over a huge yard where a pool was being built for their son who was a freshman in high school. He was already known as one of the finest swimmers in the state and Mina was so proud of him that she beamed whenever she talked about him.

Her husband is a lawyer, and their story is really poignant in that they met right after college and dated a couple of years before finally getting engaged. Mina was busy dancing and was on the road often, so Jon didn't want to rush her into anything she'd regret. They'd been married fifteen years now, and she seemed to be happy with her life.

As we sat in the den drinking iced tea, I couldn't help but ask, "Will you guys be skinny-dipping out there when that pool is ready?"

"Girl, you know I'm not going skinny-dipping in my own backyard. My neighbors' houses aren't that close, but you know some people are nosey as hell. I don't want nobody to see me back here naked and start watching me every night. We really only got that pool for our son. He's always complaining that he needs to work on his technique, so we figured we'd get our money's worth if we put one in. We even had to have heaters put in the damn thing so he can use it in the wintertime. But that Jacuzzi, that's my new toy. That's why it's over there by my bedroom. I can get in, relax, get out, and go to bed."

"Ummhmm. I'm sure you'll get good use out of it if you can slow down long enough. Let me get started so I won't take up all your free time. I know you don't get to have the house to yourself often, so I don't want to stay too long."

"Oh, no, girl. You don't have to be in a hurry. We've got at least three hours. I'm a little anxious to see what you're going to ask me so I'm ready if you are."

"Okay, then. I've got lots of questions, but you can start by telling me if you think there's a difference between making love and having sex."

"Of course, there is a difference. Making love starts when you get up in the morning, even if you're not in the same house with that person.

"If they call you to say, 'How are you doing this morning? I just called you to say I was thinking about you and I can't wait to see you tonight,' that means a lot. It sets the mood for how you'll feel when you see him because by the time you get with him you already feel like you're in the mood to make love.

"Making love is a gift two people give to each other, but sometimes when you're married it doesn't seem like that because you don't make the phone calls or leave the little notes like you did at the beginning of the relationship. When you really care deeply for a man you want to give him something that he can't buy—you can't put a price on it. A woman giving her body to a man that she's really in love with is the ultimate gift and it should be the other way around with him giving his body to her as well. There's no gift greater than that. That's the difference between having sex and making love—it's the way you feel about each other and how much you're both willing to give of yourself.

"Now having sex, on the other hand, can be whatever. There doesn't have to be any emotion involved. You can have sex with anybody, no strings attached. You might even just do it because you're attracted to each other and want to see what the other person has to offer.

"The problem is that sometimes people have casual sex and it turns out to be more than they bargained for. I was engaged to and totally in love with my husband sixteen years ago, he was my best friend and I just knew the sun rose and set on him. One night we had gone to the movies and out to dinner, but the whole time I could just tell that something wasn't right."

She crossed her bare arms and rubbed them like she'd caught a chill. "Most women I know have that sixth sense. I think, whether we want to deal with it or not, we always know when things aren't the way they're supposed to be. Every time I asked him a question I had to repeat myself because he wasn't listening.

"When I asked him what was wrong, he just mumbled something about stress on the job. He was a rising young lawyer, and he's always been an overachiever so I guess that's why he's so successful now. I asked him earlier if he'd spend the night with me since he'd been away for the last week and I was pretty horny, but he declined and gave me some lame excuse about having to be at the office bright and early. He pulled into my driveway, turned off the ignition, and said he had something to tell me. Now, I was sure something was wrong because he could be as sick as a dog and still want to make love. When he wouldn't look me in the eyes I started thinking all kinds of things, like maybe he'd discovered he was gay or maybe he decided he didn't want to be with me anymore, but it wasn't anything like that.

"He started off saying how much he loved me and that he wouldn't want to hurt me for the world, and in the very next breath said he'd gotten another woman pregnant."

Mina paused like she was reliving the hurt. "Do you know how it feels to be in love with someone and have him tell you some other woman is going to have his baby? I felt like my heart had split in two. He went on to say that the woman was an ex-girlfriend that he'd run into at his college reunion, the same reunion that I couldn't make because I was on the road with my dance group. He told me that it all began with them getting together for old times' sake, and if you ask me, that was his first mistake. Ain't no way you're going to get together with an ex-girlfriend while you're out of town and be surprised when you end up in bed with one another. Of course, he went on to say, as they all do, that the sex meant nothing. But how can sex mean nothing? And if it meant nothing to him with her I had to wonder how soon it would mean nothing to him with me. The sad part was that it truly didn't mean anything to him. She was just something to do at the time, but you could best believe it meant the world to her. Otherwise why would she take the chance of getting pregnant? Once again, another prime example of how differently men and women look at things.

"I don't know about you, but there aren't very many women I know who can sleep with a man and keep it strictly on a sexual basis with no feelings attached. He tried to explain to me that the woman was making a big deal out of nothing and to him it wasn't a big deal until he got caught, because until she called him and told him she was pregnant, he'd forgotten all about that one night. Once Jon told her he was in love with me and had no intention of marrying her, it was too late to abort the baby, so she carried him to full term and gave him to Jon when he was born, saying, 'If I can't have you, then I don't want your son either.'

"I felt our love could handle anything, so I forgave him, married him, and decided to be a mother to his son. It hasn't always been easy, but the things we went through made our marriage stronger. Of course, since that happened, I don't believe in casual sex and I know that's a fact because I've been involved in an affair with another man for the past five years now so to me sex is definitely not a casual thing.

"I've been married for fourteen years and I dated my husband for five years before we got married, so I've been with him for a long time. I hate to say it, but sex for us has become too routine, it feels like a chore and it's not because of me. You can look at me and tell I'm not prudish. When I'm working I love wearing three-inch heels with my business suits, and when I'm playing I love my miniskirts and crop tops, and when I'm horny I want to be satisfied.

"I used to enjoy spontaneous, passionate lovemaking at least three times a week with my husband, but when we haven't spoken any kind words to each other all day and saying only enough to run the house, I can't get in the bed, roll over, and just open my legs. The desire isn't there, so now I guess it's just sex for us.

"I guess men can have sex and not be into it emotionally, but most women can't because we have to make a conscious decision to make love and our emotions are very much involved. Men can get in, come, and be satisfied because they don't have to make a decision; it's usually made for them with their penis.

"To me, making love involves mind and body. I want a man to make love to my mind so I can feel free to scream, grunt, talk dirty, or do whatever turns me on, without worrying if he's thinking, 'Damn, she's a nymph.' I want to feel completely satisfied when we're finished, and I want to be able to make him feel the same way. But it's just too much work when you're not in tune with each other anymore. I truly wish sex could always be exciting like it was when we first started dating, but when he treats me like I'm just there to fulfill a need, I don't even feel like going through the motions."

MISS NORA, SIXTY-SOMETHING

"I don't remember what sex or making love feels like anymore because it's been so long since I've had any good loving. I wouldn't know what to do if I got some, but it don't bother me to be here alone, because ain't no man getting nothing free from Nora. Uh-uh, baby. He's got to bring some good loving and some cash or credit cards. Now that I think about it, I can't really say that I've ever made love. I honestly can't tell you that. There have been times where the sex has been good and I felt good afterward, but I just treated it the same way men do because I had needs that I wanted fulfilled."

MACY, FIFTY-SOMETHING

"I made love with my first husband, but he broke my heart. So now I'm just having sex. I've been married twice now but I don't get my heart all involved anymore, so to me it's always just sex."

KIANA, FORTY-SOMETHING

"I think making love is something you do with someone you are in love with, where you feel like you're one when you're together. You're connected. I think when you're having sex you care about that person and it feels good, but you know it's not going any further than that. You want him, and he wants you, but you understand that tomorrow he may be gone and if that's the case, then so be it."

PORSCHE, THIRTY-SOMETHING

"You make love with a man when you really love and care for him, and you want to give him the ultimate satisfaction, but sex can be altogether different.

"I've experienced making love, and I've experienced having sex. When I'm with my husband, I feel like I'm having sex just because he wants to and I feel like I have to fulfill an obligation. Once we're through I go to sleep, happy that it's over. When I'm with my lover, I feel like I'm making love because he does all he can to please me and vice versa. When we finish, I always cry because I can't believe how good he makes me feel and I hate for it to be over."

MARCELLA, FORTY-SOMETHING

"Making love is not about pleasing yourself, it's about pleasing your mate while enjoying yourself at the same time. It's the ultimate fulfillment for two individuals who are deeply in love and sexually attracted to each other.

"Sex, on the other hand, is usually just sex."

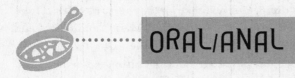

ORAL/ANAL

PORSCHE, THIRTY-SOMETHING

"I think it's great to give and receive oral sex, but I'll always think receiving is so much better. I guess it's because that's when I have my most intense orgasms. There isn't anything like good oral sex.

"I like giving and receiving it as a matter of fact. My lover is very good at performing oral sex, so I don't have to tell him what to do and that's nice. But I don't understand it when other women say: 'I would never kiss him afterward.' Those are the most intimate kisses you'll ever have. If you know you're clean, what's the problem? If you're not, he shouldn't be down there in the first place.

"I had anal sex a few times while I was in college," Porsche said, looking around like she thought someone might walk up behind her and hear. "I probably would have kept on doing it because I enjoyed the way it felt and it was something different which is probably why guys enjoy doing it so much but I interned at a hospital and I've seen a couple of women who experimented with anal sex regularly and had to have surgery because their assholes were so huge because they'd done that for so long that they'd lost all the elasticity. I didn't think it was worth taking a chance like that, so I gave it up."

MINA, FORTY-SOMETHING

"I think oral sex is wonderful if you know that person is clean. I use oral sex as my opportunity to put on a show. Men like to watch, and I'd rather give than receive because some men don't really know how to hit the right spot anyway. It's not the ultimate for me, but if I'm with a man that I care very deeply for, I really enjoy making him feel good.

"My lover enjoyed being on the receiving end of oral sex and he never did return the favor but that really didn't bother me because when I saw how much I could turn him on with just my lips and tongue I would have numerous orgasms. He didn't just sit back and watch me do all the work, believe me he kept his hands quite busy working my clitoris and fingering my vagina. I would have several orgasms before he even thought about coming once. Sex is totally mental.

"Sad to say but women will look at their husbands and go, 'Uuuhhh . . . Suck his dick? I don't think so,' while at the same time another woman is looking at that same man and saying, 'I love the ground he walks on and I'll suck his dick anytime.' I know it for a fact because I'm doing it to somebody else's husband myself.

"We almost had anal sex once, and I say almost because he didn't get all the way in before he came and that was pretty unusual for him so he must have been turned on. We weren't in one of the most private places anyway, as a matter of fact, we were outside and I was bent over the trunk of his car and we were just caught up in the heat of passion. I would like to experience it fully because it's something different. It seems like it would be exciting with the right person."

JEWELL, SIXTY-SOMETHING

"I can take it or leave it, and I'm probably the worst at giving it because I'm not swallowing nothing. Shit, there ain't that much love in the world for me. When he feels like he can't hold back, it's time to either get a towel or change positions because I'd hate to have to get ugly and ruin the whole damn mood.

"Receiving is okay, but my body chemistry is weird. If it goes on too long, I get dry and end up with a yeast infection, so I'd rather not even do it. Now, if it's real quick, just to get the juices flowing so we can move on to the next thing, then I'm all right with it, but don't kiss me afterward. Don't even put your lips on my face. I might not even want him to breathe on me because I don't want to smell or taste myself."

BIANCA, THIRTY-SOMETHING

"I used to love oral sex until I dated a guy who had a big old gap in his teeth." Bianca closed her eyes and shook her head as she thought back. "I'd been dating him for about two months and finally decided to let him have some, and I told him we could skip the oral sex because I didn't really feel like I knew him well enough. But he insisted, saying I didn't have to do it for him, but he just had to taste it because the taste of a woman turned him on. Now you know when a man loves the way a woman tastes, he usually knows what he's doing because he's not inhibited.

"Well, let me tell you, the brother did know what he was doing, but he got carried away and my clitoris got caught in his gap—just for a second—and it hurt so bad that I got pissed off and told him to stop. Of course, he was upset because he wanted to finish what he'd started, but I dried up so there was no turning back. I told him to get his shit and leave and I never saw him again after that.

"Needless to say, I don't date men with gaps anymore."

MISS NORA, SIXTY-SOMETHING

"Oh, no, honey. Miss Nora's not into that at all, and I'll tell them that straight from the beginning when they start talking about it. If they want to perform oral sex on me, that's their business but don't ask me to return the favor. If I'm gonna make love, I'm gonna make love the old-fashioned way because I'm from the old school. Besides, I've had these dentures since high school, and I don't even like the way I look without them myself. I sure as hell don't intend to let a man see me without them in."

JACKIE, FORTY-SOMETHING

"I like oral sex as long as I don't have to do it. Hey, I'm being honest. I'll receive it, but I don't want to give and I don't make that no secret. I've got a weak stomach. I don't like swallowing nothing slimy, and I gag too easily, so I don't even fool around when it comes to that."

LADY, FORTY-SOMETHING

"Girl, I love oral sex, but let me tell you a really funny story. One time this guy I was seeing called and said he was on his way over and caught me off guard. He'd been out of town on business, so I wasn't expecting him back for a day or so. I'd just taken a bath, and a vinegar douche, so when he called I had to scramble to figure out what I was going to do because I didn't want him to taste that vinegar.

"Well, I'd gone to this little lingerie party about a month before and bought some of this stuff that looked like chips of ice that you were supposed to put in your mouth while performing oral sex on your partner. The girl who was selling the stuff said it could be used by men and women so I figured I'd use it on my man, and then get him to use it on me. I wanted him to think I was being freaky, but what I was really trying to do was camouflage that damn vinegar.

"As soon as he walked in, he was all over me. I said, 'Ooh, you missed me, huh? Well, hold on, baby. I've got a little treat for you. Why don't you go take your shower while I get it ready.' He was grinning from ear to ear as he headed for the bathroom. When he came out, I worked him over good with that ice or whatever that shit was called. He was moaning and moving around so much I had to tell him to be still before I lost my rhythm, but I was enjoying the hell out of making him lose control.

"Well, when it came time for him to use that stuff on me, I couldn't wait." Lady looked at me with a smile forming at the corners of her mouth. "When he first got started, it was nice and cool, like chocolate ice cream in your mouth. But, girl, about thirty seconds into it that shit mixed with that vinegar and I thought I was on fire. I was still trying to be sexy, whispering, 'Wait, baby, wait. Slow down. I'm not going nowhere,' but he wouldn't stop because he thought it was getting good to me. He grabbed my hips and held on like he was in a damn pie-eating contest because I was squirming, trying my best to get away from him. And . . . I can't believe you're laughing at me."

Lady started to laugh herself. "You know I played it off. I told him I guess that stuff wasn't meant for men to use on women, and he believed me. Soon as he left I threw that shit in the trash and I've never tried anything like that again. I figure if a man catches me in a situation like that again, I'll just have to be honest with him and we can move on to something else."

EBONI, FORTY-SOMETHING

"Anal?" Eboni looked confused for a moment then the light came on. "You mean in the ass? Oh, hell no, shit no, Eboni don't do that. I got hemorrhoids. My tolerance level for pain is zero, and I don't want nothing back there that wasn't meant to go there. I can eat a hot link and that will mess me up for the next two days, so I don't fool around with that. If a man wants some from the ass, he needs to get a man. Hell, I'll even watch as long as it's going to keep me from doing it. I went to the hospital and had an enema one time, and I hope I never have to have another one of those. That was enough. I almost did it one time with my ex-husband. He said if we used Vaseline it wouldn't hurt, but I just couldn't get past the thought of it. I know a lot of people are into it, but not me."

SADIE, FIFTY-SOMETHING

Sadie paused before answering me when I asked her if she'd ever tried anal sex, and I immediately felt like I'd gone too far. Just when I was about to retract the question she said, "I've never tried it, and I don't want to because I know I wouldn't like it. I don't think I've ever loved a man enough to let him stick his penis in my butt. There are too many other ways to have sex that feels good. But I think anal sex would be way too painful, and I'm not into pain with sex, period. If it's hurting me, I ain't doing it, that's the bottom line."

She stopped again to sign some receipts and then waited until the waiter was out of hearing distance before speaking. "I had a friend who tried it, and she said it was very uncomfortable. I don't see how it can give women any pleasure because we don't have any lubrication there and there's no stimulation for us. Besides, you can make your vagina just as tight as your ass if you know how.

"I had a lover who wanted me to experiment with anal sex one time and I politely told him, 'Let me put my legs on the inside and cross my ankles and that should feel tight enough for right now, but don't be asking me to do nothing crazy.'"

AYOKA, THIRTY-SOMETHING

"I think if I could ever get over my fear of pain, I might like it. I tried it with my lover but I was almost knocked out with liquor so I really don't remember whether or not it was painful. Men like it because it feels so tight, but I think it's a mind thing with women. When you start thinking about doing that, your body just tightens up, and that's probably why so many women say it hurts so much. You've got to relax.

"I've heard that it helps to push as if you're forcing something out of your body until he gets in. Then once he's in, you can relax. I'd like to try it again, but it's not something I'd like to do on a regular basis."

GIOVANNI, FORTY-SOMETHING

"Oh, Lord, I knew you were going to go there," Giovanni said, trying to look all innocent. "Yes, I tried it one time with my lover and to me it felt like I was trying to push something big out and he was trying to push it back in." She made a funny face, looking embarrassed. "I was very uncomfortable, but he was back there talking and shit, saying, 'Ooh, baby, that feels so good. You're so tight.' Shit, I guess his ass would be tight too if all he used it for was its intended purpose, which was exactly what I intended to keep using mine for once it was over. I only did it because he wanted to. That's probably why I can't get rid of his ass now. He thinks I'm going to let him do it again, but I've got news for him."

JESSICA, THIRTY-SOMETHING

"I'm not down with anal sex. No. My husband used to ask me to do it but I wasn't going there. He'd say, 'Jessica, you're always willing to try something new. Why won't you at least just try it? As long as we've been together you know I'm not going to hurt you.' But you know how I broke him from asking me?

"I told him, 'I'll make a deal with you, baby. Let me go to the store and buy a dildo or a vibrator and when I get back, let me screw you in your ass first. Then you can screw me in mine.'

" 'Oh, hell no,' he said, looking at me like I was the one who was crazy. So, I don't have to worry about that anymore because he knows I'm for real. That's how you break him. Turn the tables on his ass, and he won't ask you anymore. Not unless he's a freak for real."

SOUTHERN FRIED SHRIMP

3 cups large peeled and deveined shrimp

1½ teaspoons salt

¼ teaspoon pepper

1 egg, well beaten

½ cup half and half or milk

½ cup yellow cornmeal

½ cup flour

½ teaspoon baking powder

¼ teaspoon salt

Oil for deep-frying

Season shrimp with 1½ teaspoons salt and the pepper; let stand at room temperature for 10 to 15 minutes. Combine egg, cream, cornmeal, flour, baking powder, and remaining salt in small mixing bowl; mix until well blended and smooth. Heat oil in deep fryer to 350 degrees. Add batter mixture to shrimp; stir until shrimp are well coated. Drop shrimp in deep, hot fat in batches. Fry until light golden brown, about 2 to 4 minutes. *Yield: 4 to 6 servings.*

·············· # AFFAIRS

AYOKA, THIRTY-SOMETHING

"I'm separated now and his wife has found out about us. Because of those two things the dynamics of our relationship changed and he is more cautious about where we are, when we see each other, etc. . . . But let me tell you how she found out. We were in New Orleans together and he'd left his Viagra at home. Let me also say that any couples that have given up on getting busy due to lack of an erection should definitely try the stuff. I mean, damn, if they ever ask me to donate money to keep research going for Viagra, I would have them automatically withdraw that shit out of my checking account every payday because it's just that wonderful. I kid you not, that little blue pill can make a man perform like he's twenty-one years old again. One time after he'd taken it, we couldn't get to the room fast enough and started fooling around in one of the stairwells at the hotel. He was so hard I thought he was going to burst right through the crotch of my panties, I am not lying." Ayoka held both arms up over her head and made a "V" sign.

"But anyway, let me tell you what happened. We don't always use the Viagra but he wanted it since we were going to be there for a week. He called in the prescription to the pharmacy at home, and asked them to call the pharmacy in New Orleans where we were so he could get a refill. I don't know why, but for whatever reason, the pharmacy at home called his home phone number to verify that he actually wanted it filled in a different city, and his wife was the one who got the call." Ayoka made a wry face. "Of course she called him and asked him why he needed to get his prescription refilled since he was out of town, and then she implied that she already knew we were seeing each other, so he confessed because he figured he was caught anyway.

"We found out later that she'd called my office pretending to be my sister and they told her that I was in New Orleans. She knew what hotel he was in, so she called and asked for my room and that's how she found out I was there, so by the time she called him she'd already put two and two together. When his cell phone rang, we had just come out of the Red Fish Grill, and it was misting rain like it always does in Louisiana and were standing in the middle of Bourbon Street kissing, and he got this 'Oh, damn' look on his face. I walked away so he could talk, and when he got off the phone, he never said a word. It was a few days later, in the limo on our way back to the airport, before he told me the shit had hit the fan.

"At first I was shocked, but then I got angry because he immediately started withdrawing from me, like our relationship didn't really mean anything—like I wasn't important to him. What neither one of us knew was that she'd torn the whole damn house apart going through stuff in the attic and in the storage room, looking for any little proof she could find. She did find some receipts for items he'd bought me, but what really implicated him were the cell-phone bills from the past year, where he'd been calling me and I'd been calling him each and every day, and a few receipts for some high-dollar items like diamond earrings and a diamond bracelet. I just could not believe he got that messy and I still talk about his ass for not being more careful, but that's what happens when you don't care anymore, you get careless.

"I had no sooner settled in and unpacked when my phone rang.

She had somehow gotten my private number and called me. When I answered the phone she started yelling at me and asking me why I was trying to break up her family, and then in the same breath wanted to know all the details like how long it had been going on and all that. He'd told her it had only been going on for a year. When I told her I'd been seeing him for ten years, I thought she was going to come through that phone, but I remained calm because there was nothing else for me to do.

"I don't know why he won't leave her. I don't know what kind of hold she has on him. She doesn't lift him up; she calls him dumb while he is one of the most successful marketing reps that I know. He was trying to explain to her why we were still friends even after she found out about us and he'd supposedly put a stop to the affair. He tells her that we help each other professionally. He tells her, 'I might be dealing with a specific issue or she might be dealing with a specific issue and we just might need to bounce something off each other.' One time when he told her that she said, 'Well, if you're too dumb to do your own job, you need to talk to her.' Instead of his just dismissing the put down he will start to think, 'Maybe I'm not smart, maybe I shouldn't talk to her 'cause I'm not smart.'

"When I ask him about it he says to me, 'Remember how your husband had a way of making you feel bad about every little thing?' Even when we're out of town together if she calls he'll ask me to leave the room because he doesn't want me to hear him talking to her. He said, 'She has such a way of demoralizing me when she starts in on me and I don't want you to see that side of my personality.' I still don't know why he stays with her. I used to think it was because of their child. Their child is about fifteen years old and he literally mediates their arguments. When his wife starts screaming at him, his son will look at him and whisper, 'Don't say anything. If you don't yell back then Mom can't fight by herself.'

"Well, she's the type who's going to keep on yelling until he yells back. She's like, 'You know I hate him. He cheated on me and I can't trust him.'

"The whole family was watching some movie where a married man was seeing a prostitute and she said, 'That's what your dad did to me.'" Ayoka grimaced. "I asked him if he sat there and watched the movie with them and he said, 'Yeah, I sat there and watched it with them because I hadn't seen the movie,' because he tries to circumvent what she might be saying to his son. He'll tell him, 'You know that wasn't what really happened' and that's the reason he gives me as to why he won't get up and leave because he's afraid of what she might be telling the child.

"He said after they watched the movie and he and he and his son were alone, it was obvious that the child had never really understood what an affair was, but after watching this movie he did. His son said, 'I'd always wondered what an affair was and what Mom was talking about when she said you had an affair. After watching that movie it finally clicked.' He asked his dad, 'So you had sex with that other woman, that's what an affair is.' And his dad said, 'Yes, that's what an affair is.'

"All this time he had been freaked out by the word 'affair,' he hadn't even known what it meant but he knew that it had to be something really ugly and terrible the way his mom ranted about it. Before he really knew what it meant he was probably thinking, 'What has my dad *done*? He had an *affair.*'

"If I were her I would've said, 'You know what? That was just some cheap, tawdry thing you did and you didn't care nothing about her,' and move on. I would have certainly not said, 'Oh, you made love to her,' and dwelled on it. She even calculated the number of times we might have had sex. She actually sat down, took out a pen"—Ayoka rattled some papers and acted like she was writing and goes—"'Sooooo, if ya'll got together on the average of four times a month and there's twelve months in a year'"—Ayoka sat back wide-eyed and viewed her pretend calculations with amazement—"'why that's forty-eight times a year times one year. You've had sex with her forty-eight times.'

"He had lied and told her the affair had gone on for one year when in reality it had been going on for ten. I shouldn't make fun of her because I don't know what I would do if I was in the same situation. I don't think I could put myself through that. That's crazy. If my husband was having an affair with another woman for ten years, then she can have him because that's obviously where he wants to be. Why would I want to stay with him and put myself through that misery?

"But instead she threatens him. She tells him that I"—Ayoka pointed to herself—"don't want to do nothing but destroy his family and take his money, so if he thinks he wants to be with me then just go, but he'll never have a relationship with his child.

"I told him again, 'You know sometimes divorce is better for the child.' He gets mad when I tell him that because he wants to believe that it's better that they are staying together. I said, 'Don't you realize that your son probably sits on pins and needles the whole time you're home? When you're out of town your son is probably thinking, 'Great. There won't be any fights so I can relax.' Those weeks when you're in the house, your son is wondering, 'Am I going to come home from school today and have to mediate my parent's arguments, am I going to have to hear them screaming at the top of their lungs at each other saying all this terrible stuff?'

"Finally I told him, 'I don't care what you think, I don't care if you never speak to me again but surely you don't honestly think that his witnessing mess like that isn't any worse than your being absent from the house.'

"I just want to tell her sometimes, 'Even though you hate for him to be with me, you're the one who keeps him coming back. You say you want the marriage to work but then you just keep bitching and nagging, and because you refuse to forgive and let go, you keep giving him a reason to come to me, even though he's tried to leave me alone.'

"He's been going to church and trying to get his life together too and he really wants to be a good leader for his family, but he made this mistake that she will never let him live down so he's constantly trying to do what's right but feels like he has no reason to. Our relationship is definitely not right, it's an extramarital affair and we both know that, but at least when he's with me he can laugh and have fun and talk about his hopes and dreams and other things that are important to him. All married people need to be able to do that with their spouse and they both need to realize that if they don't have a relationship where that's possible, and all they're doing is fussing and fighting all the time, one of them will eventually end up in a relationship with someone else where they feel more loved and accepted, that's just human nature," Ayoka stated.

"The last time I told him it was over and didn't give in to being with him for like two months, we would still speak to each other in passing but I wouldn't have sex with him. Then something happened to make me fall off the wagon, a bad day or something and he comes over and kisses me on my forehead. I guess I was needy . . . no, actually I was horny and just wanted to fuck, so we got back into that messy relationship because I got weak. It happened in my office after hours and the very next week his wife was acting crazy again. He came to me and said, 'I don't know what provoked it, I haven't done a thing different at home but now she's acting crazy and bringing this stuff up about the affair all over again.'

"He has never told me that he didn't want to see me anymore sexually. He's never said those words to me, ever. It's always: 'I can't help the way I feel. I don't know what to do about my situation but I'm not willing to leave her; I'm not willing to make that sacrifice.' He's honest with me about that. He says, 'I care for you a lot but I can't say I care enough to make that sacrifice.'

"If I was her I would just say, 'I love you but I can't live like this, this is killing me, literally. Let's just let it go. If you really want to be with her, why don't you just go?' but I think he's scared to do what his heart is telling him to do.

"The rest is a long drawn-out story and I had to get a new phone number but we're still seeing each other. He's still one hundred percent attentive when he's with me, and he still does all the wonderful things for me that he's always done, but we both try to be more realistic about our future at this point.

"So, with all of that said, let me tell you what I've learned. It's true that you really should not get involved in an affair, it's not good and nothing good can come of it. It's a painful journey, especially for me because I'm not just having an affair. I fell in love, which was a mistake because I should have kept them separate. I often think of all the times that my mother used to tell me, 'Regardless of what happens, if he's not able to commit to you, don't bring your heart to the party.' The problem is that I don't know how to be involved with someone and spend time with them and have sex with them and keep my emotions and my heart out of it. There are many women who can do that, but for me, if my heart ain't at the party, then there's no reason for me to go.

"Even though I've been separated for a good little while now, I have never been so needy a woman that I can just have sex with anybody. I mean, there have been times when he and I haven't been together intimately for four or five months, trying to break this damn thing off, but even then I miss sex and I miss him, but I'm not going to go out and find somebody to just have sex with because that's all it is and I don't want that. I could never be the type of woman who would purposely go to a club and bring home some stranger just so I can get banged all night—what the hell is that at my age?

"The other thing I've learned is that it may not be true when people say, 'There's somebody for everybody, and you'll end up with the person who's meant for you,' because I can't imagine that we were meant for each other if both of us married someone else. I know it has to end one of these days, but I don't know when or how. I've tried, but I love him so much, and he obviously loves me, and we can't stay away from each other, so what am I to do?"

GIOVANNI, FORTY-SOMETHING

"You know what I think?" Giovanni pulled off her gold hoop earrings and laid them on the table next to her. "I think people have affairs because they get plain old bored. If you get married before you're twenty-five or thirty, you don't really know what those vows mean. I know I didn't. It was years before I realized what 'in sickness and health, till death do us part' meant. It means that you stay together no matter what. You stay together if he doesn't have a job, if he's broke, if he's sorry, lazy, not the perfect lover, or not a good provider." She rubbed her earlobes. " 'In sickness and health till death do us part' means that regardless of the circumstances, you're supposed to be true to your spouse. The only problem is that most of us aren't really prepared for marriage. People grow and change so when the 'poorer' times or the 'bad' times come around, we're not prepared to deal with them and we look for a temporary escape.

"I'd been married a good two years when I realized what I was in for, and I must admit that it scared the hell out of me. I think I spent an hour just sitting there on the edge of the tub saying to myself, 'What have I done? I love this man but I swear he already works on my last nerve with some of the shit he does, but I made a commitment. How am I going to stay with him for the rest of my life—and does that mean he's the only man I can ever have sex with—forever? Oh, damn, that could be a problem because he's very comfortable with things the way they are but I'm already getting bored.'

"I got on the phone and called my aunt and told her about my concerns and she laughed so hard she could hardly talk. She said, 'Baby, let me tell you something. When I first got married, I went through the same thing and I thought an affair would put the spark back in my life. The man I was having an affair with was the only thing that kept me coming home because it wasn't long into my marriage before I discovered that marriage is not all it's cut out to be. It's work. You've got bills that don't get paid on time, your in-laws are getting on your damn nerves, maybe the baby's keeping you up at night, and that shit gets hard. But if you're smart, you'll realize that home is permanent. You and your husband might argue, but in the end you know he's going to be there for you. Sex with my lover was wonderful and we could talk about anything under the sun, but I had to realize that just like he walked into my life, he could also walk out the same way and I'd never see him again. So always remember what me and many others had to learn the hard way, an affair is just a fantasy. It's what you wish your marriage could be, so don't think that getting involved in one will make the rest of your life easier to deal with because all it really does is make things more complicated.' "

Giovanni continued. "For the next eight years, I stayed busy with my job, had children, and thought I was okay. But I finally let my guard down and ended up getting involved anyway because I was at a point in my life where I wasn't satisfied with marriage or myself. I'd been flirting with this guy at work for several months, just playing around like I thought he was. But then, we started having more serious conversations and I was becoming more and more attracted to him. One day, out of the blue, he told me exactly what he'd like to do to me, and invited me over to his house. I took him up on his offer because I was horny as hell just listening to him, but warned him up front that I didn't have the most fabulous body in the world.

"I was self-conscious because I'd had babies and hadn't been with another man since I'd been married, and that had been ten years. Well, why did he say all the things my husband hadn't said in years like, 'Damn, you've got some beautiful, big, sexy legs . . . Your eyes are so pretty . . . I love the way your ass moves when you wear a dress with heels . . . Don't worry about your body. I've been watching you for months and I like what I see because I'm into women, not little girls.' What did he tell me that for? 'Cause when he said that, I got to thinking . . . ooooooh . . . I'm a woman." Giovanni sucked her teeth and rolled her eyes toward the ceiling. "Like I didn't know that already.

"He turned me on, completely. I would've been happy just to sit down somewhere and stare up in his face all day and probably would've left my husband for him if he'd treated me halfway decent because I was crazy about him. I went to his house that Friday evening after work. An hour after I'd arrived, I was sitting in this plush armchair that was wide enough to seat two people and was sipping on this marvelous strawberry daiquiri he'd made with fresh strawberries and Jamaican rum. He turned the lights down, took off his shirt, sat down on the floor between my knees, and handed me some massage oil and asked me to massage his neck and shoulders because he was kind of sore from an earlier workout. I was only too glad to oblige because I'd been waiting for a legitimate reason to get my hands on him since the first time I'd seen him. I knew I was in trouble when he took that shirt off, and I got a close-up of his chest and stomach. There wasn't an extra ounce of fat anywhere. His chest was wide and the muscles firm, and the muscles in his stomach just rippled when he moved. He looked just like one of those underwear models, but ten times sexier.

"Now, I hadn't really gone over to his house with the intention of having sex with him that first evening, but I must've been expecting something, or why else would I be wearing my sexiest underwear?

"After I'd massaged his shoulders for a while, with both of us pretending to watch TV, and I couldn't tell you if you offered me a million dollars what it was we watched, he got up and walked around the chair to stand behind me. He started to caress my neck, arms, and breasts, and by the time he leaned down and bit me on my neck and started to suck on my earlobe I lost all sense of time. I managed to stand up, and we kissed all the way to his bedroom.

"First, he took all of his clothes off. His body was like black silk—skin so smooth that the thought of it gives me chills. And his ass? Two words describe it—taut and fine. I hadn't seen an ass like that before, and I haven't seen one like it since. He had these big, muscular thighs and a stomach that looked like he spent an hour a day doing sit-ups. And I'm not even going to talk about his arms and

shoulders, but I will tell you this, he could make me wet just by licking his lips. He was six feet two inches, 180 pounds, bowlegged, and
had the sexiest mouth I'd ever seen." Giovanni pushed some books
off the table that were marked for clearance, propped her feet up,
and sneaked a peek at me to see if she might have shocked me.

"When he lay me on the bed and began to undress me, he took
the time to fold every piece of my clothing, then got on his knees,
pulled me to the edge of the mattress, and began to give me the best
oral sex I'd had in my life—and not one time did I think about my
body not fitting a perfect image. I was too much into how he was
making me feel to even begin worrying about stuff like that."

Giovanni reached for a paperback book similar to the ones that
she had placed on the floor, noticed that the sale price wasn't
marked, and put it in a different stack.

"He said, 'Talk to me. Tell me what you want.' Now I wasn't much
of a talker, but before we got done, I must've talked and hollered up
a storm. I have to give it to him, he was damn good and he had the
perfect dick. When we finished, he left the bed to go clean himself up
and that's when all hell broke loose.

" 'Damn,' I heard him say. I got up and grabbed his robe that
he'd left at the foot of the bed for me and ran into the bathroom to
find out what was wrong.

" 'Look what you did.' He was staring at himself in the mirror
and pointing at the large purplish hickey on the side on his neck.

"Now, since I hadn't read the manual on the dos and don'ts of
having the perfect affair, it was obvious that I'd made a pretty big
mistake. Since then I've determined that the ten big *Don'ts* are as
follows:

1. Don't bite or suck too hard.
2. Don't scratch.
3. Don't wear perfume.
4. Don't wear lipstick.

5. Don't plan on doing it in the bed after the first time because that's where I do it with my wife/girlfriend, and I do have some morals.

6. Don't plan on using the good towels and if you insist on washing up afterward or if you must take a shower, please make it quick.

7. Don't plan on staying around too long after we're through screwing because my wife or girlfriend might come home unexpectedly.

8. Don't expect me to call you tomorrow—or maybe not even the next few days—unless I feel the urge to get with you again.

9. Don't expect me to take you out to lunch or dinner or be seen in any public place with you whatsoever.

10. Don't fall in love with me because you will definitely be hurt when you find out that I have no intention of letting myself feel the same way.

"Simply stated, I was way out of my league, totally confused and humiliated. I never had to worry about holding back when having sex, and hadn't he just told me to talk to him and tell him what I wanted? What I wanted was to be able to have sex without having to worry about remembering not to suck on his neck or grip his shoulders too hard. After all, he was a single man. I had more to lose than he did, so why was he the one with all the damn rules?

"It went on that way between the two of us for a whole year. We'd have this wild, crazy intense sex, but after each encounter, he'd act shitty until he wanted to have sex again. And I was so infatuated with him that I went along with it." Giovanni got up and started to rearrange books on the shelf directly in front of us.

Talking over her shoulder she continued. "He actually said to me one time, 'I like you and I really want to be with you, but I constantly have to remind myself that you're a married woman and I can't have you. I can't just let myself go because when it's over it's got to be over. I can't let myself fall in love with you.' But still, like a fool, I allowed myself to fall in love with him.

"What finally ended it was that he asked me when I was going to come over and cook for him. I could have jumped for joy when he asked me, but I just played it cool and said something simple like, 'Sure, what would you like me to cook?' " Giovanni rolled her eyes, ashamed of what she was about to confess.

"He told me that he liked fish and asked me to come over to his place to fry him some fish. And in case you didn't know, I happen to make some of the best fried catfish this side of the Mississippi," Giovanni boasted proudly. "Anyway, we agreed that the next Friday would be good, so everything was set.

"Well, child, that Thursday evening I bought some fresh fish, took it home and put it in my freezer, and the next morning I took it out and carried it to work with me. I didn't want my staff to see it and start asking questions, so I'd wrapped it in plastic, put it inside a brown paper bag, and stuck it in the refrigerator at work so it would be thawed out by the time I got off. Girl, I kept waiting for him to call me and let me know what time to come over, but he never did call. And there I was wondering what happened and what I was going to do with all that fish thawing out in the refrigerator.

"By the end of the day, I was pissed—not because of the fish I had spent money on, but because I wanted to see him. I must've called his number thirty times between noon and six and he never did answer. I stayed late after work, waiting for everybody else to go home before I dragged all that damn fish out of the refrigerator. It was well thawed out by then and I should've thrown it out right then, but no, I was still hoping that he'd call. I wanted to think he'd just misplaced my number or something, but I knew that wasn't the case. And I couldn't take the fish home because my husband didn't even eat fish, so I never cooked it for him."

Giovanni started to pace. "I was so mad I didn't know what to do. I had all this damn fish, and the Negro didn't even try to call me and lie or nothing.

"I finally got him on the phone after probably the fiftieth try at

7:00 P.M. I'd set him up on speed dial because my finger was sore from dialing his number over and over.

"I told him I'd been calling him all day, and you know what he had the nerve to ask me?" Giovanni paused dramatically. "He asked, 'What are you calling me for?' Can you believe that shit? Those were his exact words. I'm sure the only reason he finally answered the damn phone was because he was tired of listening to it ring.

"I said, 'Didn't you ask me to come over tonight and cook for you?' I knew I hadn't completely lost my mind and imagined the conversation. I had wanted to see him, but not so badly that I'd dream the shit up, but you know how a brother can make you second-guess yourself.

"So he said, 'I told you . . .' Now notice he didn't use the word 'ask.' He said, 'I told you I wanted you to come over and cook for me, but I didn't say I wanted it to be this Friday. If I had known you was gonna make such a big deal out of cooking for me, I wouldn't have asked you to do it in the first place.' Now, this Negro was acting like he was doing me a favor to let me buy the food, bring it to him, and stand over a hot-ass stove and cook it for him. And to top it all off I had planned to fuck him after I fed him.

"Baby, I proceeded to tell him exactly what I thought about his selfish, inconsiderate ass and slammed the phone down so hard I was hoping I busted his eardrum. To this day, every time I think about fried fish, I get pissed off all over again, but I guess I didn't learn a thing from that experience because I got bored again about four years later and became involved in another relationship that started out the same way that first one had. I swear I'm not good at just being friends with men, even though I trust them more than I do women. You know, you can talk to them, you can laugh with them, you can bounce questions about other men off of them, and you can tell them personal things that won't be repeated. But there's still that fine line you have to walk, especially if you're even slightly attracted to them.

"I still have men who I consider to be really good friends, but

I always remind myself that I have to keep things in perspective, no matter how rough it gets at home. If I start getting bored in my marriage, I do a self-check to see if I'm doing my part to keep things spicy, rather than looking at my husband and expecting him to read my mind. If I think I'm doing all I can and he's not, or if he's doing something that really turns me off, I let him know. Also, I've enrolled myself in a women's self-awareness program at the local college, and that is helping me to be a better person and feel more fulfilled with my life no matter what state it's in. See, I finally realized that the men I'd had affairs with didn't really make me all that happy. They only helped to create a facade which kept me from looking at the root of my problems, which involved being from a broken home.

"I finally realized that I'd always felt I had to give a guy what he wanted in order for him to like me, even as a teenage girl, because, even though it wasn't true, I somehow felt that I had something to do with my father leaving us. For me, having many male friends filled a void in my life that my father had left. As long as I had enough men in my life, I never had to worry about feeling that loss again. That may seem crazy, but for me, it was reality and I needed to understand that to be able to keep my male-female relationships in the right perspective.

"Still, I can't say those experiences were wasted because I learned a good, hard lesson. I learned that an affair just creates another problem on top of the one you're trying to get away from. It's a dead-end street from the very beginning, so don't think it's going to amount to something one day because it won't. Even if you end up with the person you have an affair with, you probably won't trust him and he probably won't trust you either, so why bother? And now that I know I'm ultimately responsible for my own happiness, no matter what state my marriage is in, I don't feel a need to have other men in my life *just in case*. My friends are just that, friends, and that makes me feel a lot better than having an affair ever did."

PORSCHE, THIRTY-SOMETHING

"Women are romantic, emotional creatures and tend to have affairs for far different reasons than men," Porsche said. She and I were both silent as we watched the ducks lazily circling the pond from our place on the blanket. She inhaled deeply and closed her eyes to relax. She'd stated earlier that she knew her husband was going to pick a fight about something when she got home. It never failed. He'd bought her a birthday cake one time and some sleazy outfit that she'd never think of wearing and when she didn't show the proper appreciation for it, he picked up the cake and threw it at her. He'd belittled her more times than she could even remember. She'd married him right out of college, but it had been the biggest mistake of her life, and she paid for it every waking moment.

"Your lover will tell you things your husband doesn't. Things like, 'You have beautiful teeth, sexy legs, you smell so good, you look so pretty.' I like to be complimented. I like to feel special. I like excitement, so the affair becomes thrilling because it's something forbidden, something new and different. My affair has made me feel like a teenager all over again. It's been so long since I had butterflies in my stomach that I'd forgotten such a feeling existed."

Porsche set her drink down and pulled her knees to her chest, curling her arms around them and resting her chin there. "I think a man has an affair because he enjoys the feel of a different woman, he enjoys the sex. He might not be getting any at home or if he's getting some, it's not as often or as freaky as he likes. The other woman might make him feel like the world revolves around him, the same way his wife used to make him feel before the kids, bills, and problems with the in-laws came along.

"My affair began over a business lunch. My lover, who is a physician like I am, was thinking about consolidating his practice with three or four other successful physicians and wanted to know if I was interested. We'd known each other for a few years and had run into one another at various social and professional functions over the years. While I wasn't willing to consolidate my practice, I did have to tell him something that had been on my mind for quite some time, so when I couldn't take it any longer, I put my fork down and said, 'I need to tell you something and I hope I don't embarrass you.' He asked what it was and kept on about the business of eating. I guess he thought the business portion of the meal was over because I'd said no to the consolidation for the fourth time.

"I said, 'I am very attracted to you.' I'll never forget the expression on his face when I said that. He looked halfway shocked and totally serious because he immediately laid his fork down and replied, 'Well, what the hell are we going to do about it?'

"I was stunned when he asked me that because I'd expected him to respond, 'Well thank you, that's very nice.' I wasn't prepared for a 'Well, what the hell are we going to do about it?' I got real nervous and stammered out, 'We're not going to do anything about it. I just wanted to tell you how I felt.' " Porsche began to twist a braid around one finger, as was her habit as she stared unseeingly toward the pond.

"Now remember, this was coming from a woman who had never even thought about being with someone outside of her marriage.

"He said, 'So you tell me you're attracted to me, make me lose my appetite when I got all this food on my plate, then go on to tell me you don't want to do anything about it?' I was almost tonguetied by then, but I seriously hadn't expected him to respond that way. We tried to finish eating lunch but ended up only moving the food around on our plates, so we gave up and slowly walked back to his car for the ride back to my office. After he'd parked the car in front of my building, he turned and asked me for a hug. He said, 'I just want to feel you, I want to see what you feel like.' I nodded, but I was stiff and nervous. He gave me this tender hug, and it really turned me on.

"After that we started to talk on the phone about once every other week. I'd call him or he'd call me. Then we both attended a big conference out of town.

"I'd bought all these sexy nighties and stuff, just in case, but I kept telling myself, 'I'm not going to do this. I'm not going to let anything happen. Well if anything happens, I'm not going to try to stop it, but I'm not going to initiate it.' Well, he was obviously thinking the same thing, but I didn't know it. We got there and the atmosphere was perfect for romance, but I just couldn't approach him that way. I'd never been outside my marriage before, and the idea of it scared me. Nine months had passed since I'd told him how I felt, and the fire that he had started inside of me with that one comment and that sweet hug was still there. And let me tell you, nine months is a long time to fantasize about being with someone.

"He came to my room one evening for a drink and was sitting in a chair talking to me. It was getting late, so I said, 'You've got to go. You can't be in my room.' I was getting weak and I was scared because I was still thinking at that point in time that if you have an affair and you're married, you'll have to go home, confess, and get a divorce.

"We went on a date the next night, and of course, we started talking about sex. Why is it that when you're attracted to someone the conversation always seems to turn to sex? He told me his wife withholds sex as a form of punishment when she's mad at him, and he told me all about the problems they were having. I told him my problems, too, because we all have them, but we still didn't have sex that night. We didn't make love at all the whole time we were there. We didn't sleep together until a few months later, and by then I couldn't use the excuse that it just happened. I'd had a long time to think about it. Later he told me, 'Yes, I did want to be with you, but I wasn't about to initiate it. I would've gone along with it, but there was no way I would ever initiate it.'

"Seven months later when we went out of town for another conference I finally got up the nerve to approach him. I told him that I wanted him to come to my room after dinner was over. It was hard to sit through that dinner and keep my mind on the speaker. All I could think about was the fact that I'd invited this married man up to my room. I was a married woman, and I hoped I wasn't making the biggest mistake of my life. Right after dinner, in which I could barely finish my salad let alone even touch the rest of the meal, I pleaded a headache and declined a friend's offer of getting a drink at the bar. Instead, I rushed up to my room to shower and change. About an hour later he knocked at my door, and I took a deep breath and went to let him in. He'd taken off his dress shirt and pants and had changed into a black turtleneck and khaki pants, and he was looking and smelling good. I had deliberated between wearing my robe with nothing underneath or my floor-length nightie, but I opted for a simple linen dress with no underwear. I could only be so bold.

"I offered him a drink and he sat down in the chair across from my bed while I perched at the end of the bed, making sure to keep my legs crossed because I didn't want him to see everything all at once.

"When he asked me why I'd invited him to my room I told him that it was obvious that he wasn't prepared to make the first move and that it had been over a year since I'd told him I was attracted to him. That's when he told me that he didn't want to be the one to make the first move because it was obvious that I was wrestling with the rights and wrongs of having an affair, and he didn't want to push me into doing something I wasn't too sure about. He explained that he had had one affair in the past, but that it had ended several years ago. We talked about that for a while. Then I poured him another drink and poured myself one and actually got up the nerve to go over to him and sit in his lap. When I did that I noticed that he wasn't as cool as he was pretending to be because he had an awesome erection. After I'd leaned in and kissed him he asked me if I was sure this was something I wanted to do, and when I told him yes, he took over from there. And let me tell you, it was well worth the wait—guilt and all.

"I'm so in love with him, but I hope he doesn't break my heart.

And while we may never be together as a couple, I think we'll always be a part of each other's lives. I've tried to end it several times because I know it's not going anywhere. I'm one of those people who needs a goal. I've got to be moving toward something and this relationship seems endless. I told him when we first got together that our limit was five years and if nothing materialized in five years, I was going to end it because I didn't want to do this forever. Five years is a long time to figure out if you want to be together or not. My New Year's resolution this year was that I was going to stop seeing him, and I meant that until I saw him two days later. He came all prepared to break up because I'd told him that was what I wanted. He said, 'This will kill me, but if being your friend means I can still talk to you or we can go to lunch every now and then, I'm fine.'

"It's been six years and many New Year's resolutions later, and we're still lovers."

MISS DELORES, FIFTY-SOMETHING

"If my husband had an affair I just couldn't stay with him because I could never forgive him for cheating on me. When I trust somebody, I trust them with all my heart and soul, and when they take that trust away, nothing's left." Miss Delores was adamant in her response.

"Having sex outside of your marriage is not a mistake, and I know for a fact that I could not stay with a man who betrayed me. There is no excuse he could offer me that would make it all right. To me it would be just as bad as child molestation. There's no excuse and no explanation for it.

"That happened to a close girlfriend of mine, and she didn't leave her husband. She'd told me that it had happened after they'd been married a year, she'd been young and innocent, and not too crazy about sex but doing the best she knew how. She and her husband had been at a Christmas party at someone's house when she noticed that he had disappeared a little too long. When she found him in one of the host's back bedrooms, she was confronted with the sight of him on his knees with his tongue between the thighs of a strange woman, but it was clear that the woman wasn't a stranger to him the way she was calling him by his nickname and grinding her crotch in his face.

"I don't know what makes some women stay when they find out that their man has cheated on them. Even if he tells you that the sex was meaningless, I don't understand how they can stay.

"To me sex isn't meaningless. If he took the time to have sex with her, then it meant something. It would mean a hell of a lot to me to find out that my man has been intimate with another woman, to find out that he has given her something that should belong to me only. I'm sorry, but he'd have to go because I couldn't be with him anymore. I couldn't be with him and live a life all the time wondering whether everything he says to me is a lie. When I love someone, I love with everything that I have. I can't do it halfway. If he cheats on me, he's hurt me and when he hurts me there's no going back. I just can't be with a person who would do something like that. I don't care how much I love him."

SADIE, FIFTY-SOMETHING

"I think people have affairs because they want something different. A married woman might not feel like having sex because she's tired. She'll get home from work, probably have to fuss at her kids about one thing or the other, cook dinner, clean up the kitchen, and probably wash a load of clothes. By the time it's all said and done it's bedtime and the last thing she's gonna have on her mind is trying to find some sexy negligee to drape herself in before going to bed. I'm sorry but it just ain't gonna happen. The only thing that woman's thinking about is putting on a T-shirt, some comfortable cotton underwear, brushing her teeth, getting in the bed, and going to sleep. When the woman starts doing that then her husband is going to start looking to have an affair; he is going to find some other woman that is willing to satisfy him.

"I've had several affairs myself, but I never fell in love with any of them." Sadie was, as usual, straight to the point. "Girl, that coffee isn't gonna fill you up." She motioned to a waiter and had him bring us a platter of tuna sandwiches and some fruit. He was back with the food in less than five minutes. I guess when you're the boss you get service like that.

"I'm not the type of woman to stay in an affair too long because I get bored too easy. The longest affair I had lasted two or three years, and that's a long time because it can start interfering with your married life. If you stay in an affair too long, you start comparing one man with the other and that's when you think about leaving home.

"An affair that lasts three or four months is the best kind. You don't put your heart into it, just enjoy it, and move on. Let him know you're only in it because something is missing at home, you don't have any plans of leaving home, and you don't have any plans for him leaving his wife if he has one. Really, it's better if you have an affair with somebody who's married because if a man is single, he's probably out there screwing plenty of other folks and you never know who's watching. If he happens to be in a relationship with a single woman who really wants to make your life miserable, you can best believe she'll call your husband if she finds out that her man is seeing you and you're married. You've got to watch out for all that.

"We all know why men have affairs; it's because they're dogs. It's in their nature to mess around with more than one woman. My youngest brother and me talk about everything, and he's told me straight up that one woman is not enough. He said he tried to stay faithful, but it was too hard. As a woman, I have to give it to him because when he was married, no matter how many other women he had, his wife never suspected because he loved his wife and wouldn't allow other women to disrespect her." Sadie shrugged her shoulders and cut her eyes toward me. "I know it sounds strange, but he didn't want anybody else to hurt her even though he was risking hurting her himself if she found out what he was doing.

"Some men may have three or four women, and they do it because they know they can get away with it. Some of these wives know what's going on but stay there and put up with it. The longer you put up with it, the longer he's going to keep on doing it because he feels like he can do anything he wants to. He might go so far as to disrespect you by bringing all of the signs of an affair home because you won't stand up for yourself.

"My husband has had plenty of affairs, he was the town stallion when I met him and had women galore," Sadie said. "I can never say I've seen him with someone else because he was the type that liked to party by himself. I didn't go out with him very often so I'd hear things. I was never able to catch him, and when I'd ask him about it he would deny it. Women called our house all the time and hung up on me. One woman even called and told me that the reason he wasn't home with me one night was because he was with her. I just calmly asked, 'Well, who are you, darlin'?' She said, 'His woman.' And I could tell she was surprised that I hadn't gone off on her. I simply replied, 'Well, that's fine because I'm his wife,' and she slammed the phone down in my ear.

"I can be pretty cool 'cause I'm a bitch myself, and it takes a bitch to know a bitch. So whenever somebody called me and asked, 'Is Maurice there?' I'd just say, 'No, darlin', but this is his wife, can I help you?' The bold ones would keep on and say something like, 'No, I need to speak with him . . .' and I'd be just as bold and respond, 'Well, darlin', he's not here. He's out in the streets. Check that club over at so and so. You'll probably find him there.' I wouldn't go off on the phone, but I'd cuss his ass out good when he got home. I'd never get mad at the woman on the phone; don't ever do that. If you get mad and ask her, 'Who the hell are you, goddamnit,' she'll know you're having problems at home and that you're insecure. Just be cool, calm, and collected, and say, 'Well, darlin', I'm sorry he's not here to talk to you, but he'll be home shortly. He's here every night; is there a message I can pass on to him in case you miss him?' You have got to keep your cool, and that way she'll start thinking, 'That bitch is happy. I don't care what he's telling me about wanting to leave his wife. That man is taking care of that woman.'

"The last time my husband had an affair, I found out about it and I told him, 'You've got to be the stupidest man in the world to have let me find out.' I think he messed around because he was trying to prove something to himself because he'd gone out drinking and didn't come home all night long. When I woke up and noticed he hadn't come home I got worried because it wasn't something he'd normally do. When he finally came home it was seven in the morning and he was drunk and smelling like sex because he hadn't even taken the time to shower. I said, 'Where in the hell have you been?' He said, 'Out gambling. Shit, I'm going to sleep. I'm tired.'

"When he went to bed I went through his pockets and found some matches with the name of a motel on it, so I called the number and asked for my husband. The person at the other end of the phone said, 'I'm sorry, ma'am, but he's already checked out.' I hung up the phone and thought, 'How stupid could you be to use your real name at a motel?'

"He still won't talk about it, and it's been over seven years ago. If I bring it up, he'll get fighting mad and leave because he knows I know what happened. He'd taken some whore to that motel room and I don't know what all they did, but I do know that she stole every dime he had. I think she got him drunk and when he went to sleep she took everything he had because when he came home he didn't have a penny in his pocket, and his leather jacket was missing. When I asked him about the jacket he said he was drunk when he went to this gambling shack and that somebody stole it when he hung it up. He sticks to that story to this day, but he hasn't set foot in a club since it happened."

MINA, FORTY-SOMETHING

"I've never been the kind of woman to believe that my man is so in love with my ass he'd never even look at another woman," Mina scoffed. "That's just being naive. If he's had an affair since we've been married, I couldn't prove it, and he certainly has been smooth about it because he hasn't stopped doing any of the things for me that he's always done. I know he loves me. I know that if I don't know anything else, but that doesn't mean he isn't going to mess around. He's only human. I just don't want it to be in my face.

"Don't get messy if you're going to have an affair. It's all about respect. If your spouse finds out you're messing around, the trust will be gone and when that happens, what's the point of staying together? I don't want to be wondering where my husband is every time he's out of my sight, and I damn sure don't want him checking up on me every five minutes.

"Now a few years ago, if you would've asked me if I'd ever had an affair I would've looked at you like you were crazy and replied, 'Affair? Me? No, that's the worse thing in the world you can do to somebody you love.' I knew how much it could hurt 'cause it had happened to me. There was never any doubt in my mind that I would even think of being unfaithful to my husband. I didn't daydream about other men, didn't even wish for another man. I was more shocked than anyone else would've been, had they known, when I found myself in an affair that lasted for more than five years. The experience was both good and bad, and notice I use the past tense because no matter what anybody tells you, the affair eventually ends.

"The first time we spoke to one another was on the elevator of the building where my dance studio is located. I had just left the studio, and he'd just gotten off work too. When I got outside I noticed that it had started to rain—just a light sprinkle. Well, he was right beside me as we stepped outside, so he offered me his umbrella. He is very much a gentleman. Now every time it sprinkles, I think about him. Anyway, we introduced ourselves and both went on about our business of getting home.

"After that first hello I found myself looking for him in the parking lot or getting on or off the elevator. He located my office number from the building directory and started calling. At first it was just every now and then, but it wasn't long before it was every day. I was halfway teasing when I warned him he'd spoil me if he kept it up, and I didn't know how much I looked forward to hearing from him until he didn't call for a couple of days. At that time, I was too naive to realize that I'd already fallen in love with him—or at least the idea of him.

"We met in March, talked off and on until June, and then he invited me over to his house." Mina sighed deeply as she reminisced. "We were sitting on his sofa one minute and kissing the next. It was like time slowed to a crawl because I can remember every single thing about that day down to what we were both wearing. He came toward me from his kitchen, carrying two glasses of iced tea because I'd told him I was thirsty. He was smiling. When I asked him about the smile he simply said, 'I can't believe you came.' Well I couldn't believe it either, but I'm sure he knew that.

"He sat down next to me, put the glasses on the table in front of us, then leaned over and touched his lips to mine. It was nice and gentle at first, like he didn't want to scare me off. But it wasn't long before we'd forgotten all about being gentle. I hadn't kissed like that in forever. The whole time we kissed I was telling myself, 'You can handle this. It's nothing—just an experiment.' It was a fantasy kiss, you know, those kisses that melt your insides and you get so wet you have to change your underwear? That's the kind of kiss it was. Each and every time we talked on the phone my panties got wet, and we could just be talking about something as simple as the weather, but the timbre of his voice just worked for me.

"I came from his first kiss, and the only thing that kept me from sleeping with him that day was the fact that his phone started ringing.

That's what brought me to my senses. It was like an alarm. If it hadn't been for that interruption, I would've been lying right there on his couch, making love with him.

"By the time the phone stopped ringing, I'd gotten the chance to pull myself together. I was nervous, confused, and embarrassed when I mumbled, 'I believe I'd better go.' He was a gentleman about it because he didn't try to stop me. I think he realized that this was something that I'd never done before, but I was obviously on his mind as much as he was on mine. When he called me to come back over after only a few days had passed, I went and by then we both knew what was going to happen."

Mina fiddled with her two-carat diamond wedding ring. "Before the front door closed, we were all over each other. My purse went in one direction and my shoes in another. The sex was good and from that time on, no matter when or where he wanted to make love, and no matter when or where I wanted to make love, we were always ready for each other and every time was like the first time.

"He was divorced, but he did have a serious girlfriend. What were the rules for that? What could a married woman ask of a single man? Was I supposed to give him an ultimatum and say, 'I don't want you to have a girlfriend because just the thought of you with another woman makes me crazy'? I didn't have the right to tell him that, and we never even mentioned her name. When we talked about our significant others, which was as little as possible, we just used her or him to describe them. It was like even letting their names enter into our conversation would interfere with our fantasy of one another. We were extremely compatible, but it just wasn't the right time in life for us, and he realized that from the start, but I didn't want to. I kept trying to make the relationship into something it could never be. I think I loved him as much as I'd ever loved anyone in my life, but my mistake was that I didn't try to hide it.

"I have to give it to him, though," Mina said, smiling. "He never tried to jeopardize my marriage. He never told me he loved me,

but I like to believe that he did. We were still lovers when he got engaged and married his girlfriend. You can't even begin to imagine
how much that hurt. You don't know how hard it is to have the man
you love tell you that he has asked another woman to marry him.
It's not like I didn't expect it to happen someday. I just didn't want
to believe it could. But whenever he started off a sentence with 'Well,
guess what?' I always knew it would be something that I wouldn't
like and he'd never have to finish because I would always guess. I
didn't want to picture him proposing to her over a candlelight dinner with soft music in the background or the smile on her face
when he put the ring on her finger, but I imagined it anyway, and
that time when he said, 'Guess what?' I was devastated.

"Then no more than two years after I went through the experience of him getting married, and yes, we were still seeing each other,
he again said, 'Well, guess what?'

" 'She's pregnant, right?' I responded, dreading confirmation.
But as usual, I hit the nail right on the head. And so it went. Not a
very pleasant period in my life, let me tell you, but I suffered through
it because I loved him.

"If I would've known how much hurt would be in store for me, I
wouldn't have given my heart so freely, and even though I knew
what I was doing wasn't right, the feelings I had for him were totally
honest, and I never felt guilty about being with him because I loved
him. I never got that 'it's not supposed to be this good with someone else' feeling. When I was with him I felt like it was just meant to
be. He was who I was supposed to be with.

"The last time he asked me that horrible 'Well, guess what?'
question I couldn't even begin to guess because I thought, 'What
else could there be? How much worse could it get?' He'd gotten
married, had a baby, bought a new house, found a wonderful job. I
couldn't imagine, but I knew whatever it was didn't bode well for
me. I took a deep breath and responded, 'What?' 'I'm moving to
the West Coast in three months. I got a promotion.'

"Well, that time my heart broke for good because he definitely had a choice as to whether he wanted to go or stay and he chose to go, and I had a hard time dealing with that. How could you have an affair with somebody for five years and then just up and say, 'Guess what? I'm moving.' There was no 'I'm thinking about moving' or 'There's a possibility that I might be moving.' When he told me about it, the decision was already made. He didn't ask for any input from me. His bags were nearly packed. When it came down to it, I finally realized that I had no say. I was merely the woman who had been making love with him for the last five years, nothing more and nothing less.

"To this day I still don't understand it. I don't understand how someone you've shared the most secret parts of yourself with can just out of the blue and over the phone say, 'I'm moving.' Come to think of it, anytime he had news like that to give me it was over the phone. When he dropped the news that he was leaving I felt like he was simply saying, 'The sex was good. I enjoyed the conversations, but that's all there was to it.'

"He never told me anything like, 'Hey, I really hate the fact that it's got to be this way. I'm sad that I'm leaving you, but it's really for the best.' All he said was he was leaving, and all I did was cry.

"He said, 'We'll still talk. We'll keep in touch.' We went from talking almost every day to maybe once every month or so, and I was doing good if I heard from him that often. He even came back home a few times and didn't contact me. I guess some people have to be knocked over the head a few times before they get it. I still can't believe how he took what I felt for him so lightly. It was like my love for him didn't mean a thing. I can't even begin to explain how much he hurt me and I still get angry when I allow myself to think about it because I still have strong feelings for him.

"He was on the West Coast for three years and returned to this area a little over a year ago. I had mixed feelings about his returning but so far everything has been fine. We talk on the phone a few times a week, mostly as friends but sometimes the conversation is flirtatious and it's always good to hear from him. The only reason I feel comfortable flirting with him on the phone is because there is still a good distance between the two cities we live in. Now it's not as easy or convenient to get together as it used to be in years past and until I saw him again for the first time, I wasn't really sure that either one of us wanted to get that relationship started up again anyway.

"Even if the relationship was reestablished, it could never be as innocent as it was the first time. I know that I wouldn't be as willing to open my heart up to him again because I *know* that by doing that I would be giving him the power to hurt me. He wouldn't do it on purpose but it's something that I can't allow for myself and I'm the type of woman who if my heart isn't involved, then the sex is just not happening. That's a dangerous combination, involving your heart with sex, isn't it?

"We saw each other for the first time after he'd been back over a year. Obviously we weren't in too much of a hurry to get together. He still looks good. We didn't meet for very long and the conversation wasn't about much of anything and basically we both just sat there smiling because we were happy to see each other. I really didn't know how I would feel about seeing him again after so many years had passed. After we'd talked for several minutes, he leaned over and kissed me and it wasn't just a peck on the cheek either and yes he still kisses as good as he used to and yes I was feeling it but I wasn't letting it go to my head this time. We talked a bit more before he had to leave and before he left of course I had to lean in for a second kiss because who knew when or if I would ever see him again.

"Since that meeting neither one of us has suggested getting together. I don't know why, maybe we're feeling one another out but I have to admit that it's probably for the best because I can easily see where getting with him could lead to. I don't need to go tripping down that path again."

KIANA, FORTY-SOMETHING

"My sister had a baby for a man who was engaged to be married to someone else. She never said so, but I think she was hoping he'd break off the engagement and marry her instead, but that didn't happen. He married his fiancée of two years and failed to break the news to her that another woman was carrying his child, hoping and praying she'd never find out.

"My sister was given a baby shower on the day of his wedding and after all the gifts were opened, she said to nobody in particular, 'Well, they should be married by now.' She was trying to laugh and joke about it, but I could tell she wasn't laughing inside.

"His wife must've heard rumors about the baby because she called my sister right after she'd given birth and started asking questions. Her husband had told her they were just good friends, and he helped her off and on since the baby's father was nowhere to be found. Can you believe it? This married man was giving my sister money, bought her a car, and still had the nerve to try to pass it off like he was this good guy doing a close friend a favor.

"I don't understand how his wife didn't realize what was happening. He even wrote my sister checks from a joint account that he and his wife shared." Kiana sucked her teeth. "Baby, that couldn't have been me. I would've acted like such a fool he would've been scared to sleep at night. I'm glad my sister didn't marry him because if he'd do that to his wife, he'd do it to her. She's better off without him."

KAT, THIRTY-SOMETHING

"Let me tell you something, baby." Kat dug in her purse for a cigarette. I swear, she only smoked because it brought attention to those sexy lips of hers. She lit the cigarette, inhaled, and sighed like it was the best thing she'd tasted all day. "Damn, I know I need to give this shit up, but I can't. I have so few pleasures in my life as it is." She took another deep puff, and then put the cigarette out. "I don't ever smoke the whole thing and I know I'm wasting a lot of money, but what's money when you're doing something you like?" She kicked off one of her high-heeled sandals and started massaging toes that were painted tangerine orange.

"Well, for one thing, I don't think affairs are always about sex. My husband has a high sex drive. The man would make love to me every night if I'd let him, but he doesn't have a romantic bone in his body. He's forgotten about all the sweet things that are needed to keep a relationship going. He's forgotten about the flowers, the wining and dining, the dancing. So, I for one know why I'm having an affair. I'm not going to lie. I'm doing it for the sweet things. I'm doing it for the romance, for the flowers I know he's going to show up with, and for those times when he sees me undressed, stops dead in his tracks, and says, 'Daaammnnn.'

"My lover knows a woman's body the way Mozart knew how to compose. He reads everything he can get his hands on about male and female relationships. He doesn't take it for granted that just because he has a penis and I have a vagina all he needs to do to make me feel good is put it in. He knows more about the female anatomy than a gynecologist. Whew." Kat blew out some air and fanned her face. "I know it's not just these jeans I'm wearing that's making me hot." When I asked her if he could kiss, Kat shook her head and lowered her eyes. "I can't even begin to tell you how good he kisses. He has these deep, sexy, wet, delicious kisses. You know that little piece of flesh that holds your tongue to the bottom of your mouth? It's sore for at least two days afterward, and I think about him every time I raise my tongue to lick my lips.

"I figure I can't ever take back what I give him, and when I told him that he said, 'I can't take mine back either.' That's when I told him that his could be flushed down the toilet.

"It's true. Think about it. And he knows I have certain rules. For instance, if he wants to see me and make love to me, then he needs to buy the dinner and he needs to pay for the hotel. I should be worth at least that much to him.

"He wanted to take me to Jamaica, but he suggested that I buy my own ticket so no one, meaning his wife, would get suspicious. Well, needless to say, we're not going to Jamaica." She kicked off her other sandal and began to massage that foot. "If a man wants to take me on vacation, all I should have to show up with is my purse. I shouldn't even have to carry a change of underwear if I don't want to. I want it to be like this"—she pantomimed taking out a wallet and handing it over—" 'Here, baby, if you want something, get it.'

"When he tried that thing about me getting my own ticket, I told him that for all the reading he did about relationships, he still didn't know how to carry off a rendezvous. He laughed, but you know what? He wanted to see just how far he could go with me, and if I would've bought that ticket, it would've been fine with him.

"The orgasms I have with my husband are nothing like the ones I have with my lover. I enjoy everything we do when we make love. I asked him once if the vagina felt different from woman to woman. He said that all a man feels is a soft, warm place. The only difference is in the shape of the woman's body and how you feel about her. He said that when it gets down to the sex, it all feels the same. I'd always thought that just like every man was different in size, thickness, and length, every woman was different."

CHEYANNE, FORTY-SOMETHING

Cheyanne was just about finished talking with me when I asked her about her affairs with married men. "I dated this one married man for three years, but it ended after we came back from a four-day weekend in Lake Tahoe." She adjusted the drape around my shoulders and picked up her can of Diet Coke. She drank Diet Coke like other people drink coffee.

"Of course he went and explained his absence to his wife in a way

I'd clearly warned him not to. He has a grown son from a previous marriage, and he told his wife that the two of them were going to go on a fishing trip. I told him that wasn't a good idea because she could always check that out, but he ignored my advice, shrugged his shoulders, and said, 'She ain't gonna call me.' Sure enough, the wife called the son's job, telling whoever answered the phone that she was the son's girlfriend and when he came to the phone she hung up. By the time my lover got home, every lock on every door had been changed. He was calling me no more than an hour after he'd dropped me off saying, 'She knows,' and I asked, 'Knows what?'

" 'She knows about us.' I guess she'd agreed to let him in the house once he confessed to his wrongdoing, and he called me to break things off.

"I said, 'Who is this?' The whole time I was thinking fast and good thing too, because she was on the other line.

" 'I'm telling you, she knows,' he said again, slowly this time, like I didn't understand English or something.

"I continued to play it cool and replied, 'You must have the wrong number.' Well, I guess she'd heard all she could stand, but I wasn't confessing to nothing. If he was caught, then that was between him and his wife. She didn't find out about it from me because I am not the kind of woman to be calling another woman's house, hanging up, and shit.

" 'You know who this is, bitch,' she screamed into the phone. 'You were with my husband all weekend.'

"I said, 'Look, I don't know who or what you're talking about and I told you you've got the wrong number,' and I hung up. I didn't feel bad about it because I'd plainly told him not to use his son as an alibi. I found out later that she'd become suspicious because he'd called me one time while the two of them were on vacation. I guess she found the number on the hotel bill and wrote it down. When he went on vacation with me, she called my shop, found out I was on vacation, and put two and two together.

"We broke up after that, and I eventually started seeing someone else. This new guy was divorced and crazy about me. At least he acted like it because he cooked dinner for me, washed and ironed my clothes, and everything. He was too nice, as a matter of fact, and I didn't know how to appreciate it because I started seeing somebody else at the same time. This other man lived around the corner from me, and when my boyfriend was at work I'd invite him over. It was my house, after all, and he was a damn good lover. Well, I invited him over one time too many because we'd just gotten naked when the front door opened and there stood my boyfriend. I was so scared that I started to laugh hysterically. I didn't know what else to do.

"My boyfriend finally said, 'Look, man, I don't want to fight you, just pick up your clothes and leave.' After he left, my boyfriend turned to me and said, 'If you think you need to screw around, I'd appreciate it if you didn't do it in this house.' He didn't hit me, curse me out or anything. So, I said okay and the next time I met the other man at a hotel." Cheyanne stopped talking when she heard me gasp in disbelief. "I've already told you I'm not used to a man who treats me too nice. Frankly, I was surprised that the other man was still bold enough to want to see me after that little episode, but when sex is involved, what do you expect?

"One time I'd no sooner pulled into the parking lot of the hotel before a car came speeding past, almost running into me. Well, of course it was my boyfriend. He was driving his sister's car, and he'd been following me. I parked my car, and he pulled up next to me and said, 'I really wish you wouldn't do this, but if you have to, go ahead. I'll be waiting at home so we can talk.' Then he drove off. So, what could I do? I couldn't just go up there and screw that man, especially with my boyfriend knowing that was what I was doing. So I went on home.

"Well, after that I knew for sure my boyfriend and I needed to break up because there was no reason for me to be sneaking around screwing another man while I was basically single. It was obvious this relationship was going nowhere fast. After we broke up, he moved in with a woman who lived right down the street from me and married her a month later. And he had me believing he loved me so much."

VERONICA, THIRTY-SOMETHING

"I've had one affair and my husband found out about it. Seems like the shit always comes back around." Veronica drank down some of her Big Red soda and licked her lips. "I know it's a stereotype, but I don't care. I love Big Red soda, but I guess that's okay to admit since I can't stand fried chicken.

"I had the affair a year or so after we'd been married. I was in the military and got an overseas assignment. He was supposed to go with me, but he got this well-paying job so he couldn't. We thought we could handle it since the assignment was only for a year."

Veronica picked up the tartar sauce, looked at me, put it back down, and decided to squeeze lemon juice over her fish instead.

"When I got to Germany I started going to church. I hadn't been a frequent churchgoing person at home, and by that I mean I might have gone to church once every other month or so, but I wasn't the kind of person who was in church for Sunday school, teacher's meeting, usher board meeting, and all that. I was just a plain old bench member, but I'd been brought up in the church so I knew right from wrong, which is why I was trying my best to be a faithful wife.

"I started going to church every Sunday, but I've got to tell you, when you're not having sex on a regular basis and you've been used to getting it, there's this hormonal problem. I think it's called horniness, and I got a bad case of it about six weeks after I hit German soil. There was this guy living in my building that I became interested in, and believe me when I tell you this, I'd done everything I could think of to stay away from him. I tried everything from going to the gym every day, to going to church on Sundays. I even stayed away from the NCO club at first because I knew that he and his buddies hung out there every Friday and Saturday night. But there really wasn't anything else to do on that base but go to the club and pick up somebody to spend the night with. Well, unfortunately, after a few weeks of doing without, I hit that club and started chasing him."

Veronica eyed the chocolate cake with something close to love in her eyes, and then picked it up and turned it over facedown into the turnip greens that she was through eating. "There now, I'm no longer tempted. See, I do have willpower when I want to, but at that time in Germany I didn't have any.

"One night some friends I'd met had a party with food, wine, good music, and fine men as far as the eye could see. Of course, the object of my lustful affection was there because whenever there was a party all the people in our age group would show up. Like I said before, there wasn't that much else to do. A party was always a big event, even though the same faces were always there. I knew this guy liked me because he was always checking me out, and I made it clear that I liked him because I was forever staring at him. One of my coworkers told me I should stop being so forward, but I figured she was just jealous because she'd dated him before I got to the base, but it didn't work out.

" 'Damn, why don't you go over and give him a table dance or something?' She was acting real shitty as she tossed her fake-ass weave over her shoulders. 'You acting slutty enough. I thought you was supposed to be married, but you sure ain't acting like it.' I just ignored the hell out of her and when he finally got up from his table and crossed the room to ask me for a dance instead of her, she called me a bitch and walked off.

"We left that party together and after that we were a couple the whole time I was in Germany. But it was no secret to him that I was married, so he and I were both adulterers.

"My husband found out about the affair because that jealous-ass, weave-wearing coworker of mine wrote and told him about it. When he and I got together she got pissed off at the both of us and felt like she didn't have anything to lose by writing to my husband. I didn't even know she'd written to him until I got back to the States."

Veronica finished off the rest of her soda, then picked up her water and sipped it with much less satisfaction.

"My husband waited about two weeks after I came back home before he asked me if what the letter said was true. I confessed to it because I figured he'd probably done just as much as I had if not more. I knew how horny he could be, and there was no way he would've gone for a year without having sex. After I told him the truth, I told him if he wanted a divorce that was fine with me. I've always been a very secure woman and always felt like I could get another man. I was young, the house was in my name, and I made enough money to pay the bills, so I wasn't really worried. We didn't have a lot of time invested in the relationship. We didn't have children, and we hadn't even lived together for a whole year yet.

"Although he never confessed to his own transgressions I know he had somebody else because he changed the phone number right before I moved back home. Shit, that was a sign in itself. Then some woman left a note in the mailbox for him that said, 'You changed the number. I can't get through to you.' So I knew he'd done his dirt, but he didn't confess to shit. She finally got up the nerve to come over and find out what was going on, but when I answered the door and asked her in, she was so shocked she just turned around and walked off.

"I don't think I could have another affair because there's too much baggage that comes along with it. Now that I have children I think I'd be too tired to deal with anything like that. Besides, right now I'm pretty content."

CASSIDY, TWENTY-SOMETHING

"I recently had an affair, but I wasn't looking for it." Cassidy lowered her voice. She didn't want anybody listening in on this. "I know, I know, everybody that has an affair uses that tired line. It started with a conversation, and some of the things we shared were things I'd been missing and needed to hear. He said all the right things. We'd just sit there and talk, and he couldn't believe some of the things I'd tell him about my marriage because some of the same things had happened to him.

"He's the exact opposite of what I'd normally be attracted to, but the things he said are what turned me on because for a woman, it's more than the sex. It's what a man says to her and how he treats her. Men mess up when they try to make love to a woman's body without making love to her mind, and once a man marries you he thinks he doesn't have to do that anymore.

"I care for this other man, but I don't love him. I could love him, but I think I'm just having fun playing right now. We've only had sex two or three times and each time it was planned. I was a little nervous the first time we got together, but once I got there everything just sort of naturally flowed. The first time wasn't even at his place; it was at our office building. It was late at night after everybody had left for the evening. We were on the eighth floor of the building and all of the lights in the conference room were out, but the blinds were open so we could see the whole city lit up in front of and beneath us.

"He had me turn to face the window and took me from behind. He didn't even give me time to remove my panty hose. He just ripped the fabric at the crotch, pushed my panties aside and entered me, and after a few minutes I had the most intense orgasm in my life.

"After that episode he kind of cooled off toward me, so I thought, 'Okay, he wants to play the hit-and-run thing.' So I pulled back and quit calling and e-mailing him. That next week we ended up having sex on the conference-room table, and afterward he told me he'd decided to cool it because I was becoming too needy. I wish he would've told me that sooner because I would've tried to play it cool, and I wouldn't have been so freaky. But you know how men are. Instead of coming out and telling you why they're acting the way they act, they want to play with you and make you figure it out.

"I guess it was a good thing he decided to back off because I probably would've gotten too attached if I'd let myself go more than I already had. He'd asked me if I'd be interested in having sex with him and another man and I was actually thinking about doing it until he pulled away from me the way he did. I finally decided that since he's single and I'm married and I can't even try to compete with his girlfriend, I might as well leave well enough alone.

"If I had to give a reason why I chose to have an affair in the first place, what made me take the chance, I'd have to say it was what he said to me. He said all the things I wanted to hear, and he did all the freaky shit I wanted to do. It was worth it to me, and yes, I'd do it again."

MARCELLA, FORTY-SOMETHING

"Affair?" Marcella looked at me like I'd just lost my mind asking her a question like that. "If I'm married and see another man I want to be with, then I shouldn't be with my husband, not if that's what I feel. Why do you want to stay with your husband if you want to be with another man? I don't understand that. There are lots of times you don't want to make love with your husband, but if you don't do it somebody else will.

"I was talking to a friend the other day and she said, 'All my husband wants to do is have sex.' I said to her, 'Well, what else is he going to want? Why not? He gives you everything. He does everything for you, and if he ever finds somebody else that wants to have sex as much as he does, he's going to leave you.'

"Have you ever read that book about why men cheat? What was the main reason? Sex. I understand that not having sex as often as he wants to is no reason for him to mess around, but listen, he cannot help himself. This friend of mine will only have sex with her husband once a month, maybe. I'm not saying you have to do it every day or every time you turn around. I'm talking about casual sex with your husband. You're supposed to do that. If you're married to an old man, that's different. But if you're young and your man is young, isn't that nature?

"If you're married and your husband is pleasing you in almost every way, he's treating you nice, he's not treating you like a slut, he's very courteous and considerate of you, you should be thankful.

"And he shouldn't have to buy for you in order to get sex. There's more to marriage than just buying somebody something. I get so tired of, 'Give me this; it's my birthday.' 'What are you giving me? It's my anniversary.' I don't think relationships should be like that.

"With men it always comes back to sex. If you have a husband, I'm not saying you have to screw him every time he comes to bed because there are times when he doesn't want to and you don't want to either. There are very few men who want to every night when both partners are working. But, hello. If he's the one who wants to have sex most of the time and you don't, you should still give in."

EBONI, FORTY-SOMETHING

"I've dated a married man. I'd always told myself that I was only going to see him until the right man came along and I meant that. When we first started being together, we'd see each other every day. Eventually every day changed to two or three times a week. Then it was once a week until finally he just started calling me a few hours before he got off work talking about, 'I want to come by but I can't stay.' I'd tell him he could just keep on going then because he needed to make time for me, not just stop by, have sex, and head on home to his wife.

"It didn't take long for me to find out how stingy he was with his money either. I asked him for a big-screen TV for Christmas, and he bought me a nineteen-inch. I didn't complain. He'd asked me for a gold necklace and I got him one. He opened it, said it wasn't the one he really wanted, wore it for a few minutes, then took it off before he left to go home. When he called the next day, I said, 'Look I asked you for a big-screen TV, and you got me a nineteen-inch, but I didn't say nothing about that. I got you a necklace, and you left it lying here like a piece of garbage. I'll just let somebody else have it.' He was there to pick up that necklace within thirty minutes with his tight ass.

"He'd given me a bracelet one time, and I loved it. I must've shown it off to everybody I could. Once we were all hanging out at the bowling alley with our friends and since it wasn't my turn to bowl I was playing with one of those games where you can grab a stuffed animal with those claw things. And what do you think I saw inside the machine? It was the same exact bracelet he'd given me as a gift. That Negro had won it out of a machine, found a jewelry box, wrapped it up, and gave it to me. My friends must've fell out laughing when they found out. Then I started to think back to all the other things he'd given me. He'd probably won them out of a machine, too, with his cheap ass. When I asked him about it, he didn't deny it. He just shrugged his shoulders. I paid his ass back, though. Remember that gold necklace I'd given him for Christmas? I'd taken it to a jeweler and had a fourteen-karat clasp put on it to make it look real, and the only thing real about it was that clasp. When he called me a few months later and told me the necklace had made his neck turn green, I told him he probably just had bad skin. Cheap bastard.

"He was always lying to me, so I shouldn't have been surprised about anything he did. After all, here he was cheating on his wife with me. He was always telling me he couldn't help me pay for this, or he couldn't help me pay for that because his money was tight. He kept telling me how much his wife wanted a new house, but he wasn't going to buy her one because he was going to leave her. It didn't matter to me whether he left her or not because I'd known from the start that I was just with him until the right man came along.

"Anyway, one day this woman who I thought was a good friend of mine called me and asked if my boyfriend had moved. I said no. He told me he wasn't going to move, so I believed him. She went on to say that she went to the same beauty shop that his wife did and had overheard the wife talking about getting a new house. So, I started thinking about that and about the phone calls he'd made where I didn't recognize the number on my caller ID and just assumed he was calling from somebody else's house. I decided to drive by his house. When I did I noticed that none of the vehicles in the driveway looked familiar. The next time I talked to him, I asked, 'Did you move?' He said, 'No.' So I believed him.

"This same so-called friend of mine came by my house a few days later to go shopping with me. She was driving and took a detour through a neighborhood close to the mall and started going real slow as we drove past this beautiful house, and who do you think was standing out in the front yard with his truck parked right in the driveway? It was my boyfriend with this fool look on his face. My friend said, 'I told you he moved.'

"I don't know why he thought he had to lie to me. Needless to say, my friendship with this woman ended over my relationship with this man, even though she was right about him.

"No more than six weeks later another friend of mine called and asked, 'Girl, are you and Jacob still together?' Now, I'd already learned that when somebody asked me that question it wasn't a good sign, so I sat down ready to hear the latest. Come to find out this eighteen-year-old girl he'd been seeing lived in the same apartment complex as my friend, so I went over there. The apartment had a security gate, but my girlfriend buzzed me in as soon as I drove up, then she showed me where this girl lived. Sure enough, there was his truck, parked right out in front of the apartment. I parked, grabbed my hammer off the front seat, got out of my car, and beat the shit out of his truck. I must've broken every window on the motherfucker and was screaming and cursing up a blue streak. His ass finally came outside and he started cursing, too, because he was in love with that truck.

"Then here come the girl's mama talking about, 'Why don't you leave him and my daughter alone. He don't want you.' I told her that this was between him and me and I didn't have anything to say to her or her daughter. I can't stand it when a woman tries to put another woman at fault, like a man can't do no wrong. She didn't need to talk to me. She needed to talk to him, just like I was trying to. I finally calmed down and he left with me. Everything was fine afterward, except I didn't trust his ass as far as I could throw it.

"When no more than a few weeks later that same girl called and told me he was still seeing her, I was through. I said, 'Okay, I'll fix this.' I had her come over to my place an hour before he was supposed to be there so we could talk about it. When he finally got there I made her hide in the closet and told him to go take a bath, that his dinner was nearly ready. He went into the bedroom, stripped, and was about to walk into the bathroom when she came out of the bedroom closet. You should've seen his face. I said, 'I thought you told me you weren't seeing her anymore.' I had my knife and planned to use it until she got scared and got in my way when I was trying to get at him. He hurried up and got dressed and left my house with her stupid ass following right along behind him.

"Later, he called me and said he wanted to talk, but I said, 'Hell no.' When he called back and asked if he could come get some of his things, I said, 'Hell no, motherfucker, you must be crazy.' He came by anyway and stood outside my door, talking all loud and shit, until I told him I was going to call the police. He kept talking crazy, so to shut him up I let him come in, told him to hurry and get his shit because I'd called the police, but he insisted on standing there and arguing. Then he finally went outside, took his gun out of the truck, and started waving it around. The gun is never loaded. I know because I've known his ass so long, but apparently he's forgotten I know this, and sure enough the police drove up and took him to jail.

"You know that Negro had the nerve to call me and ask me to bail him out? I told him, 'No. Call that bitch you been screwing.' He said, 'I did. She don't have no money.' And I thought, 'You sorry bastard, that's just what you get. That bitch never did have anything to offer you but what was between her legs, and now when you really need something that matters she can't help you.' Well, I bailed him out. I did do that, but I was through with him once and for all. Here it is years later, and do you know that man still calls me every year on my birthday and Christmas? He finally realized it was his loss, but that's too bad."

SELF

SELF (self) noun
selves (selvz) plural
The total, essential, or particular
being of a person; the individual.
The essential qualities distinguishing
one person from another; individuality.
One's own consciousness of one's
own being or identity; the ego.

Work like you don't need the money. Love like
you've never been hurt. Dance like nobody's
watching.—SATCHMO PAIGE

What a desire. . . . To live in peace with that word: Myself.—SYLVIA ASHTON WARNER

Can't nothing make your life work if you ain't the architect.—TERRY MCMILLAN

No one can make you feel inferior without your consent.—ELEANOR ROOSEVELT

I know God will not give me anything I can't handle. I just wish that He didn't trust me so much.
—MOTHER TERESA

Advice is what we ask for when we already know the answer but wish we didn't.—ERICA JONG

AGING

CELESTE, FIFTY-SOMETHING

"When I think about getting older, sometimes I laugh at myself. A little while back, my sister was telling me that when you get older, you can't hold your urine like you used to, and now those days are here for me. You know, when women have children it causes stress on the body, and as you get older your bladder and everything drops. Things are just not as firm and tight as they used to be. When I have to go, I have to go. Sometimes I cough too hard and almost wet myself. You just can't control it. I look at myself in the mirror and I see wrinkles that I didn't have a few years ago. My eyesight and my teeth are not like they used to be. And my weight used to be much easier to control, so I'm reminded every day that I'm getting older.

"About five years ago, I'd just finished taking a bath and was drying myself off, and I caught a glimpse of my pubic hair in the mirror. One side was just about totally gray and the other side wasn't. I thought I was seeing things. You also find that your pubic hair gets thinner as you get older. One morning I looked down there and wondered, 'Where is all my hair going? Am I just losing myself?' I looked in the bed and in the bathtub. I didn't know what was going on. It seems like it was just gone overnight.

"My memory used to be excellent, but now I find myself making more notes because I can't remember as quickly as I used to. I tried to go to someone's house the other night and turned up into the church parking lot, thinking it was a street." Celeste laughed. "But I don't feel bad about growing older as long as I grow old gracefully. I'm even getting more mature with my age, and there are still many things that I want to learn. I'm just trying to stay positive about it. What else can I do?

"I looked in the mirror the other day and said to myself, 'Girl, just took at your fat stomach. You need to go sit your little fat ass down.'

"Then I got so tickled that I really did have to sit down."

MINA, FORTY-SOMETHING

"I'm not too crazy about growing old but what's the alternative? The first time I noticed a gray hair I almost had a fit because it was not on my head, it was on my coochie. You should've seen how fast I ran and got the tweezers and plucked it. No more than a few weeks later it had come back and brought a friend with it. I've been religiously plucking those two out along with the one that has shown up on my right temple. Gray hair seems to have a different texture than the rest of your hair. I swear, I'll brush my hair back and that one gray strand refuses to lie down.

"I'd thought it was funny when a few years ago my cousin told me how she'd sit in her bathroom, mirror in one hand, tweezers in the other, and pluck out gray hairs. Now she says she don't worry about that shit no more. She said she can finally understand why some men walk around with shorts and dress socks on—they just don't give a damn about what anybody thinks, and it's a pretty good feeling.

"I also don't like the fact that it's hard for me to lose weight as I get older. I don't eat any more than I did when I was in my twenties and I swear I must gain a pound a week. I mean, it's not like I don't watch what I eat and I'm forever at the gym, but let me go without working out for two days and I'll gain two pounds. I remember how I could eat Oreos and drink chocolate milk every day for lunch and could still slip into some size five jeans. But hell, those days are gone.

"And did anyone tell you that as you get older you get varicose veins or fine hairs on your breasts, not to mention on your top lip? Well, the shit happens. I remember being a child and going over to my friend's house to walk to school with her. I couldn't have been more than nine years old at the time. Well, my friend's mother bent down to give her a kiss and her gown kind of fell open, and I could've sworn that her breasts were twisted. Now I realize she just had stretch marks.

"I used to take my breasts for granted. At a size 36D, full and standing up as perky and proud as they could be, they would've given those silicone things a run for their money anyday. Even when I laid down they stood up. I thought that was just the way breasts worked. Now when I lay down, they almost lay down before the rest of me."

EBONI, FORTY-SOMETHING

"Getting older is kind of scary to me because I don't know what to expect. It's harder to lose weight, so you attract a different kind of man. Then the men that you're attracted to may not be attracted to you because you're older now and you don't have that young, hourglass figure.

"Now, don't get me wrong. There are men who appreciate my being a 'woman' and not a teenager, but I'm just not sure I can learn to appreciate it. I find myself looking at these young kids lately and thinking about how I used to have so much energy. They want to be in the streets all weekend, at the mall and everything, but I can't go all day like I used to. My ass is tired, literally.

"I used to be able to screw a man's brains out and not even breathe hard, even if he was about to pass out. Now I've got to drink some wine and try to relax just to get wet because I don't really even feel like screwing at all most of the time.

"I noticed some girls in the grocery store the other day and their legs were so firm. They didn't have no cellulite, stretch marks, varicose veins, or anything. I looked at them and wondered, 'Did I ever have legs like that, and if so, can they ever look that way again?' That's scary for me, so I don't think I'm ready to get old yet; I really don't.

"See, right now I can still put on something sexy, put on a little makeup and the right perfume, and go out dancing, and I might be attractive to somebody. I know it shouldn't matter what men think. But what normal woman doesn't want to be attractive? But as I get older I'm not going to have as many men looking at me, and the ones who do will be old just like my ass is old, right? Shit, I don't want no old man, even if I am old.

"Sometimes when I go to a place where there are a lot of young people, like at the mall, I notice that all of them are looking at each other, but none of them really look at me. It's almost like I'm not even there. I feel invisible, like I'm in a part of the world where I'm not important anymore. These young girls are so cute with their hip-hugger shorts and halter tops—no stomach at all and firm breasts. And here I am all covered up so my stretch marks and cellulite won't show, wondering why no one even looks my way. I guess I just thought I'd always be young. I never dreamed I'd have to hang out with old ass people—people older than myself—to continue to feel that way."

JAZZ, FORTY-SOMETHING

"I think the one realization is that as I get older, the closer I get to the inevitable. Other than that, getting older makes me realize that as I'm getting older so are my parents and their parents. I need to attempt to enjoy their company more. I don't think I'm tired because I've gotten older; I'm tired because I'm worn out. When I saw that first gray hair I just thought, 'Ooh, a gray hair.' It was like reaching a milestone. I'd never thought of myself as having gray hair and I couldn't wait to call my mama and tell her about it."

SADIE, FIFTY-SOMETHING

"I don't feel too bad about aging. When I was young it scared me because I felt that it would be terrible to deteriorate and get old and ugly, but I think that as you get older you realize that time's gonna change you. You're gonna get older and you can't stop it, but it's okay because everybody else in your life is getting older, too. I see it as a challenge to be the best-looking one out of all the folks my age.

"The physical changes bother you more than anything. You look at yourself getting wrinkles and your butt getting wrinkled and your breasts sagging and white hair on your coochie. You don't feel like you're as appealing as you used to be, but you shouldn't worry about that because your husband is not as appealing either. You're both getting old together. Of course, you will have to accept the fact that it will take longer for your husband to get hard, and then he won't stay hard very long because that's just the way it is for most men.

"I think the saddest part about aging in marriage is watching a man lose his ability to get an erection because when that happens, something inside him dies. It's like he doesn't feel complete anymore. I can't speak for everyone, but that's what happened when my husband turned sixty, and I was only fifty-three at that time. Now, when I wake up in the middle of the night and feel like I want to have sex, I go to the bathroom, pee, do what I have to do to give myself an orgasm, and go back to bed.

"Since he can't make love anymore, he drinks himself into a stupor every night so I'll think he's just not interested. But we both know the real reason he drinks like he does is because he's frustrated at the situation. I guess he thinks I must be getting it from somewhere else because anytime I'm late coming home he asks me where I've been.

" 'Out screwing,' I reply. 'Where else would I be?' Of course, I'd only say that to lighten up the situation, but I know he wonders if it's true."

AYOKA, THIRTY-SOMETHING

"Just like my little throw pillow reads, 'THE BEST IS YET TO COME.' As long as I'm able to come and go when I want to and not have all those aches, pains, and cellulite on my thighs, I'm looking forward to getting older. At least that means I'm not dead."

PORSCHE, THIRTY-SOMETHING

"I like growing older. I'm more in control of what I choose to do with my life and I feel like I'm growing old gracefully. I'll be forty soon and I'll stand up against any twenty-seven-year-old any day because I got it going on, you know what I mean? When I look at myself in the mirror I don't see an old woman. I feel really good about how I've managed to take care of myself through the years.

"I've still got firm, perky breasts. I figure that since we put lotion on our legs and arms, we should take care of our breasts the same way, so I put firming cream on my breasts. You know that stuff you use to keep the cellulite down? I put that on my breasts every single day and judging by the compliments I get from my boyfriend, it must work. I was with him the other day and I was wearing these thong panties and he said, 'Porsche, do you realize you'll be forty soon?'

"In response I sashayed over to him and straddled his thighs. I love walking around him half clothed. I'm proud of my body. I had my tummy done a few years ago, and I'm happy with the results so I'm thinking about getting my breasts lifted next. I mean, why not? People who want to build a house save money for it. I ain't building no house, so I can save my money and spend it on myself because the way my body looks is important to me."

GIOVANNI, FORTY-SOMETHING

"Girl, let me tell you something about getting older," said Giovanni. "My titties are sagging, my stomach is hanging, and I hate that shit. I don't understand why gravity has to be so cruel.

"The other day while I was sitting in the bathtub, I remembered why I'd come to prefer showers. My damn stomach has gotten so fat; it felt like I was sitting in an inner tube. I used to be so fine I could get just about any man I wanted. Then I got married, got comfortable, and had these kids, and all hell broke loose. It's almost like somebody took my body and gave me another one while I was sleeping because I certainly didn't realize I was looking like this. This body just snuck up on me.

"There's this fine, young nigga at work who flirts with me all the time. He's twenty-three years old, stands about six feet three inches, and weighs about 180 pounds, and I can just look at his ass and imagine screwing him all night. But, hell, I'm so damn tired I can't even keep my husband happy, so what am I gonna do with him? He keeps telling me he loves older women, but young men also like to change positions all the damn time when they have sex, and I'm too old to be doing all that shit. I wouldn't want him to catch a glimpse of my breasts hanging down in the mirror while he's working it from the back, so I ain't even trying to mess with him because I'd be too embarrassed to look at him the next day.

"I guess that's just life. You either get old or get dead, and I'll have to admit I'm not quite ready to be dead."

RED BEANS AND RICE

1 (16-ounce) package
   dried red beans

10 cups water

1 ham bone (or ½
   pound smoked ham
   hocks)

1 onion, chopped

1 green bell pepper,
   chopped

2 garlic cloves

½ teaspoon salt

¼ teaspoon ground
   black pepper

½ teaspoon ground red
   pepper

1 teaspoon hot sauce

1½ pounds smoked
   sausage, sliced

Hot cooked rice

Bring first 10 ingredients to a boil in a dutch oven. Reduce heat, and simmer 2½ hours, stirring occasionally.

Brown sausage in a large skillet over medium-high heat; drain. Add to bean mixture; simmer 30 minutes or until beans are tender. Serve over hot cooked rice. *Yield: 6 to 8 servings.*

SELF-IMAGE

VALEKA, FIFTY-SOMETHING

"I'm a very sensitive and loving person, and I try to make other people feel special. Regardless of what it takes, I want my family and the people around me to be happy, because it makes me feel good to see them happy. I'm not moody, I try to be a good, positive person, and I love to make people laugh. One thing I really enjoy is shopping. I can shop till I drop. I try to stay focused on the positive things in life because life is too short to be negative. I don't even like to be around negative people because they take your energy and bring you down.

"I've had many obstacles in my life, but I've remained positive and kept my self-esteem high, because that's what it takes to be successful. Every morning when I wake up I give God thanks and tell him how grateful I am to be alive and kicking. Then I go to the mirror and smile at myself because I'm proud of who I am.

"There may be people out there who perceive me to be totally different from how I really am, and there may be some who don't like me and talk about me. But that's not for me to worry about because, as my mama always said, 'If they killed Jesus Christ, our Savior, what do you think people will do to you?' As long as I know who I am and I'm happy with who I am, there is no need for me to worry about what others think.

"I do get a little sensitive when people make little comments about the way I dress because I love exclusive clothes and I have expensive taste. But do people know how long and hard I've worked to have some of those clothes?" Valeka asked. "Do they know that many times I had to shop at Goodwill when my children were young because I couldn't afford to go to the mall? No, they don't know that, and I don't have time to tell them, so if they want to talk, let them.

"I got that expensive taste from my mama; she was a lady with great taste and even though we were probably poor, we didn't know it. She made her own clothes, and her own hats, but when she stepped out of the house, you would've thought she had money, and I inherited that from her. So if someone wants to judge me based on my outward appearance, that's not my problem. No matter what people say or think, I'm still going to enjoy everything that I have to the fullest because I worked hard for it, I deserve it, and tomorrow I may not be here."

JESSICA, THIRTY-SOMETHING

"I think I'm a kind, caring person, and even though I used to worry about what others think, I don't anymore. By the time I got to my late twenties or early thirties, I learned that if people like you, they like you, and if they don't, they don't, so I don't worry about it, and I don't let it affect the way I live my life.

"Now, I had to develop high self-esteem but that didn't take much because my mom taught me that I should always be true to myself. Her attitude is, 'To hell with other people, they ain't doing nothing for me.' Since I've listened to that all my life, I guess I kind of feel the same way. As a matter of fact, when I was much younger I would let people talk to me badly and I'd sit there and listen instead of walking away. One time there was a bully on the block and she called me on the phone to tell me what she thought about me and what she was gonna do to me, and I was sitting there listening to her, crying.

"My mother came in the room and saw me and said, 'I know you're not letting somebody make you cry over the phone. Are you crazy? Hang up the damn phone, what are you doing?' But the thing was, I wanted her to like me because she was the bully and everyone was trying to be her friend. Then I realized that those people were probably scared of her just like I was, so why was I so worried about her liking me. It finally took my cousin, who is younger than me, to come over one day and tell her off. She said, 'Get your big ass off my cousin's bike, you too fat and you may flatten her tires. You need to go home with your big old, bossy self.' And the girl actually looked like she was going to cry by the time she left. When I saw that, I got over being scared of her real quick.

"With that said, I hope people will always know and say that I'm a nice person, not a bitch, because a lot of times, when people first meet me, they seem to feel that way. You'd be surprised at the number of people who won't talk to me when they first meet me, probably because I don't open up to people right away, but I don't trust everybody. I may sit back and be quiet in a room with new people, while others may go up and start talking freely. I kind of sit back and watch people and then pick who I want to talk to because I don't want to share stuff with people if I don't know who they are.

"Also, because I like clothes, I will look at people from their feet up to their hair and back down, just because I'm looking at their outfit to see if it matches or something like that. I only do that to people who I think dress nicely but others who are watching me may see me do that and think I'm trying to size somebody up, but that's not what I'm doing. Then later, when they get to know me and find out what I was doing, they feel badly about having judged me, because I really am a nice person. It just goes to show you that you really shouldn't judge a person before you get to know them, because if you misjudge, you could be missing out on getting to know someone who is really wonderful."

TAMIA, THIRTY-SOMETHING

"I see myself as shy, even though most people tell me they don't see me that way. I remember that as a child in elementary school when I was probably in the first or second grade, I'd lost a coin purse at school that was full of quarters, dimes, and nickels. Someone found it because they made an announcement over the loudspeaker that a coin purse had been found and that whoever had lost it could come to the office and pick it up. Do you know I was too shy to even raise my hand and tell the teacher it was mine? I just sat there and didn't say a word, and that goes against my nature because I love money. I may appear to be more outgoing now and I probably am, but I still see myself as a shy person inside.

"I know that I am an intelligent woman and that I have a good feel for people. I can read people really well. I can tell if they don't mean me any good and when I get those kinds of vibes from a person, I keep my distance. I'm a down-to-earth person and I feel things deeply. If someone close to me is physically hurt, I can almost feel their pain myself, and because I am extremely sensitive, I take things to heart. When I love a person, I love them hard. I don't take their feelings lightly, and I would never hurt someone's feelings on purpose, but I expect the same treatment in return.

"I'm a loner, and I'm very careful about who I call my friend. I like people who are real, who don't put up a pretense. I appreciate the normal day-to-day things in life like the smell of the sky right before it rains and the way the lightning flashes across the sky before the thunder comes crashing right behind it. I enjoy those experiences.

"I think I'm an attractive woman and I don't need things like hair extensions or sculptured nails or false eyelashes to make me look better. I think that I'm beautiful just as God made me, and God doesn't make mistakes.

"My self-esteem is high because I grew up being told that I was pretty and that I was smart, and I believed that. That's why I feel it's so important to tell children positive things. Once you believe in something for yourself, you don't care what anyone says about you. People I come into contact with think that I'm intelligent and successful, and that I got it going on, but that doesn't make me the person I am because I already feel that way about myself anyway. I'm a very private person and I know who I am, so if people don't really know me, it's because I haven't allowed them to get too close. I choose who I want to know me, and I don't worry what people say or think about me. Their opinion is only as important as I allow it to be, and I simply don't take their opinion to heart."

ALICIA, FORTY-SOMETHING

"I like myself just the way I am. I feel that others usually like and respect me but lately I've been questioning myself. Now I find myself wondering what I could've done differently when raising my daughter and what could I do now that would make a difference in her life.

"I think of myself as a good woman. I'm patient and kind and I am also a very strong woman. I try to do the right things in life so when I make a decision to do something I always think of the consequences first. Oh, I screw up like everyone else does, but I'm human and at least when I do screw up I turn around and try to learn from those mistakes. I want people to like me and I value my relationships with my friends and family. My relationship with my family is the most important thing to me.

"Usually I feel good about myself but it depends on what day you ask me. If things are going good in my life, then my self-esteem is high. If I feel like I've disappointed someone who cares about me or that I haven't lived up to his or her expectations, then my self-esteem drops dramatically. I tend to be pretty sensitive about the feelings of others so my self-esteem can be easily affected.

"Because I'm sensitive to other people, it matters a great deal to me how I'm perceived. I think it's normal to want to be liked. It hurts my feelings for others to talk badly about me so I work overtime to keep them from having a reason to do that.

"Most people who know me well know that I'm a nice person and that I would do anything within my power to help others. They know I love my family and that I work hard at my job and in my home. What most people don't realize though is how strong my faith in God is. I have always kept that part of my life private but without my faith I would be nothing and I probably should share that instead of keeping it to myself because I'm sure there's someone in my life who needs to see what faith in God can do. Hopefully my faith will get me through the situation I'm in now."

AYOKA, THIRTY-SOMETHING

Ayoka stuck the tip of her tongue out and looked heavenward when asked what she thought of herself.

"Hmmmmm," she said. "I don't like that question but I'll do my best to answer it." She gave it a little more thought before replying. "I really do love myself, I really, really do and most people don't believe that when they meet me. People think that because of the stuff I've taken from my husband that I must have some serious self-esteem issues but I don't think I do. I've even been told by my therapist that the only reason I've stayed in the affair for so long is because I have no self-esteem otherwise I would've moved on a long time ago. I think I'm being treated quite well all things considering. A trip to Europe paid for by a lover wasn't such a bad deal the last time I checked."

Ayoka laughed, "I haven't stayed in this relationship because I'm afraid I can't get anybody else. I've stayed because I just don't want anybody else right now. I know I'm a damn good catch. I've decided that I want what I want and I'm not just going to settle for anything just to have a man in my life, I'd just as soon not have a man because it's too much work and I'm tired of settling. I've settled for most of my life. I think very highly of myself, maybe too highly but if I don't who will? I'm smart, I'm a good person, I don't do anything bad, all in all I think I'm pretty dull.

"I think my self-esteem is high because even when people try to tell me I can't do this or that or that something won't work out, I don't let anyone set limitations for me, my only limitations are those I create for myself. I mean truly, that's what a lot of people think. 'Well, you know you're a black woman so you can't do this or that or the other.' Well, I tell you what; my not succeeding won't be because you've told me that I can't do this or that. I'm just going to say, 'Is that right? Well, guess what, I'm going to try anyway. I may not succeed at it but it's not because you said I couldn't do it.' That attitude has helped a lot in my career and in my life so that's what keeps my self-esteem high. My parents had always told me, 'There is nothing you can't do as long as you believe in yourself,' and that definitely attributed to my self-esteem.

"As far as what others think about me, I know for a fact that most women don't receive me well and I don't know why. Maybe it's because I don't dress very conservatively. I'm very feminine and I think sometimes they worry that I might try to flirt with their boyfriends or their husbands or whatever, but when they get to know me and like me, they're cool. So consequently, I don't have good strong relationships with other women initially.

"One time I went to a luncheon with some girlfriends and the question of the day was, 'What is your honest opinion about so and so?' Well, one woman said it best about how other women receive me. She said, 'When I think of you I think of flashy.' Well, I didn't exactly know what that meant.

"I was like flashy? What does that mean? I didn't understand so I asked her to explain what she meant by saying I was flashy.

"She said, 'You seem like you're always out to be seen.'

"I was like okaaaaay." Ayoka made a face. "My personal idea of being flashy is wearing too many rings, a platinum-blond wig, or a loud-colored dress." Ayoka pointed to herself. "I shop at Saks Fifth Avenue where flashy clothes and colors don't even exist. But truly, there have been very few women who have met me and told me that when they first saw me they liked me.

"Of course men are different, I've been told by many of them that the first time they see me they think of sex," Ayoka said. "They say, 'You're very sexy,' and I don't know how to interpret that. I mean, what exactly does sexy mean? I'd like to know if I'm being complimented or if I'm being told, 'I just want to get me some of that, you sexy thang,' Ayoka teased.

"In my opinion, being sexy is about the way you carry yourself. It's like, 'I know who I am, I know what I want, I know what I like, and that's what I try to portray.' I love feminine clothes, I got these"— Ayoka motioned to her breasts as she stuck her chest out—"and I like them. I ain't going to be flashing them at any and everybody but I ain't going to be zipped up to my neck either.

"So, back to your question, sometimes it matters what people think about me but it depends on the person. In emotional relationships, male or female, it matters tremendously what they perceive. I might put too much weight on what they think because I try to become who they want me to be as opposed to being who I am but in my everyday friendships, I tend not to care.

"I have yet to meet a person who spent time in my presence, got to know me, and still didn't like me. I don't know what they think when they first see me but once they get to know me they realize that I'm a fun person and if they don't, I don't care."

SADIE, FIFTY-SOMETHING

"I'm just a good old Joe, that's what kind of person I am, and I say that because I'm very flexible. I'm my own woman and I don't pretend to be anything that I'm not. I do and I say what I like, and most people who know me know that. They may not like what I say or how I act, but this is me and people can either accept it or not.

"I don't like to but I can go down as low as you want to go and do some street talking if I have to, and then I can mingle with the classy people just as well. I'm very personable and easy to get to know, and I enjoy life and try to make the best out of it. I've worked hard all my life, and I've played hard all my life, and it all goes together.

"And don't get me started about self-esteem because mine is probably too high. I never let anyone bring my self-esteem down because I like to feel good about myself. I get so tired of hearing about women who say they feel bad because a husband or boyfriend said she's too fat, or too skinny, or whatever. You have a problem with yourself if you allow what someone else says about you bother you, because no matter what anybody says, even your significant other, you have to feel good about yourself. If someone says I'm fat, that's fine because I'll just say, 'I'm fine and fat,' you know? I don't have to lose or gain weight to impress anyone else as long as I feel good and I'm happy with myself. When a man makes a dumb-ass statement like, 'You're just getting too damn big,' tell him to let you put on the right outfit and go out tonight, and show him what other men think about your being fat. Baby, there's a man out there somewhere who likes healthy women, believe me. If the one you're with can't love all of you, maybe you need to get someone who will.

"See, my brothers and my father always made me feel like I was a princess. It has to start at home when a girl is very young. I don't care if my hair was all over my head, if I asked Daddy how I looked he'd say, 'You're just the prettiest thing that Daddy's ever seen.' Then I'd go around with my hands on my little hips and say, 'Daddy said I was cute,' and no one could make me feel any different. I've always felt like I was pretty, and smart, because of the way they treated me.

"When I got older, old enough to go to a café or someplace by myself, my daddy would always give me a five-dollar bill and tell me, 'Baby, you keep this here because you're a special, beautiful young lady, and you may find yourself in a situation where you have to get out of a young man's car and make it home on your own. This money is for you, and anytime you leave home I want you to have money in your pocket so that if the man you're riding with tries to lie about having car trouble or something like that, you can just get out and wait for the next bus, there's one coming through here every hour. I want you on one if you ever get stranded. And always remember that there ain't no man out there who's better than you, so don't ever feel like you have to kiss, or have sex, or anything else to make him accept you. If he respects you and cares about you, he won't try to talk you into doing nothing you don't want to do.' Therefore, I never felt like I should have to accept being treated like anything less than a lady at all times.

"Of course I met a few selfish men when I was a young lady and I probably cared more for them than they did for me, but that still didn't change the way I felt about myself. Maybe he just didn't want me and maybe he didn't want to give enough of himself to fully accept my love, but that's a weakness on his part as far as I'm concerned and I don't like weak men. I never have, even when I was young. I always believed that if I gave my love to a man and he didn't accept me, that was his loss because I know who I am and I know I'm good. That's life and I just kept on stepping right to the next one. After all was said and done most of them had to come back and tell me that the biggest mistake they ever made was to let me get away and marry someone else.

"As far as what others think of me, it doesn't matter. There are a lot of women who can't stand me because I have such a strong sense of self and I'm very proud. When I walk into a place, people take notice. Some women look at me and say, 'She thinks she's something,' but again, that's their problem, not mine. That never bothered me and I don't have many women friends anyway because I know women will cut your throat. My friends are my family. I refuse to let an outsider stab me in the back because that would mean I was stupid. That's why I've only had one very close girlfriend all my life, and I've known her since we were little girls. We know each other really well so we've never had any problems."

JEWELL, SIXTY-SOMETHING

"You know, people can think and say whatever they like, you have no control over that. As long as you know that your life is meaning-ful, and as long as you're doing what makes you happy, don't worry about it. In your lifetime, there will be things that you do to help people and many times you may not even know how much it helped. But there will be other times when you almost break your back for the benefit of others and get no credit for it. That doesn't matter, as long as you feel good about yourself for what you've done, no one should have to give you any recognition.

"For instance, I was very active in the Equal Rights movement. When Martin Luther King Jr. was going strong, I was very involved with that process in the town I lived in, but not many people know that. I was the first black female in most of the places I worked, but my getting the job was always geared toward helping other black people to get jobs by getting my foot in the door first, and then working hard and making a good impression.

"The grocery store in the city I lived in wouldn't hire blacks at first. The leaders of the group I was affiliated with asked all the young people who had any type of skills to go to different places and apply for jobs, and be able to handle the job once you got it, and I was one of the first females they picked. It may not sound like a big deal now, but I was the first black female hired by Piggly Wiggly back in 1959. At first my hair was very long, almost down to my butt. But I had to cut it all off because the white women working there were older, and they wore their hair short. After I'd been on the job for about a week, the manager came to me and said that for health reasons, I'd need to cut my hair if I wanted to keep my job. Of course, they were just looking for a reason to let me go anyway, so I went to a black barber on my lunch break, and had all my hair cut off. You know how black folks felt about long hair back then, so it broke the man's heart to do it, but I knew it would grow back so I didn't even think twice about it. When I went back to work, that manager took one look at my head and turned so red I thought he was going to pass out. I just smiled and went right on to my register like nothing had happened, and I worked so hard for the next six months that they hired another black girl.

"Shortly after that, the local union contacted me and told me that they'd heard all about me and wanted me to go and apply for a job as a cashier at Safeway which was a newer, larger chain of grocery stores, and which would also pay more. Of course I needed the money, so I went in to fill out the application and, child, it was so long and detailed you would have thought I was applying for a job as the president of the damn company. Once I finished the application, they asked me to take a polygraph, and once I completed that, they hired me on the spot. Well, honey, over the course of the next year that I worked there, I took so many polygraphs that I could almost tell you what they were going to ask next. Every time the store came up a dollar short, I had to take a polygraph because I was the only black person there. That's not the only thing I had to deal with, I can remember that when I first started people wouldn't even come through my line. I heard one white lady say, 'I'm not letting that nigger touch my stuff.' I didn't even care because whether her wrinkled old ass came through my line or someone else's, I was still getting paid.

"That's only a little of what I went through in order to help open doors for other black people, but still, people who don't know me look at where I am now and say mean things. They don't know the struggles I went through, so I don't care what they think because they really don't know anything about me. You can't just look at a person and envy them because of what they have because you don't know where they've been or what they've gone through to get it. I never complained about what I endured because when you tell people your business, all they do is run and tell it to someone else and they're not doing it for your good either. They're not going to do anything for you so when times got hard in my life I kicked a few walls, and cried a few tears, and kept on stepping, because that's what I was always taught to do. Hard times and mean words didn't break me down or make me feel badly about myself, they made me stronger and wiser. I used those experiences as building blocks to help myself and others, and now that I can look around me and see how far I've come, I know it was all worth it."

JACKIE, FORTY-SOMETHING

"Overall I think I'm a very nice person. I'm giving and nurturing and I like being around people and socializing but I don't like being criticized and that's only because not many people are constructive with their criticism. If they're constructive with it, I do okay but if they're not constructive, it just tears me apart. I take it personally; I'm very sensitive in that area.

"My self-esteem can be extremely high but at the same time it can be extremely low. I'm bipolar. It's a disorder that runs in my family and a lot of us have it and actually have to take medication for it. When I'm high, I'm high. I talk too much, I'm extremely friendly, I spend a lot of money, and I want to give as much as I can to whoever I think needs help. But if I'm low, I isolate myself, I don't want to be around people because I feel like I'm not up to par.

"My lows aren't so bad that I might want to commit suicide or so low to where I can't get up in the morning and get myself ready. It's like I'm on a lower middle ground but not below the line which is kind of normal but to me that feels abnormal because I prefer being high. Who wouldn't feel good being up all the time and doing stuff?" Jackie asked. "So I have to take medication to keep myself on the midlevel and then sometimes the medicine just makes me feel weird. It makes me feel funny, so I don't like to take it.

"Sometimes it doesn't feel like it works at all, anybody who's bipolar will tell you that. My problem is making myself take the medication. I can feel so good that I forget to take it." Jackie chuckled. "Then if I forget to take it, I get higher and higher and higher but then I get real low. It's a gradual decline but I don't like that feeling so I just make sure I take the medication. I hate the fact that this is something I have to live with all my life. I also hate the fact that it's not something I can talk about.

"Sometimes my husband has to remind me to take my medicine. He'll just ask me casually, he knows not to pressure me. If he says, 'Did you take your medication?' I'll ask him, 'Did you take yours?' because he has high blood pressure. He knows that I need to take mine so I can go to work because if I get to the point where I'm real low, it may affect me. Therefore, I've got to take it all the time.

"I just wish I could talk about it. I don't want to have to go to some mental group or psychiatric ward or something to talk about it because to me, it feels like I have it under control. It would be nice to talk to somebody about it every once in a while whether it be my sister or my brother, it doesn't have to be a doctor. Even if I could just say, 'I've been having a hard time this week trying to stay up because I missed a few days on my medication' or something like that, it would help me. But because I can't talk to people about it, it's like I'm on my own. If I'm not talking to my husband about it, I'm on my own and that's hard.

"People think you're crazy," Jackie stressed. "People hear the words 'bipolar' or 'manic depression' and they right away think that you're mentally ill or mentally disturbed or whatever and it's really just a chemical imbalance. My brain just doesn't produce enough salt, so that's what causes it and if I take the lithium everything is fine. I'm able to work and have a normal life, but who do you tell that to? If you discuss it with someone at work, they look at you funny so I just live with it without talking about it. It's like a secret I have to keep.

"I've had it all my life but I was diagnosed sixteen years ago. My oldest brother also has it and my niece was recently diagnosed with it but I still don't talk to *anyone* about it, not even them. That's a burden I carry. It's so private and so personal that I don't talk to anybody about it except for my husband. A couple of times I've talked to a friend about it. She can't do much but at least she can listen, all I need to do is unload and get it off my chest and that seems to help me. But as far as just talking to people about it, I just don't do it.

"Instead, I pray and talk to the Lord. I ask Him, 'Help me to be able to deal with this, and help me to not read so much into things.' I ask and He helps, so that's what gets me through.

"I know that people don't understand the disease so I say I don't care what people think about me but, *baby,* I care. I care and I'm very sensitive although when somebody hits me with something you could not tell. I will not let on that you hurt me or did something to me to make me feel sad, but I take it straight to heart and sometimes things like that cause me to become very depressed. It just depends on what it was.

"Your manic depression cycles can sometimes depend on how bad an incident was. It could cause you to go into a deep depression or start you on a cycle to go up or down so I try to monitor who I'm around. I don't want to be around people who are constantly criticizing because I know how it affects me, even though they don't mean any harm, I just prefer not to deal with that. I know I can't live in a world where nobody ever says anything bad about Jackie but I can protect myself as much as I can, so that's what I do.

"For the most part, I just want people to say that I'm nice and cooperative. I like to talk to people on what they call the 'level of authenticity' where you're just you. Everybody can't do that because people are phony. Some people will act like they're themselves but they're really just being phony, whereas me, I try to be true. I'm trying to be me right from the beginning but when I feel them out and I'm not getting those vibes, I back away. Some people you hit it off with right away and some people you don't, but me, I'm trying to be real right from day one no matter what other people may do."

VICKY, FORTY-SOMETHING

"Let me start by telling you what kind of person I am. I'm pretty easygoing, which is something you don't often see in Leo women. I try to be professional, I'm a hard worker, and sometimes I work too much and don't allow time for pleasure. I'm very driven when I'm working on a project.

"I'm not a woman who likes to party, I'm not wild. As a matter of fact, I'm pretty laid-back. I'm into the arts, cultural things like going to museums, the theater, and the symphony. I love doing things like that.

"I danced ballet for fifteen years but I don't any longer. I had to quit when I was almost thirty and that was because it started to become painful and I found out I had rheumatoid arthritis. My feet were already messed up from cramming them into those toe shoes and my doctor just thought it wasn't a good idea to keep doing that. I hated to give it up because it's such a graceful dance and I felt beautiful whenever I did it.

"Dancing really helped my self-esteem, which although it was never as high as I'd like it to be, it wasn't completely low either. But it did hit an all-time low while I was going through my divorce. When your husband leaves you for another woman and an *older* woman for that matter, you automatically think something's wrong with you. Even though he was the one doing everything wrong you still believe that something *must* be wrong with you otherwise why would he have left? My self-esteem isn't as low as it was when I first got divorced but still it could be better.

"I keep reminding myself of the things I've accomplished and that makes me feel successful as a single mom. I went back to college and after two more classes I'll be done with my master's degree. I think that's quite an accomplishment for any woman with two young children. I've gotten A's and B's in my classes, a higher paying job, and bought a house on my own, so I remind myself of those things when my self-esteem starts getting low."

LADY, FORTY-SOMETHING

"I think I'm a nice person and now that I'm a little older I finally know who I am. I know what I want, and what I like, and I know what I'm willing to do and what I'm not willing to do. I have to admit that in the *extracurricular relationship* I'm in now, I'm putting up with some shit I don't normally put up with, but that's a choice that I make every day. I'm kind, loving, very giving—probably too much—and I really care about people.

"I don't like to see people living on the streets or begging for food, and when I watch those documentaries about people in third world countries who are starving and dying from all sorts of diseases, it breaks my heart. It brings to mind that I could have been born in one of those countries and those could be my precious children starving, and that bothers me.

"I even feel sorry for people who are addicted to drugs, I wouldn't wish that on anyone, and people who think of them as 'crackheads' or 'addicts,' who are sorry and useless, should stop to consider that they could have been unlucky enough to end up that way too. God loves that 'crackhead' just as much as He loves me, so I don't dare point my finger and judge people like that, because that could be me. If my mother had been a crackhead, or if my daddy had sexually abused me when I was a child, I could have ended up on the street as a prostitute or drug addict, any of us could have, so we should count our blessings.

"I work with kids in the alternative school and there's one kid in particular who reminds me of my nephew. He doesn't know who his father is, his mom gave him up to the state when he was twelve and he's been in and out of almost every foster home and school in the district, but I feel sorry for him because he really hasn't had a chance. Other staff members say it's useless to try to help him, but I think all the kid really needs is love and discipline.

"One day he got pissed off and said something to a teacher that he shouldn't have said, and she and another teacher were trying to get him to go to the office. I came around the corner and saw him, with that frustrated look on his face, and immediately I started thinking like a mother. He was getting loud and I called him by his name and told him to come into my office and sit down. I said, 'Now why are you out there getting all-loud and acting ignorant with these white folks?' and that kid just burst into tears and said, 'They always after me, everybody hates me and they're always on my back.' This kid has lived without love for so long that he doesn't trust anybody, not even his own mother, and he's just one of many. All I can do is try to pray for him, try to encourage him and give him some advice. He can't help who his parents are and I'm sure he wasn't born that way, so it's not his fault.

"What happens when you start treating a child bad all the time is they start acting the part because that's what they get used to. They may not be bad, but after a time, after you keep talking to them like that and telling them, 'You're stupid, you're ignorant' and this and that they figure, 'Well, okay, they think I'm stupid and ignorant anyway so I might as well go ahead and act like it.' I mean this kid cried like a baby and I know he didn't want to cry in front of me, but he was so full he couldn't help it. He just feels like the whole world is against him. He doesn't even know how to be good and make good choices because in the environment he grew up in, there were no good choices to make.

"I try to be careful with judging people but I also have to be careful not to be too soft because sometimes people will take your kindness for weakness. I've gotten to the point where even though I have a kind heart and I don't mind giving or helping other people, when it takes away from me or if I'd have to do something that I really don't want to do, I'm not going to do it, regardless. I used to

give and give and give thinking that maybe that would make somebody like me better, but I learned that some people don't care
about you no matter what you do. A lot of them care about what
they can get and that's all. I'm not saying that the majority of people are that way, but there are some people who just don't think
about other people. They'll take all you give them and then ask for
more, and get mad when you don't give it to them, so I don't waste
my time with people like that anymore. That's how I know my self-
esteem is much higher than it used to be, I think of myself more
now than I ever have, and I don't see anything wrong with that.

"I looked in the mirror one day and didn't like what I saw, so the
first thing I decided was that I needed to take care of myself better.
I started by working on my weight, not because of what other people thought of me, but because I wanted to be happy with myself. I
really don't even care what other people think anymore because
they don't have no heaven or hell to put me in, they're not going to
help me pay my bills, and they're not going to put my children
through college, so what difference does it make what they think? I
don't give a damn anymore.

"I've finally arrived at a place in my life where if I go in the store
and see a fifteen-dollar tube of lipstick and I like that color, and it
looks good on me, I buy it. But I'm not buying it because somebody
else thinks it looks good, I'm buying it because I think it looks good
and I think when you get to the place where you want to do things
for yourself rather than for other people, that's when your self-
esteem is getting to where it should be. Other people can tell you
you're beautiful, but if somebody has been telling you you're ugly all
your life that don't mean you're going to believe you're beautiful all
of a sudden. You've got to learn to care about yourself, you've got to
take care of yourself, and you've got to realize you've got one body
and one life and you need to make the most of it.

"If I step on somebody else's toes in the process of doing what I
need to do to be happy, I'll just have to tell them I'm sorry. If I say

something that hurts someone, and I didn't mean it that way, I'm not too proud to go back and say I made a mistake.

"There may be coworkers or people in my little circle of life who say I think I'm all that, but the truth is I'm not that way at all. *They* may think I'm all that, but that's their problem because they don't know the struggles I've been through. I'm a very proud and very private person, and I'm not here to impress anybody else, so I don't have time to worry about what people say. Sure, I have days where I think I'm sexy as hell and that I look good, but I also have days where I feel like I could crawl back into bed. I can't change other people's opinions of me so I'm not going to lose any sleep over it.

"It's just too bad they don't know me because I have a heart for people. If somebody asked me, 'Would you pray with me?' I would stop what I was doing right there and say, 'Yes, I'll pray with you,' even though I may not be living my life the way I should. If that's what they need, then yeah I'm there for them. I'd like people to know that I care about them because of who they are, not because of what they have or where they've been or what their title is; I am not impressed by titles at all. I'm not impressed if a person is a millionaire, I don't care.

"As a matter of fact when I see a limousine, whether I'm driving down the street or walking, I automatically look the other way. I am not going to break my neck trying to see who's in there, that person isn't any more important than me. And if I'm walking through the airport and I see somebody popular but they're dressed incognito, I'm not going to bother them because they're entitled to their space, and they're only human beings just like we are, so what?

"See, I'm just regular. I like to have fun and laugh, and be happy as much as possible, and I like to make other people happy. One time I worked with a young lady who was divorced with about four little children. She got fired because she couldn't really afford day care, and she had to take off work a lot. I figured she must be having a hard time paying her bills, so rather than giving my tithes to the church, I got money orders and sent them to her, but she never knew the money was from me.

"Now do I need to call her and say, 'You know that money you got, that was from me?" Lady asked. "I never told her that I was the one sending her money. I didn't send it to her for her to tell me, 'Oh, thank you so much.' I sent it to her because the Lord put it on my heart that she needed that money more than the church did. She had kids she couldn't take care of, so I sent it to her, and I did that several times, but I don't want to go and broadcast it to people because I didn't do it to get any recognition. It made me feel good to be able to do it for her, because she needed that money more than I did, and I have faith that God will send someone to do the same for me if I ever find myself in that situation.

"I'm willing to go all the way if someone I know needs me, but as far as letting people hurt me over and over again, not anymore. If I can't tell you how I feel, I don't need you in my life. Nobody has the right to force their opinions and their views on me and then not give me the right to say what I feel, that's not fair and it's unhealthy to be in a relationship like that.

"If I can't express my feelings, then I'm holding all this stuff in and I've got all this animosity, and nine times out of ten I'm taking it out on somebody who doesn't have anything to do with it rather than directing it to where it needs to be. I decided a long time ago that I wasn't going to hold my feelings in anymore and even though I tell people how I feel, I don't think that makes me a bad person. I have a heart of gold, but I'm not going to let other people keep chipping away at it until there's nothing left for me, not anymore."

············· # SPIRITUALITY

ALICIA, FORTY-SOMETHING

"To me being spiritual means to live your faith. It's wonderful to believe in God, that's all well and good, but I believe that you actually have to walk the walk and talk the talk. If you actually live and breathe what you believe, then that's being spiritual. Just going to church and mouthing the scripture doesn't make you a Christian and neither does singing in the choir and working on the usher board. You can practically live at that church, be there all day Sunday and go back for Sunday evening prayer meeting or whatever, but if you aren't actually living like a Christian in your everyday life, you're talking about people, being hateful, being mean, if you're going to church but you're still doing all that you're just wasting your time.

"As a Christian I know that I need to go to church more and talk to God more often. It's amazing how we don't turn to God the way we need to unless it's in times of trouble. As long as things are going well, I barely talk to Him but as soon as something bad happens like this thing with my daughter, I find myself talking to Him every day and you know what, He's always there, just patiently waiting for me to come to Him with my troubles. He never ever gets tired of listening to me. It is so much easier for a person to ask for help than to remember to thank God for the many good things in life. I guess I need to learn how to complain less and count my blessings more. I'm sure God would appreciate that."

VALEKA, FIFTY-SOMETHING

"Being spiritual is being God-fearing and loving other people as God loves me. It means caring about others, even when they don't measure up to what I think they should, and it means helping those in need when I have the ability to do so.

"It doesn't mean you have to go to church every Sunday. You can still be Christ-like by doing the things the Bible says you should do. Doing little things like making a phone call to an elderly or sickly person is a demonstration of being spiritual. When I do something like that, it just makes me feel good, and I know that I get that good feeling because the Holy Spirit is pleased with me. I feel that God has a purpose for my being here; He created each of us for something specific, and our lives are much fuller and happier when we are participating with Him to accomplish that purpose.

"I could always focus on trying to do better in my spiritual life, all of us could. I probably should make more of a commitment to community service, but you know how it is, we're so busy that we have to make time for those things.

"I'm always prepared to have prayer with someone if that's what is needed. The Bible tells us that there will always be those among us who are less fortunate. I try to always keep in mind that I'm wonderfully blessed, and not because I've done anything special, but because of God's grace and mercy. I never want to look down on anyone and think that I'm a bigger or better Christian, because I'm not. I'm still working toward being more obedient to God's will each day, and sometimes it's not easy because I'm human and I want to do things my way. There is always room for improvement."

TAMIA, THIRTY-SOMETHING

"I think being spiritual is believing there is someone or some being out there who is more important than anyone else, who looks out for all of our needs and even our wants. He's someone to talk to when you can't talk to anyone else, and I try to talk to Him every day. I'll say, 'Thank you for my job, even though I'm complaining that these people are getting on my last nerve, thank you for letting me have a job to come to,' or 'Thank you for my family and thank you for my health,' things like that. I may not get on my knees and pray every day, but I still talk to Him and usually I don't ask for things, I'm mostly thanking Him for what He has already given me.

"Even though I don't go to church, I know that I'm a spiritual person. I know the difference between right and wrong, good and bad, and I have high standards and good morals so I'm at peace with myself. That's more than what some people who live in the church can say. I'm a black-and-white type of person meaning, if I'm doing something I shouldn't be doing on a daily basis, then I'm not going to be going to church and trying to teach Sunday school. That causes too much conflict and I don't like to have conflict within myself."

SADIE, FIFTY-SOMETHING

"I believe you need a higher power to keep you going. Everyone needs that because otherwise you'd be walking the line, and you can't survive living that way. I'm a very God-fearing person. Although I'm not perfect, I'm a God-fearing woman and God knows that so I don't have to pretend. I can sit right here and talk to God just as I would if I was in church, so I don't think I need to go to church every day. That's not necessary, but many people get so caught up in the building and the activities and all that go on in the church that they feel they need to be there every time the doors open. God is not concerned about how many times a week you go to church,

He's concerned about what's in your heart. He's not going to bless Sister Tina, who goes to church three nights a week, any more than He's going to bless me if I only go on Sunday, because we can't work for our blessings.

"All you have to do is believe in Him, really and truly believe in Him, and believe that with Him in your life, running things His way, all things are possible for you. I definitely think that every member in the house should be a member of a church, especially the children, because things in the world have gotten so bad these days that if they don't know God, they'll have nowhere to turn if they mess up and Mama and Daddy aren't around to tell them what to do. I know that for me, my relationship with God has helped me through many tough times. No matter when I need Him, He's always there, never asleep, never ignoring us, always forgiving, and always loving us unconditionally, even when we mess up really bad. What more can we ask for?

"Even though my husband never sets foot in a church, I tried to make sure my kids were there because I never wanted them to say that I didn't try to make sure they were spiritually grounded. That is a huge responsibility, which I think more parents should take seriously.

"Don't get me wrong, I have a lot of growing to do myself, and I could always improve on a few things. A good example is my interpretation of the Bible. Sometimes I read things and think I understand, and then I go and hear someone else explain it and it's not the way I thought it was at all, so I'd love to go to some Bible classes so that I can have a better understanding. You know how it is when you're talking about something in the Bible with someone at church, and one person will say one thing that just messes up what you thought, and then you get all confused. You hate to ask too many questions because you don't want people to think you're stupid. So you just sit there and think, 'I'd better keep my mouth shut because that's not what I thought about this thing and I'll look like a fool if I start telling them what I thought.' Just like when you're in church and the pastor tells you to turn to a certain book of the Bible and you don't know exactly where it's at. You might ask somebody, 'What did he say, which book?' like you really didn't understand him, and the whole time you're looking to see what page they're on so you don't have to go to your index to find it. There have even been times I've wanted to say, 'You sure that book is in my Bible,' because I just couldn't find it."

JESSICA, THIRTY-SOMETHING

"To me, being spiritual means having a strong faith in God and believing and acting, as His word says that we should. When I was young, one of my parents was Catholic and one was Methodist. They combined and became Lutheran, but I don't know how that happened. The first church experience I can remember is when we went to this white Lutheran church, and they sang songs like 'Michael Rowed the Boat Ashore, Hallelujah,' and that was hard to get into because it was so boring. My mom said I enjoyed going to Sunday school, church, and Wednesday night service, but I really don't remember that part. I do remember the church and what it looked like because it wasn't your traditional church. The outside looked like an office building, but when you went inside there were chairs instead of pews. I think it was called an interdenominational church, which meant that when you walked through the front door, the different religions went into different rooms to worship. You know the Baptists went to one room, the Jewish were in another area, and so on. There were pulpits and a choir stand in each room, but because of the way it looked, it was just different. By the time I was in junior high school, we still went to church but we didn't go every Sunday, and we never read the Bible at home or had family prayer time and stuff like that, so it's not like I've practiced religion my whole life.

"When I was in high school I started dating this guy who was Methodist, so I went to church with him and I was like, 'Ooh, thank God, this is my kind of church.' It was a black church and I loved to go because the singing and the music was good. I did listen to the word when I went, but most churches don't speak directly to the different age groups and you kind of get lost in what the sermon is about. Most of the time I would listen to the sermon but when I walked out I couldn't even tell you what it was about, because they never made it relative to my life on terms I could understand. But it was still nice because of the atmosphere in the church, and because after church we'd go out to eat and stuff like that, so I enjoyed it. Then when I graduated from high school I went to a college where the only time I even read or talked about church was when I had to take religion as a freshman. I didn't have a car and none of the kids I hung out with belonged to a church off campus, so I never went. I didn't even start attending again until after I graduated from college. I really didn't have the normal, African-American, go-to-church kind of upbringing that most people my age had.

"I do attend church now, but I really should go more often. I'd like to find a church with children's services so that my children could go and get something out of it too, and not have to put them in a nursery or have them sit there and sleep through church because they don't understand what's being said. I don't think it's important to go to church just so people can say you came if all you're doing is sitting there babysitting your children. When I do go, I barely hear anything because I'm too busy telling my kids to sit still, or sit up, while I'm passing out Cheerios and juice to keep them from acting wild. I can actually just stay home and watch church on TV and get more out of it, so that's usually what I do. I watch it on TV and read my Bible, and I feel more satisfied than I do when I actually attend church. So what, I drive way across town to go sit in the church and not hear anything, just so I can say I went. What good does that do?

"I've tried taking my kids to Sunday school so that at least they'd get something out of the experience, but they told me they only like to go to Sunday school if they don't have to stay for church, because it just lasts too long. I can't get mad at them at all because it really does last too long, even for adults, but my husband doesn't want to

RECRUIT CARE KIT   3160028020
                                7.99
M290P M L/S TEE SAND LARGE
    4794748385   7.00
M290P M L/S TEE SAND LARGE
    4794748385   7.00

TOTAL $21.99
CASH $40.00
CHANGE $18.01

ITEMS 3
10-12-2006   16:09
1401 01 000111   5413

change churches, which I think is a little selfish. I told him that if it means we have to go to different churches in order for the entire family to get what we need, then that's what we need to do because the church we go to now is the one he grew up in, and I just don't get anything out of it. We are a family and we should be attending the same church together even if it means he has to move.

"I mean they almost hold you hostage. You're there all day because they don't have an audience until Sunday. They hold church until 1:30 P.M., then have the nerve to want you to come back for something else at 3:00 P.M., and I think that's ridiculous. You know, you spend all day Saturday grocery shopping, washing, cleaning, and stuff like that to get prepared for the next week, so Sunday is really the only day you have to spend with your family. It's nice to start the day with your family in church, but I just don't think it needs to take all day. I look at some of my white friends who go to church and they're there an hour, hour and a half max, and then they're out of there for the rest of the day. They heard the same word and can apply it to their life the same way we do, but it didn't take them all day. You go to my church, which starts at 11:00 A.M., but the pastor doesn't even get up to speak until 12:30 or 12:45 P.M. They take up two or three offerings, then ask you to give money for something you've never even heard of, but we never build a bigger church, and the parking lot has so many holes you could almost fall into one with your nice heels on. Why can't we do things with the tithes we give like other churches do? I don't understand.

"Like I said, the part I like is the singing and the music, so I don't want to lose that by attending a church where the music is monotone and boring. But it doesn't take an hour to do announcements and thank you's and all that kind of stuff. Why can't people just read the program for themselves anyway? Then, when they open the doors of the church for people to join, they need to understand that if someone wants to come, they're coming. You don't need to stand up there and say, 'I know I'm feeling somebody out there who wants to come. Don't be ashamed, just get on up and let the Lord have His way,' and all that. Sometimes I get so mad I feel like standing up on the pew and yelling, 'Hey, they ain't coming so let's just move on 'cause it's time to go home.' So, why should I go sit up in the church if I feel like that?

"The other thing is that I know we're not supposed to be judging other people, but I've heard so many bad things about some of the people in that church that it's hard for me to sit there and look them in the face. What good is it if I'm sitting there thinking negative thoughts? One of their associate pastors has such a bad reputation for being a womanizer that I don't feel he can tell me anything. That's like the blind leading the blind so it would be better if I didn't even know about his past. I'm not perfect, I can't judge anybody, and I know God forgives you for these things, but still, I think that's so hypocritical.

"I sit close to the back of the church since I have little children who always need to go to the rest room, and the teenagers sit right in front of me and talk through the whole service. They ain't hearing nothing nobody is saying except their little friends next to them. The parents are making them come every week and what for? That's why they need to have programs for these kids, they need something to do and they need to learn something too, otherwise they don't feel like a part of the church. Last year someone got smart and decided to let the teens do their own program for Christmas and it was just fabulous. No adults involved, just the kids, and they did a wonderful job because they felt like they were contributing. There was none of that old boring stuff that the old folks in the church are used to, acting like they were never kids and like they never had any fun.

"And finally, what really gets to me is you can't even wear pants. Why? They say, 'Come as you are,' but then turn around and say, 'But women can't wear pants, or shirts with no sleeves, and don't dare come in here without any panty hose on because we might not say anything to you but we'll talk about you so bad behind your back that you'll probably feel the knives sticking you.' Girl, I have heard them talking, right there in the church. I mean, does wearing a pair of pants mean that you can't hear what the pastor is saying? Sure, we need to be mindful of the fact that we are in a place of worship and we should be respectful and use good judgment in the way we dress, but are we really going to hell if we wear pants? I don't think so.

"Then again, these young girls are out there so bad I can sometimes understand why the dress codes are so strict in some churches. I recently visited a church where the pastor either closes his eyes during his entire sermon, or wears a blindfold. He explained it by saying, 'We say come as you are, but, ladies, I'm a man, and there are other men in here, and you can't be coming up in here with the same dress on that you wore to the club last night. You know, the one that's cut so low you have to keep pulling it up, and then it's so short that you can't even cross your legs, and the back is all out with them cute little strings crisscrossing everywhere? That's the one I'm talking about. If you don't have any respect for yourself, at least have some respect for the house of the Lord and for your sisters and brothers in Christ. It's just a shame the way some of ya'll dress on Sunday mornings, then you wonder why you can't find a respectful, churchgoing man who wants to marry you. Don't get mad now, you know I'm telling the truth and the Bible says the truth shall make you free. If you want to get free from pulling at your clothes, buy some that fit right and not tight.' Girl, everybody in that church fell out laughing because even the ones he was talking to couldn't deny that he was telling the truth."

AYOKA, THIRTY-SOMETHING

"Now that I'm a Christian, I've decided that I'm going to try to the best of my ability to live according to God's word, and that's a tall order. See, once you have that knowledge, it's hard because you can't use the excuse that you don't know better. You feel really guilty when you do something wrong once you know better, so I'm working on that right now. I've been so blessed, but I know that this relationship with my boyfriend is not right, even though I love him, so that's my biggest hurdle.

"I would like to honestly say that I don't want a relationship with him, but I'd be lying. Even if we continue to see each other as friends, I know we'd end up doing things that go against the word and knowing all that it's still hard for me to walk away. I don't want things between us to be the way they are, I want to be able to go to church with him, stand next to him, and hold his hand, and I don't want us to have to hide our love for each other, but I know that's not in line with the word. To want what we have is wrong, but how can being this much in love with someone be so wrong and how can it be such torment?" Ayoka asked.

"The more I grow in the word the more my spirit hurts, it tears me up. I keep telling myself I won't make love with him again, no matter what, but when we want each other, I can't say no. The people I'm really close to in my church who know about him tell me all the time that if I'll let it go, God will bless me with a wonderful relationship with the right person, but that's easy for them to say. How do you let go of something that's in your heart, do you just say it's not there and expect the feeling to leave? I've even discussed it with my pastor and he says it's a choice and that I've first got to get him out of my head before I can want him out of my heart but my pastor is a man and it's much easier for men to remove emotions from their relationships than it is for us.

"My pastor says that as soon as I make up my mind that it's done and over with there will be nothing my lover can say to me to make me want to stay in this relationship. So, I constantly pray and ask God to remove the feelings I have for him and when I ask, I mean it with all my heart and with every fiber of my being. But I also have to be honest with God and say, 'I'm asking you to help me do what's right, Lord, but you know that's not really what I want.' I don't know if it's worth it to give up on something you've wanted for so long, especially when giving it up means you could possibly be alone forever. I just don't know if I can do that. I mean, I love God, but I know that this man is the one who makes my heart smile—it just seems so natural.

"I realize that God gave His son for me and that He loves me more than any human being ever could, but I feel sad about the possibility of losing him. But why has my road been so rough? I'm not trying to become a nun. I'm just trying to live my life one day at a time and be happy. Why is my journey so hard? I often hear people in the church say, 'There are people who were on crack and they gave it up for God,' but that crack was hurting their body and destroying them so I can't compare that to my situation because he makes me happy. The only time I'm not happy with him is when I let my guilt get in the way; otherwise, he really wouldn't cause me any unhappiness at all.

"Of course there are other things I have done wrong that I can accept the penalty for, such as getting a divorce, because I know there are scriptures in the Bible that say divorce is wrong. But then another scripture makes it clear that God loves me and never intended for me to be treated the way my husband treated me, so does that mean I won't be punished? I even went through Christian counseling when I first got separated because I started going to church and I felt so guilty about filing for the divorce. The minister told me, 'I don't condone divorce and I'm sure I could provide you and your husband with some counseling to help you work out your marriage, but he's already said he's not interested in counseling and God never intended for you to be physically abused or spit on and called anything less than His child, so you don't have many options.' "

JACKIE, FORTY-SOMETHING

"For me being spiritual means believing in God, believing in somebody superior so that when all else fails, you can go to Him and know that He is truly there for you. You don't guess it, you don't think it, you know it, you know that He's there and when you pray you ask the Lord to help you be the best mother and be the best wife you can be. When you constantly confide in Him and let Him know how you feel about different things, and when you pray and talk to Him, asking Him to always give you the strength to handle whatever comes your way, that's being spiritual in my opinion. It's about having a personal relationship with God.

"I read the Bible all the time but I don't go to church all the time. I've never felt like you have to so I can't say that. My desire is to be more vocal if the situation presents itself, to let people know that I do believe and by being vocal I don't mean while I am at work I'll blurt out something like, 'Oh, the Lord blessed me with this.' I mean just to demonstrate it through actions, just regular everyday stuff. I don't want to be one of those people who go on and on and on, that's just a turnoff. Stuff like, 'Girrrrl, the Lawd is really using me.' I don't like that kind of lip service."

VICKY, FORTY-SOMETHING

"For me, being spiritual means believing there is a higher power—that there is somebody, something, or some spirit out there who created everything, and that we owe Him. I believe He is the one who helps you to direct your life and the one who you can bare your soul to without worrying about Him telling your secrets. I call that higher power God, even though I know people call Him many other names, because I was brought up Catholic. I went to Catholic school and I still go to Catholic church, but that is not what made me a spiritual person. In fact, going to Catholic school turned me away from the church for a long time because it was an awful experience.

"Back then, it may not be that way now, and this may not include all Catholics, but the majority of Catholics think that their religion is the only religion in the world, and that nobody else should ever believe anything else. Even though I was raised that way, I don't feel that the person sitting next to me has to believe the same thing. However, when I was a kid, they told you exactly what you had to believe in, and if you didn't believe in it, they'd tell you that you were gonna go to hell, which is crazy to me.

"I still get together with some of my friends from grade school and we laugh about this; we had to go to confession once a week. We had a funky old gymnasium/cafeteria/church, all in one room, and we'd have to line up in the hallway for confession and tell what our sins were that week, even though we were only in the second grade. Here we were going to confession for our sins, even though we didn't even have any, and we'd stand there and make up a sin because the nuns would say, 'You're all sinners and you have to go to confession and talk to God and ask Him for forgiveness.' So me and my friends would get together and decide who was gonna say they lied, or stole, or this and that, this week, so we'd have something to confess. We would just make it up, we still laugh about it.

"And those old nuns were so damn mean, probably because they never got to have sex. I mean, I saw them lock other kids in closets, and I was so scared that I never said a word in school. Boys would act up or do something, just being boys, and they would lock them in the closet and leave them in there all day sometimes. They were just so cold, they shouldn't have been teaching. There's this one nun I'll never forget, her name was Sister Mary Ann Carmelita. She was an ugly, mean, old woman, and she used to fall asleep at her desk every day.

"She would make kids sit under her desk if they did something bad, and she would kick them while they were under there. You could actually see her feet under there kicking them. And of course we wouldn't dare tell our parents because then we'd get spanked for being in trouble in the first place. That's the reason a lot of the abuse and stuff that went on then is still going on now. We were afraid to tell on anybody, so there was physical, verbal, and sexual abuse going on all the time. I can remember that one of our priests was there one day and gone the next, and it wasn't until years later that I found out they moved him because he was having sex with the boys. One of my best friends had a brother it happened to and his parents forbid him to tell anybody. To this day, that guy is just messed up. Someone that you trust is not supposed to do that to you, you know? Here these people are teaching you about God and His grace and mercy and then warping your mind with the physical and sexual abuse they inflict on you. That's enough to drive anybody crazy.

"So, when I got out of school and was on my own, I didn't attend church. I stayed as far away as I could from it until I was older and had met my husband and started dating him. I started going back to church with him because I figured we'd get married someday and we wanted it to be in the church, and that's the first time I can remember being able to enjoy being in a church, which is a shame when you consider that I was in church for most of my life.

"Because of my Catholic upbringing, I know now that there are some changes I need to make spiritually. I think I could probably do a little bit more with the church, be involved a little more, and get my kids involved so that they'll have a foundation. I would also like to understand what all of this is truly about by studying the Bible more, and that's something you have to really want in your heart. It's important to me, and I'll do something about it soon, but when I do, I'll have to find a different faith because I refuse to subject my children to what I went through. There are enough things they'll have to deal with out in the world, but when they're in the church, I want them to feel loved, and safe, unconditionally."

LADY, FORTY-SOMETHING

"Being spiritual means that you have a relationship with God, and that relationship impacts the way you live your life and the way that you treat other people. I think it impacts everything else in your life.

"It's not so much about going to church every Sunday, even though I enjoy going to church, but if I'm going to go to church and saying I'm saved, I can't live like hell Monday through Friday because I'm playing with God and I don't like the way that makes me feel. If I'm going to be spiritual, then I need to do what the Bible tells me to do but sometimes it's hard. I mean, how can I go to church and serve on the usher board when I know I'm having an affair? That's so hypocritical.

"See, you have to die to your flesh and that's hard. That doesn't mean that you don't get to do what you want to do or that you don't get to have fun, but you do have to be willing to give up your desires for what God has planned for you, and the only way you know what His plans are for you is to communicate with Him every day. You have to say, 'Lord, order my steps in Your word, help me to do what You want me to do today, let the words of my mouth and the things that I think about and the things that I do be a good reflection of me as a Christian,' because when we say we're Christians and then go out there and do things that are not Christ-like, that's a bad reflection on God. Other people who might want to get saved will figure they may as well keep doing what they're doing when they see a Christian living the same way a non-Christian is living, so we have to be careful not to mislead people by our words and actions.

"If He's my Father in Heaven and if I go out and do things that I shouldn't, then I make Him look bad just like if my kids go to school and act a fool, the teachers are asking themselves, 'What are these kids' parents teaching them at home?' I know how much I love my children, I can't even imagine somebody asking me to let one of them die for any reason. I can't imagine it, and I wouldn't do it, but yet God did that for us. I feel like I owe Him the respect and that I should obey His word, but my flesh is so weak sometimes.

"It's not like you get saved and then you live perfect the rest of your life, it don't work like that. But it could be easier if I was willing to give up my will. I think part of the reason I have a hard time with that is because I come from the era where what my parents said went, they had the last word. It was always in the back of my mind that I was going to do whatever I wanted to do once I became grown, but now that I am grown, I realize it's not that easy. I'm a born-again

Christian and I'm supposed to do what God wants me to do, so I'm right back to square one, I'm not a child anymore, but I'm *His* child.

"Sometimes you want to do something and you know it's wrong no matter how you look at it. You try to rationalize it by saying, 'I'm just going out to dinner with this really nice guy I met the other day, there's no harm in that.' But you know it's wrong if you're sitting there grinning up in his face and you'd rather eat him than eat the food on your plate, so you can't question God and say, 'Why does something so innocent seem so wrong,' you already know why it's wrong or you wouldn't have to ask. God only wants us to be intimate with one person because our hearts can't be divided.

"The Bible says you can't serve two masters because you love one and hate the other and it's the same way in relationships. If you start falling in love with another man, you don't want your husband to touch you and that's the reason God designed us that way. You cannot serve two masters and you cannot love two men, I don't care what nobody says. It's too hard.

"Being spiritual also means you're supposed to willingly obey God's word. You're not supposed to do it out of obligation, and it should make you feel good when you do it, if you're doing it for the right reason.

"If paying your tithes is important to you and it means you have to pay a bill a few days late, you have to have enough faith that God's going to take care of you. But then on the other hand, that doesn't mean go crazy and give all your money to the church and then expect God to miraculously come pay your house note for you. That's not going to happen, so don't be silly and act like you don't know better, and don't use God as an excuse for not handling your business. He's not going to send you to hell because you missed tithing that week. If the electric company is getting ready to cut your electricity off, use your own common sense.

"One of the things I try not to do is look down on others who are not as spiritually mature as I am. I've been saved a long time, but I still struggle *daily,* so I'm in no position to judge or criticize anybody. I think that's one of the reasons some people stay far away from church—there is so much criticism. If God says, 'Come as you are,' what's the problem with people accepting that? It's pitiful that some of the older ladies in our churches act the way they do toward the young girls in the church, acting like they've never cursed or had sex outside of marriage. You know some of those old heifers used to be so hot that it truly was a sin and a shame, but now that they're old and can't do anything, they want to judge these young girls rather than help them and that's sad.

"Don't get me wrong; I'll be the first to tell you that I can't throw any stones. I need to give up those people and those habits in my own life that keep me from having the relationship with God that I'd like to have, so I try not to judge anybody else, *lest I be judged the same way,* like the Bible says. I'm no fool, I know that God has real jewels for me, probably more than I could ever even imagine, and one day I'm gonna use my head and get rid of the fake ones I've been holding on to, because they're not worth a dime."

OLD-FASHIONED BREAD PUDDING

1 (16-ounce) day-old French bread loaf, cubed

2 (12-ounce) cans evaporated milk

1 cup water

6 large eggs, lightly beaten

1 (8-ounce) can crushed pineapple, drained

1 large Red Delicious apple, grated

1 cup raisins

1½ cups sugar

5 tablespoons vanilla extract

¼ cup butter or margarine, cut up and softened

Bourbon Sauce

Combine first 3 ingredients; stir in eggs, blending well. Stir in pineapple and next 4 ingredients. Stir in butter, blending well. Pour mixture into a greased 13 x 9 inch baking dish.

Bake at 350 degrees for 35 to 45 minutes or until set. Serve with Bourbon Sauce. *Yield: 6 to 8 servings.*

BOURBON SAUCE

3 tablespoons butter or margarine

1 tablespoon all-purpose flour

½ cup sugar

1 cup whipping cream

2 tablespoons bourbon

1 tablespoon vanilla extract

1 teaspoon ground nutmeg

Melt butter in a small saucepan; whisk in flour, and cook 5 minutes. Stir in sugar and whipping cream; cook 3 minutes. Stir in bourbon, vanilla, and nutmeg, and simmer 5 minutes.

Best Advice Received

GIOVANNI, FORTY-SOMETHING

"Unfortunately, there aren't many ladies in this world anymore, at least as far as I can see from the way some women carry on—cussing up a storm, drinking like a sailor, or laughing and talking louder than any man in the room." Giovanni went to the small refrigerator located in the storeroom of her bookstore and brought out a bottle of Kendall-Jackson chardonnay. She also unearthed some very expensive-looking wineglasses, uncorked the bottle, and began to pour. "I keep this stuff here for book signings and such. I also have some cheese and crackers. Would you like some?"

I declined, and then asked her how she'd learned to be so lady-like. "Not a day went by that my mama didn't tell me how important it was to look, act, walk, and talk like a lady, so it's a natural part of me, and I taught my girls the same thing." She sat down on one of the three plush sofas stationed around the store.

"I absolutely forbade my girls to call boys. And don't tell me how things are different today because they don't have to be. The rules have not changed when it comes to the fact that a man should treat a woman like a lady. I feel the same way about that now as I felt about it twenty years ago. If a man is thinking about you and wants to talk to you, then let him pick up the phone and call you.

"My brother, who is divorced and way too old to be dating by the way, told me that just yesterday in the span of two hours the same woman called his number twenty times, and he didn't bother to answer the phone because he just didn't feel like talking to her then. So, who's the fool? A man likes to be the one to do the chasing, so what's wrong with letting him? It's gotten so bad now that some men won't even take a woman out to dinner without expecting her to pay half, and if she doesn't pay half he's expecting sex. Now, why is that? Because women have allowed it, that's why. Women just don't seem to place much value on themselves anymore, and by value I'm not talking about how much she can get out of a man. I'm talking about respect." Giovanni leaned back on the sofa, crossed her legs, and held up her glass of wine. "Take a glass of wine, for instance. You've seen how some women will guzzle it down like Kool-Aid?" She shook her head in disgust. "A lady should always leave a few sips in the bottom of her glass."

I nodded my head in agreement, making a note to myself to remember not to drain my glass dry like I usually did. I like to believe I'm a lady, too, but there haven't been too many times when me or my girlfriends have left perfectly good wine sitting in a glass, especially when we were often the ones having to pay for it. I couldn't remember how many waitresses my good friend Tina had cussed out because they'd picked up her glass too soon when she still had one good sip left.

Giovanni didn't get in a hurry when she talked, either. She talked the same way she drank, slowly, like she was relishing the taste of her words. "My mama said that a woman should never try to measure arms with a man either because she'd lose every time." Giovanni could tell from the look on my face that I had no idea what she was talking about.

"A man can sleep with his wife's best friend and all his male friends will congratulate him on the conquest, while the women, when they find out, will shake their heads and say, 'That's a man for you.' But turn the tables for a moment and say that the wife decides to sleep with her husband's best friend. The conversation would be totally different. The men would think of her as easy and try to figure out how they could get some, too, and the women would label her a no-good, lying bitch who couldn't be trusted around their own men." Giovanni picked up her wineglass, took another small sip, and looked me dead in the eyes as she smiled slightly. "Did you ever notice how much more of an impact curse words have when they come from the mouth of a lady?"

MISS NORA, SIXTY-SOMETHING

"My grandmama's name was Emily, but everybody called her Ms. Emma and I called her Mama. She raised me and always told me how important it was to get a good education. She'd always say, 'If you get a good education and put God first there is nothing you can't do.' Well, I didn't finish school like she wanted me to, but I still put God first in my life.

"Mama was able to send all her children to college and her only skill was in knowing how to sew. If she made you something, you could turn it inside out and wear it on both sides." Miss Nora pulled a handkerchief from her pocket. "See these stitches?" The stitches were so tiny you could barely see where one ended and the other began and as straight as any I'd seen done by machine. "Mama made this handkerchief a long, long time ago. It's one of the few things I have left that was hers, and it means a lot to me." Handling the cloth as if it were made of gold, she brought it to her nose and inhaled deeply, and you could tell by that simple act that she was picturing her grandmother all over again.

"She also taught me that a man should take care of his woman," Miss Nora said. "I don't believe in giving men stuff. I was raised to believe that the man buys the food, the man buys the drinks, whatever."

"Look, baby, if he don't give you much when he's dating you, he's gonna give you even less when he marries you." She folded her handkerchief. "Now don't get me wrong; it works both ways. When my man got sick, I took care of him. I managed his checkbook, I paid his bills, I carried him to the doctor, and I got his medicine, but there ain't no way in the world I'm gonna let a big, strong, healthy man lay up in the house with me and do nothing except be there and then have the nerve to think I'm happy just because he's there.

"Mama was the same way, and she said time and time again, 'Ain't no man gon' come in here, lay in my bed, and eat my food if he ain't spending no money on me.' When Granddaddy started messing up with the money, she packed his clothes in a tin suitcase, took that suitcase out to the porch, and threw it up in the air. When that suitcase hit the ground it burst wide open and his clothes went everywhere. Mama then turned around and looked right at me and said, 'If a nigga care anything about you he'll do something for you.'" Miss Nora put the handkerchief back in her pocket, still reminiscing. "That was the best advice she ever gave me, and it's still good advice to this day."

BIANCA, THIRTY-SOMETHING

"Don't let nobody make a fool out of you," Bianca stated firmly. Her attitude indicated that she was not a woman to be messed with. No wonder men hesitated to come over and ask her for a dance whenever we went out. She was also slowly coming to the realization that she might not ever get married.

She tucked a strand of hair behind her ear and lay her tortoise-rimmed shades on the bar. Staring at herself in the mirror that covered one wall of the bar, she checked to make sure that her makeup was still perfect, and it was.

"There was this one man in my life I was crazy about," she said. "There was nothing I wouldn't do for him. If he just happened to mention that he'd like a steak, when he got home a thick juicy T-bone would be coming hot off the grill along with a potato, green salad, and red wine. If he wanted to see his favorite team play basketball, I'd get tickets to the game and they'd be the best seats in the house. When his birthday came, I had a limousine take us to the most upscale restaurant and nightclub in town. And he still broke up with me. And you know why? He said I didn't need him. I had a good job, I had a nice house, I vacationed at places that most people only read about in books, so what could a man do for me? He wanted a woman who needed him."

Bianca swung around on the bar stool and faced the dance floor where couples were grooving to Maxwell. One brother with a gold tooth winked at her. She scowled and quickly turned her stool the other way. "Shit. See? That's the kind of brother I get. I swear. Just last week I went to Harold's Barbecue in the old neighborhood and I guess the brother working inside called himself trying to flirt with me because he not only gave me an extra hot-link sandwich, he also threw in a bag of barbecue seasoning. He had a gold tooth too."

"Like I was saying, I don't get it. Wouldn't you think a man would want a woman who had something to bring to the relationship instead of one who can't keep a job, always walking around with her hands out, begging for shit? I ain't never wanted no sugar daddy. I just want somebody who I can love and who will love me in return.

"The best advice I can give other women is don't be buying and doing everything for him when all he's done for you is tell you how good you look, if he's even taken the time to tell you that." Bianca frowned as she looked toward the entrance of the club. She was watching that door like Mr. Right was going to step through it any minute.

She glanced toward the dance floor again. "I learned my lesson. I cooked for his ass, bought him shit, gave him these thoughtful cards just to let him know I was thinking about him, and you know what I got in return?" Bianca shredded a napkin between her fingers. "All I got was a hard dick and a broken heart."

"Something as simple as a card would've had me on cloud nine for days, but he didn't have a clue. So I finally got to thinking, if I don't even rate a birthday card, why am I wasting my time? I'd handed my heart over to him on a silver platter with a glass of champagne on the side, and he hadn't even noticed."

Bianca twisted back and forth on the bar stool, bracing herself against the wrought-iron railing at the bottom. "How can a man who can't help but know how much you care about him because you've made sure he knows it think it doesn't matter that he can't even take the time to buy you a cheap-ass birthday card? And hell, even if he don't care about me the way I care about him, the least he could do is pick me a flower every now and then. If he likes me enough to screw me, it's the least he can do."

EBONI, FORTY-SOMETHING

"If a woman's satisfied, she should never let her man know it. If he takes her shopping and spends $1,500 on whatever it is she wants, when they get home she still needs to ask him some shit like, 'Who in the hell was that bitch you were staring at in the mall?' They like it when you act jealous anyway, and believe me, if you're too gentle with a man, he'll mess you over every time.

"If I let a man stay at my house for a day or two and I say, 'Baby, I need some lunch money . . .'" She stuck her hand out, palm up, and I could actually picture some man pulling out his wallet and handing the whole thing over to her. "I'm talking about at least fifty dollars because the whole time he was staying with me, the lights were on, the air was on, and the water was running. All those things add up to bills." Eboni gave an exasperated sigh. "It's amazing the things a woman will do just to say she's got a man. She'll let him drive her car, and she'll not only cook his dinner and wash his clothes, she'll buy the shit. My advice to a woman like that is, 'Stop acting so hard up. Men have been chasing women for years, but if you don't give them a chance to chase you because you're so eager, chances are you'll stay single.' "

MINA, FORTY-SOMETHING

Mina got up and started pacing again. "When I found out that my fiancé had gotten another woman pregnant, I was this close to breaking up with him," she said and held her thumb and index finger an inch apart, "but my mama said to me, 'Baby girl, let me tell you something about life. That woman knew exactly what she was doing when she came up pregnant. She knew you'd leave him as soon as you found out. Now if you love that man the way you say you do, then keep him. Don't let her have the upper hand. I'm not saying he didn't make a very big mistake, but he loves you and you love him so stay with him and prove her wrong.' Believe it or not, that was very good advice because I've been with that same man now for seventeen years. When his ex-girlfriend found out that I wasn't going to just toss him out of my life, she told him he had to take his son, so we did." Mina stopped pacing, looked down at me, and shrugged. "Now I know that a lot of women wouldn't have done what I did. A lot of women would call me all kinds of a fool, but until you're in a situation, you don't know what you'd do."

SADIE, FIFTY-SOMETHING

"I'll give you some good advice all right," Sadie said as she poured more coffee in my cup without me asking. "I know about relationships if I don't know nothing else because I've been married over half my life, and one thing I know for sure is that a woman should never put sex first in the relationship. When a woman puts sex first, it overpowers everything, especially her common sense, and you know some people don't even have common sense. That woman will end up blocking out the important things she needs in life just because some man is able to make her have an orgasm. I ought to know because I've done some stupid shit behind men who know how to make love." Sadie nibbled on a sandwich. "Sex has definitely got to be the last thing on your list.

"The questions you should be asking yourself are these: Is he a good provider? Is he willing to take care of you, not just financially but emotionally too? If you can answer yes to both of those questions then you're lucky because that kind of man doesn't come around very often. It's much easier to overlook mediocre sex than it is to overlook a man who treats you badly or is unable to provide for you and your children. It's easy to find a man who's good in bed, but that only takes you through to your next orgasm and if that's all he's good for, in the long run he ain't gonna do a damn thing for you."

MISS DELORES, FIFTY-SOMETHING

"Remember your family because that's who you're always gonna have. You're gonna have that family if you don't have anything else. If there's a fire, you're gonna have that family; if there's a flood, you're gonna have that family; if there's fighting, when the fighting is over, you'll still be family."

JEWELL, SIXTY-SOMETHING

"When I was in high school my daddy told me, 'No matter what you want to be in life, be the best. If you want to be the town whore, be the best whore in town and you'll be respected for it.' That advice has always stuck with me, and I'll tell anybody, no matter what I do, even if I'm a nurse's aide cleaning shit, I'm going to be the best shit-cleaner you can find."

PORSCHE, THIRTY-SOMETHING

"I've been on this earth well over thirty years now and I've finally re-alized that nobody can make you happy but you. A man can change into everything you thought you wanted him to be, but his changing won't make you happy and you can't waltz through life blaming your unhappiness on someone else's actions. I don't know how many years I've spent crying and saying to myself, 'I don't understand why I can't be happy, all I want is to be happy.' Well, I've finally decided that nobody has any control over my happiness but me. I've finally decided that if someone is making my life miserable, it's up to me to change things."

Advice to Younger Women

CHEYANNE, FORTY-SOMETHING

"Stop running after men," Cheyanne advised. "I just can't stand to see a woman running after a man. I had this one girlfriend who could not take no for an answer. The man had told her that he wasn't ready to settle down and get serious with anybody, didn't bother to return her phone calls, and when she did luck out and happen to catch up with him he acted like he wanted to be anywhere else except around her. He finally had to come right out and tell her that she just wasn't his type before she got the hint and left him alone.

"Don't put up with a man's shit just because you're afraid he'll leave you if you speak your mind. If you do that and he knows it, you better believe he's gonna start thinking, 'She's got to have me.'

"A man ain't a necessity like food or water. And don't even let me start talking about those women who complain about some woman stealing their man. Somebody please tell me . . ." Cheyanne put both hands together as if in prayer and raised her eyes heavenward. "Somebody please tell me how you can steal a grown man?" She sucked her teeth. "Nobody can tell me how because it ain't possible. There ain't no way in this world you gonna steal a man unless he wants to be stolen and believe me, if it was that easy, I'd be Mrs. Michael Jordan by now."

VERONICA, THIRTY-SOMETHING

"I went to this women's retreat that my church held, but I only took the fun courses. I wasn't about to take some serious course that would scare me or make me think too hard. They were offering this one course on Revelation. The Book of Revelation scares me to death. I steered clear of that course and enrolled in one about the Other Woman and how she seduced your man. It was all based on the Bible. There are things in the Bible that surprise me. There's stuff about how ladies perfumed their sheets and covered their bodies with oils and powder. Women need to do those same types of things today. Now I know that sometimes we're too tired to even begin thinking about some oil or powder, but if your man likes a red light in the bedroom, buy a red lightbulb and screw it in. Your bedroom should be the best place in the house. The best place shouldn't be the living room or the kitchen. A lot of us use the bedroom to watch movies or sleep and leave sex as an afterthought.

"Before that retreat I hadn't bought new sheets in five years, but afterward I went out and bought some silk ones and some Egyptian cotton ones. If you've never slept on a silk sheet, you definitely need to try it because it's very sexy.

"I also learned that a woman should dress to please her man. If he buys me a short, sexy nightgown that I really don't even want to see myself in, let alone somebody else, I dim the lights and wear it anyway. Don't worry about no cellulite, that poochie stomach, or the fact that your breasts are sagging a little. Wear that gown and wear it with an attitude, an attitude that makes him think that he's lucky to even get the opportunity to see you wearing something like that. And believe me, if he didn't want to see you in it, he wouldn't have bought it for you in the first place."

Veronica spied a couple at a table a few feet away from us, so into each other that the woman pouring the tea had to ask them twice if they wanted a refill since they hadn't even noticed her coming up beside their table. "Now those two look like they could be having an affair," Veronica whispered. "That's the way a married woman should treat her husband, like she's having an affair with him. Slap him on the butt sometimes, tell him how good he looks or smells, and most of all, keep your eyes open for the small things, the little things that don't add up. You know what I'm talking about. If you can't do nothing to please him, then something's wrong. If the only time he seems to be halfway satisfied is when you're in bed making love, something's wrong. And when he starts picking at every little thing, asking, 'Why you doing this . . . I don't like the way you're wearing your hair . . . you need to lose some weight,' you need to sit up and take notice because he's trying to tell you something important. There's something going on that's much deeper than a hairstyle or a few extra pounds.

"I didn't realize that all those hints meant something until I found out my husband was cheating on me with my best friend. A woman needs to take care of herself, and by that I don't mean she needs to concentrate on getting her hair done or her nails polished, even though that's all well and good. But she also needs to hit the gym a few times a week or find a track and go walking every other day. Remember that whatever it took to get him will be the same thing it takes to keep him."

SADIE, FIFTY-SOMETHING

"These girls need to let these boys know they want to be treated with respect," Sadie stated firmly. "If a boy isn't willing to respect a girl, he needs to move on. I'm a true believer that if you don't have your self-respect, you don't have nothing.

"There are a lot of young girls and grown women who give their bodies away as if it doesn't mean anything, and that's unfortunate. If a girl wants a boy to respect her, she needs to respect herself. She needs to stand out from the others and be different.

"Men were made to be conquerors, so let them do the chasing. I tell young women all the time, if a man has ten women chasing behind him and you're the only one who's not, you're going to get his attention.

"Don't start off doing nothing you don't plan to keep on doing because the way you start out is the way it's gonna be. A man goes into a relationship expecting the woman to stay the same, while a woman goes into a relationship expecting the man to change. If you draw his bathwater every evening and then one day stop because you're tired of doing it, there's gonna be a problem. All he's gonna care about is the fact that you stopped doing what you used to do and wonder why you changed."

MISS NORA, SIXTY-SOMETHING

Miss Nora was always one to give out free advice, whether the person she was advising wanted to hear it or not. She was just like my mama, forever telling you some shit you don't want to hear about, especially when you know she's telling you the truth.

"Now I know about men, and a woman needs to be careful when a man starts asking her about where she works and what kind of car she drives," Miss Nora said. "He don't need to know nothing about all that unless he's trying to be a bo-weevil. You do know what a bo-weevil is, don't you? A bo-weevil is an animal who's always looking for a home and somebody to take care of him." Miss Nora crossed her legs and kept on talking, aware that my ears had perked and that I was nodding my head in agreement. She was in her element.

"I never let that happen to me. I wasn't no young fool, and I sure ain't gonna be no old one. If you went in there right now and looked in my bedroom you could see that I sleep on one side of the bed and I got my Bible, newspapers, and bills on the other." She sucked her teeth. "Ain't no man just gon' come in my house, lay up in my bed, or eat at my table without contributing nothing. If I'm seeing a man, he's gonna have to spend some money on me. I ain't talking about taking his whole paycheck, but at the very least take me out to dinner before you even think about taking me to bed.

"It's not that I can't cook. I just cooked some corn bread and a big pot of mustard greens this morning—six bunches and they taste damn good, but a woman should never allow herself to be used. Yeah, I got a house and I got a bed, but if he wants to sleep with me, he needs to spend his money. Don't try to use what I already got. I don't mind standing up on my feet for hours and cooking for him, but if he wants me to cook, we need to go to the grocery store so he can buy whatever it is he wants to eat. And I'm not gonna cook for him too many times if he don't put some money in my hand. You got to have money for almost everything. You can't do nothing without it."

KAT, THIRTY-SOMETHING

"My mom used to tell me all the time, 'Life is not a fairy tale.' Kat wiped off the lipstick she was testing and reached for another shade. She was totally ignoring the man at the next table who was staring at her like he'd never seen a woman so beautiful.

"I didn't believe her then, but I do now," she continued. "Wisdom definitely comes with age. You have to work hard to make a relationship work because it just doesn't happen all by itself.

"I'd always fantasized that my marriage was gonna be this wonderful Cinderella/Snow White/Prince Charming thing but it's nothing like that. Mothers should make it a point to tell their daughters that life is not always going to be Disney World, and sex isn't always gonna be fireworks and shooting stars. I'd always looked forward to being swept off my feet like that woman in the movie *An Officer and a Gentleman*. Remember the part at the end of the movie where he comes striding into the place where she works, sweeps her off her feet, and rides off into the sunset with her to live happily ever after? That's what I imagined because that's all I saw. I never thought about what happened to Cinderella and Prince Charming after they'd lived together for a few years and had a couple of children. I think that's why women get so frustrated after being married a few years. They don't try to see past the sweeping-off-the-feet part in the beginning. All of that shit changes after four or five years, when you've gained five or ten pounds and he couldn't sweep you off your feet if he tried.

"A woman should put her happiness before anything else, and she should never be afraid to let a man know how she feels. If he wants to have sex in the park but you'd feel more comfortable in a hotel, tell him. If you don't tell him and you go ahead and have sex in the park, jumping at every strange sound, he's gonna think you're okay with it. If you think your honesty will run him off, you don't need him. If he leaves you because of your honesty, he was going to leave you anyway. You shouldn't have to bite your tongue or get all stressed out because you're afraid to let your feelings show. Stop hoping and praying that shit will change and he'll suddenly wake up one day so totally in love with you he can't see straight. It's never gonna happen that way."

EBONI, FORTY-SOMETHING

"Why does a woman always try to change a man?" Eboni asked. "The reason so many women lose sleep behind a man is because they are lying up wide awake trying to figure out how to make him change.

"And what's the first thing a woman will cut off when she calls herself trying to punish a man? She'll start rationing her coochie out to him like it was some kind of endangered species, like he couldn't get it from somebody else if he wanted to." The phone started to ring again and Eboni ignored it. It was clear that she was still bitter about her divorce, but apparently she hadn't had a problem getting a new boyfriend. Men had always been crazy about her. "Withholding sex is not the answer. What a woman needs to do is just take him the way he is or move on to somebody else."

PORSCHE, THIRTY-SOMETHING

Porsche took a bite of chicken salad, hummed, and closed her eyes tightly like it was the best thing she'd ever tasted. It was pretty good. You can't go wrong with grilled chicken breasts, fresh squeezed lemon juice, walnuts, olive oil, and mayonnaise.

Porsche swallowed, then took another sip of wine. "That salad is delicious, girl. Okay, let's see, what kind of advice would I give to a young lady?" She thought about it for a few seconds. "I'd tell her to never put all of her eggs in one basket. Women have this tendency to go into marriage or a relationship with a mentality of 'This will last forever. I'm so happy. My husband would never leave me.' I mean, it's fine if she wants to think positively, but she still needs to be realistic. She still needs to take care of business.

"A woman should always put something aside for herself; I don't care if it's just five dollars a week. If saving that five dollars a week means not buying that Blue Bell Homemade Vanilla ice cream on your grocery list, then that's what you need to do, because, believe me, baby, when a man decides to leave, he leaves." Porsche took another bite of salad and chewed thoughtfully.

"I've personally witnessed three divorces of close girlfriends. All were middle-aged and not one of them had put anything aside for a rainy day. One woman had to sell her house and move into an apartment because she couldn't afford the house note. Her alimony payments didn't even come close to covering the mortgage. This woman hadn't worked a day in her married life. She had a master's degree in business administration, but when they got married she decided to quit her job and stay at home and be his wife. That was her job. He handled everything else. He left her when their youngest child was a senior in high school."

Porsche reached for a few of the purple grapes that I had brought along. "I would tell a young woman that she should never give up herself so completely. Sure, it's nice to be somebody's wife, but that doesn't mean she has to become a complete extension of that man. She should be able to say, 'Hey, I love you with all my heart and soul, but if you feel like you need to go I'll fix you a lunch because I don't want you to go hungry.' "

MISS DELORES, FIFTY-SOMETHING

"The advice I'd give to any woman is that she should test a man to see if he really cares about her. Start asking him for things. If she asks him three times and he still hasn't given her anything or he always has an excuse for why he can't, then she needs to let his ass go because it's clear he ain't about nothing but the sex. If he can't give her some little thing that might cost ten dollars or he can't find the time to take her somewhere when she needs a ride, but then he can turn around and ask for a blow job, he ain't worth it.

"My daughter met this guy and they had been talking off and on by phone for about two weeks, and you know what he asked her? He said, 'I been talkin' to you for two weeks, tryin' to get to know you and stuff. When I'm gon' get to know the cat?' She hung up in his face and when he had the nerve to call back, she told him not to call her anymore because he couldn't do anything for her if that was all he wanted. She'd already seen what happened to her other girlfriends when they slept with a boy too soon.

"Then there's the situation with my niece, who would meet a boy one day and be in bed with him the next. A woman should not take her body and sex so lightly. Now how long you think a boy's gonna stay with a girl that gives it up that quickly? You'd think she would've figured this shit out by now. It's not like it's rocket science or anything because it happens over and over again. Unfortunately, she grew up in a family where her mother and some of her aunts went from man to man. So, if that's all she had for role models, then what was she supposed to do? She was fighting an uphill battle anyway. She wasn't taught any better, so that's all she knows."

FROM THE AUTHORS—
A FINAL NOTE OF ADVICE

Life is short, and tomorrow is not promised to anyone, so we must make the best of each day. The gumbo of your life can be full of laughter, fun, and happiness, or sadness and disappointment; it's all in what you choose. Each of us has a spirit within: a light that will shine to show us the path we should take. But only when we stop trying to find our happiness in a man, or a new hairdo, or dress, and look within will we find that light. We often shortchange ourselves when looking too hard to find what we already have, and that's our God-given gift of wisdom and discernment.

Isaiah 30:21 says: "Whether you turn to the right or to the left, your ears will hear a voice behind you saying, 'This is the way, walk in it.'" If you simply ask and are willing to listen, that voice will always tell you the right way to go.

IN CLOSING . . .

We hope you enjoyed the read. Did you find yourself in any of these stories? Did you reminisce about some of your own escapades and find yourself smiling or maybe even feeling sad? Well, happy or sad, it's always good to know you're not alone when facing the things that life throws your way. It's good to be able to nod your head in agreement and think, "Girl, I know exactly where you're coming from." And the sex . . . the toe-curling, make-you-wanna-holla' sex . . . isn't it good to know that chemistry like that doesn't exist just in romance novels?

Do you plan to take some of the advice you've read and pass it on to another sister who's struggling with a situation similar to yours? If so, our mission has been accomplished. We just want you to know that you're not alone, no matter what you might be going through. No matter what you might be facing, you can best believe that some other woman has faced that same thing. And guess what? They survived.

Always remember, your gumbo or your life is what you make it. Even though you may put in too much of one thing or not enough of the other, rest assured, in the end it will all come out fine.

Please write us with your comments regarding *Sister Gumbo—Spicy Vignettes from Black Women on Life, Sex and Relationships.* We look forward to hearing from you. You can reach us at www.SisterGumbo. com or write to Sister Gumbo, P.O. Box 19252, Fort Worth, TX 76119.

We are currently at work on our next book, *Mister Gumbo* from the male point of view. Maybe you can let us know what it is you want to hear from the men. It's gonna be interesting.

Thanks for picking up *Sister Gumbo*.

Be blessed.

Sincerely,

Ursula Inga Kindred and Mirranda Guerin-Williams

ABOUT THE AUTHORS

Sister Gumbo is the work of two sisters, originally from Baton Rouge, Louisiana, who are lucky enough to be able to talk to each other and their friends about anything. No subject is taboo. Throughout all the listening and talking, it finally occurred to them that women shared a lot of similar life experiences.

Both are voracious readers who realized that bookstores and library shelves were missing fun-filled, enjoyable books that all women could relate to. They decided to write *Sister Gumbo* to give readers a book that was a pleasure to read and not peppered with words you had to look up in a dictionary to understand—a book where the reader could point to a paragraph, nod her head, and say, "Girl, I've been there."

Ursula Inga Kindred has a bachelor of business administration degree in finance from Texas Christian University. She is employed as a senior cost analyst for a large aeronautics company, and has future aspirations of becoming a full-time author. She lives outside of Fort Worth, Texas, in the country with her husband, Wade, and their two sons.

Mirranda Guerin-Williams spent six years in the U.S. Air Force; worked as a licensed cosmetologist; and is now employed by the federal government. She is pursuing a bachelor's degree in sociology, after which she plans to become a speaker and counselor for teens and engaged couples. She resides in a small town just outside of Fort Worth, Texas, with her husband, Jerome, and their daughter and son.